The Transformation of Old Age Security

The Transformation of
Old Age Security

CLASS AND POLITICS IN THE
AMERICAN WELFARE STATE

Jill Quadagno

THE UNIVERSITY OF CHICAGO PRESS

Chicago and London

JILL QUADAGNO is the Mildred and Claude Pepper Eminent Scholar in Social Gerontology at Florida State University. She is the editor of *Aging, the Individual, and Society* and *Social Bonds in Later Life* and the author of *Aging in Early Industrial Society* and *The Family in Various Cultures.*

The University of Chicago Press, Chicago 60637
The University of Chicago Press, Ltd., London
© 1988 by The University of Chicago
All rights reserved. Published 1988
Printed in the United States of America

97   96   95   94   93   92   91   90   89   88   54321

Library of Congress Cataloging in Publication Data
Quadango, Jill S.
    The transformation of old age security: class and politics in the
American welfare state / Jill Quadango.
        p. cm.
    Bibliography: p.
    Includes index.
    1. Social security—United States. 2. Social security—Europe.
3. Old age pensions—United States. 4. Old age pensions—Europe.
I. Title.
HD7125.Q46 1988
368.4'00973—dc19   87-18754
ISBN 0-226-69923-4   CIP

TO JENNIFER AND BRYAN

Contents

Preface

When I began thinking about this project more than five years ago, I believed I would be tracing the development of programs for the aged in the context of state expansion. Indeed, the first draft of a first paper, prepared for a Rockefeller Foundation Conference, focused primarily on the transition from poor laws to pensions as wider government units usurped the welfare function. As a consequence of my interest in the state, I turned initially to government records, specifically the enormous collection of papers, official correspondence, statistics, and letters of the Social Security Administration, housed in the National Archives and Records Service in Washington, D.C., and the Federal Archives and Records Center in Suitland, Maryland. My first impression, of a strong state bureaucracy determining the directions of program expansion, was quickly qualified as I noticed the tremendous pressures southern congressmen exerted on the Social Security Board. The southern states simply were not cooperating with the law, successfully foiling the bureaucracy's attempts to gain compliance.

At this time I knew little of southern history, and so I devoted the next several months to reading and studying, trying to understand why one region so adamantly resisted national welfare legislation. The answer that gradually unfolded convinced me that both the theoretical and the empirical issues were more complex than I had anticipated and that I needed to be attuned to all possible influences on social policy. The vast theoretical literature on the welfare state directed me toward other factors that might have shaped American programs. Intrigued by the ability of the social democratic model to explain the origins of many European welfare programs, I began to explore labor history to see why organized labor had apparently been so ineffectual in the United States.

The search, which led me to the proceedings of labor union meetings, the papers of union leaders, and then the records of their employers, convinced me that at least part of the explanation of public sector program development lay in the private sector, in the struggle between labor and capital. Thus I moved back and forth between theory and archival materials, with each new set of empirical observations guiding my generalizations about the factors shaping welfare policy.

To a large extent my central question, why the American welfare state developed later and less comprehensively than its European counterparts, determined my approach—what Charles Tilly calls "individualizing comparison."[1] The basic purpose of this approach is to account for the peculiarities of individual cases. Although the method of individualizing comparison is limited in that it can illustrate theories but not test them, there are times, as Tilly argues, "when what we need most is a clear understanding of the singularities of a particular historical experience."[2] Given the extensive debates regarding the failure of the American labor movement to take a radical course and the implicit encapsulation of the working-class power thesis within this debate, I felt that individualizing comparison was justified, indeed mandated, by the issues I wished to address.

The one problem with this admittedly ex post facto justification is that this book contains only an implicit comparison, at least at the level of the nation-state. Although the core question is undeniably comparative, I use that question merely as a takeoff point for a detailed archival analysis of American welfare state development. And though this method is undoubtedly less powerful in terms of theory testing, nonetheless the lack of original historical research on the American case, compared with, say, Sweden or Great Britain, convinced me that the need for basic data more than compensated for the absence of direct comparison.

When I begin to delve into the complex factors affecting American welfare state development, however, the approach becomes explicitly comparative, not on the level of nations, but in terms of variations between theoretically relevant factors. I suggest that three crucial factors affected the structure of the American welfare state: first, the power of private sector initiatives; second, differences in the material interests and relative access to power of the two segments of the labor movement, mass-production and craft workers; and finally, the impact of the existence of two economic formations—the North and the South—within the boundaries of a single nation-state. This approach can best be categorized as variation finding, that is, "comparison establishing a principle of variation in the character or intensity of a phenomenon having more than one form by examining systematic differences among instances."[3] The advantage of this method is that it allows me to draw conclusions—that the late unionization of mass-production workers impeded the development of American welfare programs, for example—that can be readily extended to new cases and tested against additional evidence.

Historical research requires extensive travel, and I am grateful to the American Philosophical Society, the Henry J. Kaiser Family Foundation, and the Hall Center for the Humanities of the University of Kansas for providing me with the funds to examine various archives throughout the United States. Historical research also requires large blocks of time, and research grants from the General Research Fund of the University of Kansas and from the Kansas Committee for the Humanities, an affiliate of the National Endowment for the Humanities, as well as a sabbatical leave, provided some of that time.

If, on my trips to those archives, I had had to rely upon my own ability to track down useful materials, this book would have been at least another three years in the making. Aloha South, judicial, fiscal, and social records librarian at the National Archives and Records Service, helped me determine which of the vast files of the Social Security Administration it might be worthwhile to examine, taught me the filing system, and often, after a letter or phone call, prepared materials ahead of time so that I could begin working as soon as I got off the plane. Marion Howey, the recently retired documents librarian of Spencer Library at the University of Kansas, spent hours helping me track down legislation, showing me how to trace the fate of a single bill through the enormously complex system of government documents. Her help was invaluable. Warner Pflug, Thomas Featherstone, and the other archivists at the Walter P. Reuther Archives of Labor and Urban Affairs also gave freely of their time and energy to help me locate material on labor unions and pensions, and I am grateful to them as well.

Two conferences to which I was invited during the preparation of my manuscript proved highly stimulating, and comments I received from fellow participants refined my research and moved my analysis in new directions. The first, "The Elderly in a Bureaucratic World," organized by David Van Tassel and funded by the Rockefeller Foundation, was held in 1983 at Case Western Reserve University. David Hackett Fischer, a fellow participant, gave me detailed comments on my paper at the conference. Upon my return home, I subsequently found myself bombarded with papers and data from historians all over the country who were working and publishing on the development of the poor laws. David Fischer is a man of enormous energy, and I am grateful that he chose to expend some of it for my benefit.

At this conference I also had the good fortune to meet John Myles. No other individual has had so great an impact on the arguments presented in this book. Through numerous conversations with him and through his detailed comments on several drafts of the manuscript, I was able to shape and refine my ideas. He helped me recognize the theoretical significance of the historical materials and continually forced me to move beyond the narrative I found so enticing to interpret my findings and place them in a broader explanatory framework. Another conference participant, Brian Gratton, has also been very influential in the development of the manuscript. A relentless critic, he read each chapter with a historian's eye for detail, always tempering his sometimes biting criticism with wit and humor.

In 1985 I was invited to participate in another conference, "The Politics of Social Policy in the United States," funded by the Project on the Federal Social Role and held at the University of Chicago. This conference proved equally valuable, both for the comments I received on my work and for the opportunity to listen to the research findings of others engaged in similar endeavors. The organizer of this conference was Theda Skocpol, and her help and encouragement have been most significant in the development of my ideas. Although she often disagreed with my conclusions, she has read and commented on the entire manuscript, forcing me to sharpen my arguments and document my findings more precisely. Her ability to separate personal relationships from intellectual disagreements has made her an invaluable critic.

Numerous other friends and colleagues have provided helpful comments on various chapters of this book. They include Neil Fligstein, Ann Orloff, James Schulz, Alex Keyssar, Georgia Walker, Scott McNall, Warren Peterson, and the faculty and students associated with the Midwest Council for Social Research in Aging, who criticized drafts of various chapters at numerous seminars. I would also like to thank Charles Perrow, whose insightful comments as one of the University of Chicago Press reviewers caused me to restructure a major argument that was not fully supported by my evidence. D. Ann Squier was my research assistant for a semester, and her diligence in tracking down obscure trade journals was invaluable in helping me trace industrial pension history. Karyn Davis, who was department secretary when I began the manuscript, not only typed the whole first draft but frequently babysat for my children. Peggy

O'Connor finished typing the manuscript, and Pat Johnston provided the final polishing as well as completing the enormous task of typing the Bibliography. During the preparation of this book, my husband David did more than his share of maintaining a household and raising a family, while my children, Jennifer and Bryan, grew into independent teenagers. It is to my children that I dedicate this book.

Fig. 1 *The Eagle Magazine*, January 1925, p. 10.

1

Theorizing the Welfare State

As the Roaring Twenties drew to a close, Americans faced the first bleak years of a depression that was to deepen rapidly. People who had taken pride in their economic independence found themselves drawn into the ranks of those forced to rely upon the state for protection against the ravages of poverty associated with unemployment and old age. Yet in contrast to its European counterparts, the American nation-state was entirely unprepared to assume responsibility for buffering its citizens against the exigencies of a market economy.

In previous decades other Western nations had created national welfare legislation to provide a floor of protection for those at greatest risk. Germany legislated a contributory national pension in 1889; Britain passed a universal Old Age Pensions Act in 1908; the Swedish *folkpension,* available to everyone upon reaching age sixty-seven, was adopted in 1913.[1] Although the United States had a military pension system that provided generous old age benefits to more than half of all native-born white men outside the Confederate South and many of their widows, Congress never acted upon proposals to convert it to a national old age pension. Until the 1935 enactment of the Social Security Act, individual states sporadically provided the only public pensions for older people.[2] Thus, though there was great diversity among nations in this developmental period, the United States lagged far behind even the minimal efforts of European nations in legislating a national program.

In the post–World War II era, welfare benefits were transformed from minimal relief systems into comprehensive, universal programs that guaranteed workers a basic standard of living, not just an income floor.[3] Sweden implemented major pension reform immediately after World War II, replacing its earlier means-tested program with a universal demogrant. As subsequent inflation reduced the value of the pension, in 1950 the Riksdag indexed pensions to consumer

prices and then to the increase in real wages.[4] In England the
Beveridge Report of 1942 proposed a national minimum benefit to
guarantee all citizens freedom from want. By 1950 the British
government had higher social insurance expenditures than Sweden,
Italy, Canada, or the United States.[5] German pension legislation
enacted in 1957 contained three programs that covered the vast
majority of the West German population. Although the legislation
did not include automatic cost-of-living increases, in every year
between 1959 and 1977 pensions were increased by a percentage
close to the increase in average gross wages.[6]

Unlike the European pattern of development, the United States
implemented a joint system of social assistance and social insurance in
a single piece of legislation, the Social Security Act of 1935. Old age
assistance was a traditional relief program that included local
administration, means tests, and stringent eligibility criteria.[7] Old age
insurance did little more to meet the criteria of a true social security
doctrine. Its benefits were lower than those in the assistance program
for more than twenty years, and coverage, initially extended to less
than half the population, expanded only gradually. Not until a series
of acts passed between 1969 and 1972 increased tax rates and indexed
benefits did the American social insurance system provide a full
retirement wage.[8] Even then the quality of benefits varied, not only
along lines of class but also by race and gender. By the 1980s, 82
percent of the United States population was fully insured under old
age survivors and disability insurance (OASDI), including 92 percent
of all men and 73 percent of all women. But in 1980 the average
monthly benefit for white males was $432, for black males $351, for
white females $279, and for black females $245.[9] Thus women and
minorities have been unable to share fully in the economic rights of
citizenship.

The conversion of the federal-state program of old age assistance
into Supplemental Security Income (SSI) in 1972 further reinforced
the class-based bifurcation of benefits. Available only to those
ineligible for adequate old age insurance, SSI became a separate
national old age poverty program. Thus the segregation of benefits
for the poor and the middle class, embedded in the Social Security Act
from its inception, remained a characteristic of American welfare
policy.[10]

Why, compared with other Western capitalist democracies, was
the American welfare state so late to develop, and why did the
programs that were legislated retain a dual structure with a
traditional relief component? To understand the reasons for
American exceptionalism, two separate issues must be untangled.

The first task is to explain why national welfare systems arise, since it is impossible to interpret the American case without some more general understanding of the factors underlying all program development. The second task is to determine what unique aspects of American society made the United States unwilling to legislate a national social security system.

THEORIES OF WELFARE STATE DEVELOPMENT

There exist a number of explanations of the rise of national welfare states that differ considerably except for their common emphasis on some component of economic development as the motor of historical change. The simplest version of an economic explanation is the logic of industrialism thesis. Its core argument is that all industrializing nations, regardless of their historical and cultural traditions or present political and economic structures, become similar through an evolutionary process resulting from the impact of economic and technological growth on the occupational system.[11] As industrialization proceeds, it creates new needs for public spending by reducing the functions of the traditional family and by dislocating certain categories of individuals whose labor becomes surplus—the very young, the old, the sick, and the disabled.[12] Two factors make it possible for industrializing nations to develop national welfare benefits: the new wealth and expanded surplus created by the industrialization process, and the development of an enhanced organizational structure—a massive state bureaucracy—through which benefits can be delivered. Only nations at a particular level of social and economic development can develop welfare programs. As Wilensky explains, "Economic growth and its demographic and bureaucratic outcomes are the root causes of the general emergence of the welfare state."[13]

Empirically, the logic of industrialism perspective fared well in cross-national studies based on data for the 1940s to 1960s, but when research became more longitudinal and incorporated broader time spans, the argument floundered. Flora and Alber found that levels of industrialization failed to predict the timing of social insurance adoption by twelve European nations between the 1880s and the 1920s. Similarly, Collier and Messick found that neither levels nor significant thresholds of industrialization explained the timing of social insurance programs in fifty-nine nations between the 1880s and the 1960s.[14] These studies demonstrated that welfare states do not emerge merely as a by-product of industrialization. Nonetheless, the reasonably consistent relationship between economic development and the rise of national welfare states was sufficiently compelling that alternative arguments had to take it into account.

In response to the inadequacies of the logic of industrialism thesis, two somewhat competing interpretations emerged regarding the relation between economic change and the introduction of national benefit programs. According to the social democratic model, it was not industrialization per se that caused the growth of the welfare state, but the growing power of labor. At the core of this thesis is the view that labor gains strength in a series of historical stages associated with the development of capitalism. Because capitalism requires a free market where labor can be bought and sold for a wage, legal emancipation occurs first.[15] The capitalist economy then emerges from the fundamental cleavage between those who sell labor and those who purchase it. An emancipated labor force first organizes in the marketplace to demand wages beyond those prevailing in a free market. Unionized workers then carry the struggle to the state, where they win electoral victories and use the state as a vehicle to modify distributional inequalities.[16]

A substantial body of evidence supports the social democratic view. In many European nations, workers organized into political parties to aggressively implement social spending measures. Further, numerous quantitative cross-national analyses verify that nations with high union mobilization and stable leftist governments have the highest levels of welfare spending.[17] Yet contradictory evidence also exists, which undermines the power of the social democratic argument. Many studies, for example, concede that state power through social democracy is not the only route to welfare state growth and that social benefits may be initiated by any number of different political coalitions. Further, socialist impact on welfare is at least somewhat determined by economic conditions and political system characteristics. Another anomaly is that the social democratic agenda in welfare spending is not always consistent. As Parkin notes, "Social democrats have been more willing to broaden the social base of recruitment to privileged positions than to equalize rewards attached to different positions."[18]

Parkin's argument does not undermine the social democratic position so much as it reflects the political realities of mass democratic politics. When organized labor attempts to achieve socialist goals through competitive political parties, it is contrained by the need to expand the party base beyond the working class. As the party becomes more heterogeneous, it erodes the sense of collective identity of party members and limits the range of political goals. The inherent dynamic of the party system limits the content of all politics and "makes democracy safe for capitalism."[19]

Neo-Marxist theories of the welfare state carry this principle one step further.[20] Neo-Marxist theorists view social welfare programs as the outgrowth of the basic imperatives molding the state's activities in capitalist society. These imperatives consist of the need to maintain profitability and the need to ensure social harmony. Welfare programs increase profitability by lowering employers' costs of maintaining a healthy and skilled labor force and contribute to the legitimation function by quieting discontent.[21] The state can never develop a set of policies truly designed to meet human needs, because these policies will invariably encounter the constraints of the capitalist economic system.[22]

Some research supports the neo-Marxist view that the welfare state is largely a repressive social control mechanism. The German pension program established by Bismark in 1889 served a dual purpose: it checked the threat of the working class and contained the power of the bourgeoisie. Others have demonstrated that employers' organizations have sometimes initiated social benefit programs and that social expenditures by right-wing parties are sometimes greater than those under left-leaning governments.[23]

Whereas the social democratic model overstates the impact of working-class power on welfare state formation, the neo-Marxist perspective limits our ability to take working-class history seriously. The basis problem is that the theory implies that the "state and politics always do just what needs to be done to stabilize capitalist society and keep the economy going."[24] Not only is there little discussion of how the state accomplishes this task, but the "structuralist perspective often reduces working class consciousness to an abstract cipher, virtually dependent on the manipulation of elite state managers."[25] Are labor movements never able to win real victories? Why then have working-class parties attempted to obtain worker benefits that free labor from market-based criteria?

The apparently conflicting evidence over who initiates welfare programs and who gains from them can be resolved by recognizing that since these programs benefit both capital and labor, at a given historical moment either class faction may be in a structural position to establish them. From this principle a new set of issues arise regarding the functions of welfare and the determinants of the ability of different class factions to shape welfare programs.

WELFARE AND THE ORGANIZATION OF SOCIAL PRODUCTION

This book poses an alternative argument that is theoretically consistent with the economically grounded arguments described above but that subsumes them all at a more abstract level of analysis. It begins with the recognition that welfare programs are not a unique feature of advanced capitalist nations, though they are sometimes treated as such. Since at least the sixteenth century, public welfare benefits in the form of poor laws have performed two functions in most Western societies. First, they have been a source of sustenance to the vulnerable—the orphaned, widowed, and aged poor.[26] Second, in precapitalist agrarian economies these traditional relief systems, not market forces, were an important factor in allocating labor. Associated with an abundant but unskilled labor force, poor laws functioned as repressive systems of labor control. The key features of the British poor law—for example, local autonomy and residency requirements—allowed farmers, in their dual roles as poor-law authorities, to tie workers to the land by manipulating the eligibility requirements.[27] Another feature was the "roundsman" system, under which unemployed laborers rotated among the farmers of a parish, with each providing maintenance in exchange for service.[28] As wage labor developed, landlords also kept benefits below wage levels so as not to undermine work incentives, taking workers off relief whenever they were needed to work the fields or harvest the crops. Similar conditions prevailed under the American colonial poor law, where colonists farmed out the able-bodied poor as indentured servants. In a labor-sparse economy, paupers formed a cheap labor supply.[29]

The progression of industrial capitalism necessitated the free sale and purchase of labor as a commodity and the elimination of restrictions on a free labor market. Workers could no longer be locked to the land by laws that made eligibility for relief dependent on local residence. Industrialization also brought about more automatic means of work-force control—through the market and the factory. These external control mechanisms reduced employers' dependence on enforced discipline through poor laws.[30] Initially, more lenient residency requirements in poor laws freed workers to respond to market fluctuations in demand. Gradually, social security programs designed to elicit spontaneous cooperation from workers replaced the poor laws. Thus history demonstrates that welfare programs have shifted in response to changes in the social organization of production. They are not unique features of advanced capitalist nations but have always served to regulate the labor supply.

The argument developed throughout this book is that the social organization of production determines the nature and form of relief programs. If poor laws are a product of feudalistic agrarian societies requiring an immobilized labor force, then national welfare systems emerge from the conflicts generated by the commodification of labor under industrial capitalism and the need for a mobile labor force. This thesis is derived from Marx's materialist theory of history, in which "in the social production of their life, men enter into definite relations that are indispensable and independent of their will, relations of production which correspond to a definite stage of development of their material, productive fores."[31]

Even if the social relations of production evolved simultaneously in two nations, the timing and structure of their welfare programs could vary considerably. To explain welfare state variation, this admittedly deterministic vision must be qualified: the link between welfare state development and forms of social production may be modified in an advanced capitalist state if labor obtains the political resources to free welfare programs from market criteria. But even when organized labor forms a political party, it often does not attain market-free welfare benefits. It is not just the development of social programs that must be examined, but also the type of programs in terms of whether they are market based. The welfare state may be, but certainly is not invariably or even usually, in opposition to property and market forces. It is this point that social democratic theorists often fail to recognize, because of their assumption that the political and economic arenas are separate. Workers' ability to wrest social benefits from the market depends on their position in the state hierarchy. To explain how variability is introduced into program structure, the next section constructs a theory of the state that presumes the opposite of the social democratic principle—that the polity and the economy are inextricably linked.

THE STRUCTURE OF THE STATE

The initial premise of the logic of industrialism thesis was that a massive state bureaucracy, capable of delivering social benefits, developed along with an industrializing economy. It lacked any serious analysis of the state as a separate force. But critiques of the theory found that the state did not merely respond to increased vulnerability in the population, but rather had an independent impact on program development. For example, Collier and Messick found that social security was implemented at lower levels of development in later-developing countries, because the state played a larger role in initiating social security measures as an easy way to tax citizens and as a means of weakening labor movements.[32] Similarly, in a comparative study of welfare state formation in Germany, Britain, France, and Italy, Hage and Hanneman concluded that the rise of new vulnerability in the population does not in itself automatically increase welfare expenditures. These needs must be translated into policy through some mechanism, the choice of which is related to the level of political development.[33]

Although political variables increased the explanatory power of industrialization models, further research indicated that the state was not merely a neutral vehicle but responded to external pressures. Williamson and Weiss found that adding class variables increased the explanatory capacity of a developmental model. In comparing thirty-nine nations at various stages, they found that socialist party strength or labor union strength had a significant indirect effect on the growth of a welfare bureaucracy.[34] Thus, adding class and political system variables undermined the argument that economic development alone can explain welfare state formation.

The social democratic thesis clearly incorporates a class analysis into discussions about the relation between economic development and the role of the state. Its core argument is that organized labor mobilizes into a political party and works through the state either to directly initiate welfare programs or to pressure traditional parties to do so. Because of this premise, it views the state and the economy in capitalist democracies as separate. This separation allows workers to alter the distributional process in a manner independent of market criteria and the class principle; in effect, the market can be bypassed and its rules of distribution be made irrelevant.[35]

The problem is that this ideal-typical welfare state, which mitigates market forces, does not reflect the reality of most of the welfare states that have come into existence since World War II. Nor does this model help explain the conditions under which a true separation between the state and the economy might occur. In an attempt to delineate the state-economy relationship more precisely, Mary Ruggie describes two kinds of welfare states. In a liberal welfare state, "the proper sphere of state behavior is circumscribed by the functioning of market forces," with public welfare serving merely to ameliorate market dysfunctions. The result is incremental public policy measures and a fragmented structure. By contrast, a corporatist welfare state defines the parameters of market forces a priori, intervening not simply to compensate for inequality but to institutionalize equality. The result is a blurring between state and society. In a liberal welfare state, state capacity is high, in a coporatist welfare state, low. The problem is that for Ruggie what determines state capacity is the position of labor within the state.[36] None of the other factors that might affect the state's willingness or ability to create a generous welfare state are present in her model.

The neo-Marxist perspective provides clearer guidelines by defining the state as an autonomous force mediating between class factions. According to Poulantzas, the structure of the state is determined by the class contradictions inscribed within it: "Each state branch or apparatus and each of their respective sections and levels frequently constitutes the power-base and favored representative of a particular fraction of the bloc, or of a conflictual alliance of several fractions opposed to certain others." These fractions may include big landowners, nonmonopoly capital, monopoly capital, and the internationalized bourgeoisie or the domestic bourgeoisie. The contradictions between the dominant fractions embedded in the state make it "necessary for the unity of the bloc to be organized by the State." The state, then, is not a unified mechanism but rather a mediating body that weighs priorities, filters information given, and because of its autonomy from any given class or faction, integrates contradictory measures into state policy.[37]

Although Poulantzas's version of the neo-Marxist perspective provides a useful reminder to look not only to transformations in economic institutions but also to changing power formations within the political system, it never articulates the process through which political decision making occurs. Further, there is a tautological element in an argument suggesting that social policy is the outcome of state mediation between factions or power blocs.

How do we conceptualize the state, then, without reducing labor-capital relations to a preconceived set of functions? Claus Offe provides a more historically grounded analysis that involves no predetermined vision of the relationship between labor, capital, and the state. According to Offe, the political process within the state consists of three tiers. The first and most obvious is the arena of political decision making. Here the activities of politicians and political parties are observable as political elites compete for electoral victories and decide on social programs, legislation, and budgets. The second tier is the level at which "the agenda of politics and the relative priority of issues and solutions is determined, and the durability of alliances and compromises is conditioned."[38] On this level it is more difficult to identify specific actors, for the parameters of possible decisions of political elites are determined by less visible societal forces, such as events in the international environment, macro-economic indicators, changes in levels of unemployment and inflation, and changes in the cultural aspects of social life.

Although the power to shape these perceptions cannot be traced back to single actors, there is, in Offe's terms, a "matrix of social power" that shapes the "environment of decision making." The ability to affect this environment depends on the relative resources of different groups. While these resources may balance each other, they may also be concentrated in the hands of the same class or group, depending on "cyclical or conjunctural variations which may allow a group to exploit its specific social power to a larger or smaller extent at different points in time."[39]

Finally, there is a third level of politics in which changes occur in the matrix itself—that is, in actors' relative access to the power to shape the social agenda. This shift in power can occur because the resources each class controls are constantly redistributed. Thus, the most fundamental level of politics is the struggle for the redistribution of social power. The development of the welfare state can be investigated at all levels of the political process, from the visible actions of politicians to the invisible shifts that occur in the power matrix.

If the welfare state is constructed around changes in the relations of production and through shifts in the state's power matrix that determine the agenda of decision making, then explaining American exceptionalism means explaining the unique configuration of American political and economic development that might have impeded the growth of its welfare state. This task is not unique to arguments about welfare state development; rather, it is the intellectual offspring of broader attempts to explain the absence of class-based politics in America.

EXPLAINING AMERICAN EXCEPTIONALISM
The Weakness of the American Labor Movement

If, as the social democratic model asserts, the "growth of the welfare state is a product of the growing strength of labor in civil society," then the lack of a well-developed program of social benefits in the United States may be attributed to the weakness of the American labor movement. To all appearances, organized labor never formed a political party through which to press its demands, and American labor leaders adopted a philosophy of voluntarism that left them uninterested in social insurance.[40]

The question, then, becomes why a labor movement that was once the most radical and violent in history never formed an independent political party through which to advocate a socialist agenda. In attempting to understand what distinctive aspects of American political and economic development undermined a class-based political movement, social scientists have offered a number of explanations: opportunities on the frontier that diffused class conflict; the absence of a feudal past; racial and ethnic diversity that splintered the labor movement; early suffrage that demobilized working-class consciousness; the presence of an egalitarian, achievement-oriented ethos; and the greater opportunities available for the American worker to achieve social mobility.[41]

The problem with all these explanations is that they accept the initial premise of "weak labor." This general presumption precludes any serious analysis of the structural organization of the American labor movement in terms of where its political opportunities lay and negates the possibility of searching for instances of successful labor action. If we begin with the thesis that welfare is shaped by changes in the social organization of production, then the explanation for the underdevelopment of American welfare programs is not predetermined—that is, that labor was weak. Rather, the answer can be located in historical analysis of the transformation of the American working class.

A clue to how to proceed with such an analysis comes from Gosta Esping-Anderson's comparative study of political development in Norway, Denmark, and Sweden. According to Esping-Anderson, the welfare state's political effects can vary dramatically. If the welfare state is constructed along lines that strengthen the weakest section of the working class, then it will decommodify workers "so that they will possess sufficient resources to engage in broad solidaristic activity." If, on the other hand, the state becomes "the champion of the destitute or of weak minorities while permitting the majority of the population to acquire welfare and resources in the marketplace," residual welfare statism will result. In this case privileged workers will be more inclined to favor private welfare programs and to oppose increased taxation to support social benefits.[42] In Sweden and Norway a broad-based program of universal social benefits decommodified workers, whereas Denmark's welfare state was more circumscribed.

Esping-Anderson's typology is similar to Ruggie's; both recognize that either a market-based or a decommodified agenda may be legislated. But in Esping-Anderson's analysis labor was politically powerful in all three nations. Instead of his merely explaining the type of welfare state as the result of a strong labor movement, the variations between the three nations impelled him to examine labor's actions more closely. He concluded that what determines the structure of the welfare state is the relative access to power of the two core components of the working class: skilled craft workers as opposed to unskilled industrial workers. Each faction of labor varies in its relative capacity to demand universal benefits. Although skilled craft workers were the first to form unions in all three nations, the Swedes and the Norwegians, whose working classes were not dominated by skilled labor, moved toward vertical, industrial unionism. In these nations the industrial proletariat was "better situated to invoke broad class solidarity." In Denmark, by contrast, where narrower and exclusionary craft interests maintained control, horizontal, craft-based negotiations predominated. Thus the historical development of unionization in the three nations had significant implications for subsequent welfare policy. Unskilled industrial workers are more likely than skilled craft workers to support an agenda that removes benefit programs from market criteria.

What implications about American underdevelopment can we draw from this analysis? Clearly, Esping-Anderson's evidence would direct our attention toward the relative influence that skilled artisans as opposed to the industrial proletariat have on welfare legislation.

In the United States initial unionization was restricted almost entirely to craft workers, whose central goal was to preserve craft autonomy.[43] Preserving the prerogatives of craft could be achieved by a dual agenda: maintaining unions along a strictly craft basis to maximize bargaining power with employers, and resisting encroachments of the state into union affairs. Although an unskilled proletariat emerged during the earliest phases of factory production, the craft unions exhibited no interest in recruiting these workers. In fact, the American Federation of Labor (AFL), the strongest craft union, overtly rejected any organizing attempts by unskilled workers and strove to repress "dualism." All attempts by the unskilled to organize on a mass basis failed except for the miners, the reservoir of the one strong union of industrial workers.[44] Until the mid-1930s, the vast numbers of unskilled and semiskilled workers in the core mass-production industries remained unorganized. Not until after 1935, when the basic form of the welfare state was already established, did large-scale mass-production unionism arise.[45]

Instead of attempting to explain the delayed development of the American welfare state as merely the outcome of a weak labor movement, this book will take labor history seriously. A core line of argument will be to explore the relative impact of craft and mass-production workers on the timing and structure of the programs that did arise.

The Power of Private Sector Initiatives

An underlying assumption of the "weak labor" thesis is that government activities are expressions of or responses to social demands. An alternative perspective views the state as the locus of autonomous action, independent of the demands of groups and organizations in civil society. From a state-centered perspective, states are "first and foremost sets of coercive, fiscal, judicial, and administrative organizations claiming sovereignty over territory and people," which affect policy as "the sites of autonomous official action." If a "given state structure provides no existing (or readily creatable) capacities for implementing a given line of action, government officials are not likely to pursue it." The appeal of certain policies, then, depends on "how well groups think they could be officially implemented."[46]

These two concepts, weak state capacity and a subsequent lack of citizen confidence in the state's ability to pursue a particular policy agenda, have been used to explain the late onset of the American welfare state. In America the early democratization of the electorate created a patronage system in which government outputs took the form of distributional policies. Patronage spending peaked under the Civil War pension system, when a substantial portion of the federal budget was expended on a corruptly administered program. With the central government weak and the state bureaucracy virtually undeveloped, reformers doubted that social spending measures could be implemented honestly. Citizens' fears of further patronage abuses in benefit programs undermined public confidence in the state's capacity to carry out national welfare programs and delayed legislation for social benefits.[47]

A lack of public support is one potential outcome of a weak state capacity; an alternative possibility, which is not incorporated into the state-centered approach, is that such weakness reduces the state's ability to intervene in the private sector. If we understand welfare programs to be a public-sector response to the problems of the commodification of labor under industrial capitalism, then an equally logical consequence of a weak state capacity is a powerful private sector initiative. When state capacity is low, one could argue, the state never gains the opportunity to adjudicate the battle between capital and labor.

In moving from absolutism to constitutional democracy, nineteenth-century European states retained the concept of the state as the embodiment of the public interest. As they developed frameworks of public and private law to govern interactions among state institutions and safeguard the public interest, the laws determined that autonomous concentrations of power intermediate between the state and private citizens were unacceptable. In the United States, by contrast, the system of federalism, which ensured the survival of regional governments, inhibited the development and extension of central power. State authority in the United States was thus diffused to an extent unparalleled in Europe.[48]

In the vacuum created by the lack of centralized government, large corporations unregulated by the state came to dominate the economy, beginning in the late nineteenth century. Although state governments had the authority to outlaw restraints of trade, in 1886 the Supreme Court ruled that only Congress had the authority to control interstate commerce. This ruling limited states' ability to regulate the activities of corporations within their boundaries. State governments further abdicated their control over the growing concentration of corporate power by passing generous incorporation laws, allowing corporations within a state to acquire companies outside the state.[49] Such laws encouraged the growth of oligopolies.

With states unwilling or unable to regulate the large corporations whose jurisdiction extended beyond their boundaries, the regulatory authority should have passed to the federal government. A Supreme Court ruling, however, determined that regulating business activity was not a function of the law and that the business corporation was a real entity with the same rights and privileges as an individual. This legal decision left the federal government incapable of taking responsibility for incorporation, virtually ensuring the security of the large business corporation.[50]

In this setting of freedom from government intervention, the large corporation grew increasingly prominent, and in many sectors of the economy oligopolistic competition and price-fixing replaced the individualism of the free market. When pools and voluntary agreements among corporations failed to reduce the fierce business competition that characterized the last decades of the nineteenth century, corporations, spurred by the growth of the capital market for industrial stocks, entered into a series of mergers. The merger movement began in 1897 and culminated in 1901 with the formation of the U. S. Steel Corporation.[51] During this period, 35 percent of the assets of American manufacturers were involved in mergers.[52]

Although the merger movement consolidated corporate power and led to the emergence of a few large firms in many manufacturing industries, it failed in its most fundamental aim—to control internecine competition. There are a number of reasons why the merger movement failed. One factor was that business often achieved no economies of scale by forming large combines, and in many management difficulties actually increased production costs. Another factor was the ease with which competing firms could enter, making it impossible for trusts to control the market. Finally, attempts to enforce monopoly and prevent the etnry of other firms often led to antitrust suits.[53] The failure of the merger movement is nowhere more evident than in the fact that in subsequent years the market share of large corporations in most of the manufacturing industries decreased.[54]

With efforts at self-regulation a failure, large corporations turned to the state for help in reducing competition. Much of the Progressive Era regulatory legislation either was initiated by or had the support of the manufacturing corporations being regulated. As Gabriel Kolko explains, "It is business control over politics . . . rather than political regulation of the economy that is the significant phenomenon of the Progressive Era.[55]

An equally significant spur to business involvement in the state was its hostility to organized labor. As stronger unions organized more strikes around the turn of the century, businessmen formed antistrike and antiunion leagues. Although many of these began as local organizations, businessmen recognized that they could attain greater influence by joining together, and local organizations combined to form state and then national associations, culminating in the formation of the Chamber of Commerce. These associations lobbied successfully for laws to impede unionization.[56]

Organized labor achieved some influence on local and regional politics during the Progressive Era, and in this period states did pass some legislation favorable to labor. But the "large business corporations were the central actors in the emergence of the modern American state, dominating its institutional and ideological configuration," and organized labor never achieved more than marginal status in the national polity.[57]

Given the heavy hand of business in defining the boundaries of corporate activity during those crucial years when other nations were initiating welfare states, it is clearly important to explore whether private sector welfare activity could have formed a serious impediment to public sector action. Understanding the eventual emergence of public benefits requires analyzing how the private sector dealt with the issues resolved elsewhere by social programs.

The Dualism of American Economic Development

There is one final aspect of political and economic development in the United States that virtually all accounts of American exceptionalism ignore: that though the United States apparently had all the characteristics necessary for a class-based political movement by the late nineteenth century—industrialization, democracy, political parties, and an organized working class capable of pressing for social benefits—in fact two distinct economic formations existed within the boundaries of a single nation-state. Although industrial capitalism had spawned strong and sometimes violent conflicts between labor and capital in the North, until well into the twentieth century the South remained primarily agricultural, a labor-intensive agrarian sector within the boundaries of an industrializing nation. It was not just the agricultural nature of the southern economy, however, that distinguished it from the rest of the country, but rather a particular mode of production characteristic of the cotton-growing counties—a plantation mode of production, neither feudal nor capitalist in the organization of relations between planters and workers. Before the

Civil War the plantation mode of production functioned on the basis
of coerced labor under slavery. Shortly after the war it was reestablished under a system of sharecropping, which guaranteed planters
great control over a subservient, primarily black labor force.
Sharecropping remained in place through the 1940s and in some
areas until the 1960s.

In addition to its economic underdevelopment, the South also
lacked a second key condition for creation of a welfare state—an
organized working class. Although the general pattern of union
growth in the South between 1890 and 1930 resembled that of unions
throughout the rest of the nation, strikes in the South were much less
likely to succeed, and during the antiunion open-shop drive of the
late 1920s, few of the existing unions survived. Further, the official
AFL policy of not admitting black workers greatly weakened
southern unions. In spite of a more rapid rate of union growth in the
South between 1939 and 1964, at its peak in 1953 only 17.2 percent of
southern workers were organized compared with 34.1 percent of
workers outside the South.[59] The lack of unionization in the South
also affected union strength elsewhere. Employers used blacks as
strikebreakers and moved plants to nonunionized southern states as
an antilabor tactic. Thus the major force for welfare state initiation in
European nations was almost nonexistent in a significant portion of
the United States, and the lack of unionization in the South weakened
the national labor movement.

The South was politically as well as economically distinct. Although
the United States was a democracy, a condition that most theories
assume precedes the onset of national welfare states, the South
initiated democratic institutions later than northern states and had
stripped most citizens of the right to vote by the end of the nineteenth
century.[60] This right was not reinstated until the 1960s. Through a
series of disfranchising conventions held in the 1890s, all southern
states reduced their electorate from as high as 70 percent in many
states to less than 20 percent, and in some instances as low as 12
percent.[61] Motivated primarily by the desires of southern planters to
keep political power out of the hands of blacks and thus ensure that
the plantation mode of production remained intact, suffrage
restriction had the secondary consequence of keeping poorer whites
from voting.[62]

What disfranchisement also accomplished was the reduction of the
opposition to the Democratic majority so that, aside from a few
pockets of Republicanism, the South was completely dominated by
one party for nearly seventy years. Between 1876 and 1944 not one of
the eleven southern states went Republican more than twice, and four
of these states—Alabama, Arkansas, Georgia, and Mississippi—

never voted other than Democratic.[63] Thus, in contrast to the rest of the nation, in the South politics were conducted without benefit of political parties, carried on by amorphous factions within the Democratic party. The result was a system in which all political choices were restricted to the primary elections and in which leaders were chosen on the basis of personal appeal rather than a programmatic party agenda.

The South, which contained less than 25 percent of the total population until 1969, was able to exert a controlling negative influence on national legislation because of the organizational and procedural structure of Congress and the particular circumstances of the Democratic party.[64] Early in the nineteenth century the House and Senate began establishing standing committees to process the mass of legislative bills that were proposed. In 1822 the House adopted a rule granting these committees the right to report a bill out of committee. The effect was to give committees important powers, particularly negative powers to obstruct legislation, since a bill could not be brought to the floor of the full House without favorable committee action. At midcentury a new procedure was established— using seniority as the basis for selecting committee chairmen. As early as 1858 senators from the slave states controlled the chairmanship of every major committee, and though this domination was interrupted during the Civil War and the Reconstruction period, southern dominance was rapidly reinstated. Between 1877 and 1963 the Democrats organized the House of Representatives twenty-six times, and during this period there were few important committees that the South did not control. The two most powerful House committees are the Ways and Means Committee and the Committee on Rules. The last northern chairman of Ways and Means completed his term in 1893, whereas Rules had only three northern chairmen for ten Congresses.[65]

Southern control of committee chairmanships during periods of Democratic control of the Senate were equally striking, even though these periods were much fewer, since the Senate remained a Republican stronghold. The powerful Committee on Finance, for example, remained under southern control for seventy-three years. With the exception of two periods when Republicans were dominant, the South maintained control of the presidency or the House of Representatives for the fifty-eight years between 1875 and the New Deal.[66]

The South was able to dominate the Democratic party and thus Congress because the party's southern wing was always larger than its northern wing, making it dependent on its southern contingent. For example, with the exception of 1912, 84.5 percent of the total electoral vote cast for all Democratic condidates between 1886 and 1928 came from southern and border states.[67] Further, because the South remained a one-party region, Democratic congressmen, who often ran unopposed, gained seniority by consistently being elected to office.

The South's ability to exercise negative power was curtailed during the New Deal when Franklin Delano Roosevelt was elected to office by a Democratic landslide. Although he secured the support of southern states, his electoral victory was not contingent on this support. For the first time, the South became a minority faction within the majority party, since fewer than half of all Democratic congressmen came from southern states.[68] Although the South did not lose power all at once, its position within the Democratic party became more precarious, culminating in its 1960s defeat over civil rights legislation.

Although considerable regional diversity existed in the South throughout this period, it was the cotton-based economy and the interests of the politically dominant planters in maintaining, initially, the value of slave property and later coercive control over a subordinate black labor force that imposed an organic economic unity.[69] Through their control over the region's wealth, planters were able to control its political institutions as well, and while northerners devoted their energies to transportation, immigration, town building, and the politics of local development, southern planters were much more concerned with the international cotton market and with national legislation that might damage international trade or interfere with local control of black labor. Thus, the preeminence of cotton focused southerners' attention on national politics.

This does not mean that southern politicians were always successful at or even desirous of halting the advance of social policy initiatives, or that they did not often find themselves aligned in curious ways with northern industrialists or organized labor over particular issues. But most discussions of American welfare state development proceed as if the necessary preconditions were universal and neglect the very salient fact of southern underdevelopment. This book will examine key turning points in the history of the welfare state to determine whether the South was a factor in impeding social benefits.

CONCLUSION

American welfare programs have all the characteristics of a liberal welfare state: public policymaking has proceeded incrementally, a dual-benefit structure exists, and the main function of most programs is to alleviate poverty rather than to institutionalize equality. This book will analyze the origins and development of old age benefits under Social Security. Old age benefits are crucial to any analysis of American welfare state development for several reasons. First, they now constitute the largest share of welfare state expenditures, both in the United States and in other Western, capitalist democracies. Their economic cost makes them an important program and one that requires explanation. Second, old age benefits became an important neo-Keynesian measure for regulating the labor supply. Removing older workers from the labor force as a means of coping with high unemployment in the 1930s was a primary justification among policymakers for legislating Social Security, a function similarly performed by pensions in the private sector.[70] Finally, old age benefits represent the best case for analyzing the structure of the American welfare state, because economic security for the aged was the only welfare issue resolved by legislating two programs—universal old age insurance for wageworkers and means-tested old age assistance for the aged poor. Old age benefits embody the dualism of American welfare in their basic structure.

In tracing the historical development of Social Security, I presume that public welfare is a product of two processes—the development of markets and the expansion of the state. Each chapter will analyze whether changes in the social relations of production shaped the program's structure or delayed the introduction of a national pension. Because of this theoretical thrust, the primary focus will be upon labor-capital relations, although activities by actors outside the economic arena will be part of the analysis where relevant. Throughout, this central thesis will be tested against alternative explanations derived from other theories of welfare state development.

I will define the state as a three-tiered structure that includes the arena of political decision making, the matrix of social power, and changes within that power matrix. In this conception the state becomes not a static entity, but a historically grounded force in which different class factions vie for access to the environment of decision making. In the American case, these class factions are likely to include skilled craft workers, industrial workers in mass-production industry, monopoly capital, competitive capital, and southern planters. Each chapter will analyze the policymaking process at all levels and consider the interaction of the relevant class factions as they gain or lose power in the state hierarchy.

Fig. 2 *The Eagle Magazine*, August 1925, p. 16.

2

Old Age Security in Industrializing America

At the beginning of the twentieth century when European nations were beginning to institute national programs of old age security, the United States was spending more than one-third of its small federal budget for a system of national military pensions. In addition, a network of poor laws provided minimal protection for those who fell outside the coverage of military pensions or private charity. Given the high level of national spending for military pensions, the United States clearly had the economic capacity to support a national pension system. Further, by any measure of economic development, America had surpassed the level of industrialization reached by such nations as Sweden or New Zealand, which had already instituted old age pensions. How then can we explain the failure of the United States to pass a national old age pension at this critical turning point in history?

One theme predominant among historians has been that ideological conservativism impeded program initiation. David Hackett Fischer, for example, argues that though older people were in financial need in the early decades of the twentieth century, "an ideological obstacle lay squarely in the way," the gospel of thrift, which had been "central to the system of secular morality in America since the Puritans." According to Fischer, the hostility of Americans to compulsory old age insurance was rooted in "the deepest political and moral principles."[1] Similarly, W. Andrew Achenbaum asserts that the federal government evinced little interest in national old age pensions before World War I because "professional opinions about old-age dependency were not significantly altered by late-nineteenth century theories, organizations, and legislation reshaping the ways Americans perceived 'poverty' in general." It was not until the crisis of the depression "provided the context in which prevailing ideas about older people's status and their actual conditions" could be reassessed that "Americans could create a novel solution to the plight of growing old."[2]

Yet in the thirty-five years before the Social Security Act was passed, forty-seven bills providing for public pensions were introduced in Congress. Some came from socialists interested in protective measures for workers, others from reformers with a less radical vision who recognized that military pensions already served as de facto old age pensions for a substantial proportion of citizens. But none of these bills were ever reported out of committee.[3] The factor to be explained, then, is not a lack of public interest but the failure of the state to act.

In analyzing the state's failure to enact a national pension system, one argument locates the explanation in the legacy of nineteenth-century patronage politics. According to Ann Orloff and Theda Skocpol, the early democratization of the electorate created a patronage system in which government outputs took the form of distributional policies. Patronage spending peaked under the Civil War pension system, when a substantial portion of the federal budget was expended on a corruptly administered program. With central government weak and the state bureaucracy virtually undeveloped, reformers doubted that social spending measures could be implemented honestly. Citizens' fears of further patronage abuses in benefit programs undermined public support for national social programs and directed public attention toward political rather than social reform.[4]

The problem with this explanation is that though civil service reform did occur in the Progressive Era, it was carried out sporadically. When the Social Security Act of 1935 was passed, many patronage-based abuses of old age assistance occurred, similar to those that wracked the Civil War pension system. No merit system in federal welfare programs was initiated until 1939.[5] The lack of citizen confidence in government may have been a factor, but it does not completely explain the delay of a national pension, since Congress legislated Social Security while government reform remained an issue of public concern.

The next three chapters will analyze three alternatives to explanations for the lateness of the American welfare state that focus on beliefs and attitudes. These include the dualism of the American economy, the pattern of unionization of the working class, and the power of private sector initiatives. This chapter examines the argument that the dual pattern of American economic development, an industrializing North and an almost feudal South, affected the timing of a national old age pension. The first section traces the differential development of poor relief in North and South. It demonstrates that whereas the poor laws evolved to reflect the changing labor needs of an industrializing economy in the North, the political economy of the cotton South impeded the expansion of relief in this region. The second section reexamines the premise that a lack of citizen confidence was the primary impediment to proposals either to convert the military pension system into a national old age pension or to legislate a universal pension for all "soldiers of industry."[6] Instead it traces the pattern of economic development in North and South that gave politicians from these regions separate agendas for state policy. Like other public policy issues, pension proposals reflected the sectional conflict that arose from the different economic interests of northerners and southerners.

ECONOMIC DEVELOPMENT AND
SECTIONAL CONFLICT

In the United States a capitalist mode of production based on com-modity production, the concentration of productive assets in the hands of a minority class, and the simultaneous development of a "propertyless class for whom the sale of their labour power was the only source of livelihood" emerged in one sector, the expanding Northeast.[7] By contrast, a plantation mode of production, neither feudal nor capitalistic in its nature, characterized the nineteenth-century South. According to Mandle:

A plantation economy is defined as one in which the state of technology allows profit-maximizing, large scale farmers to produce a staple primarily for an external market. That same technology, however, requires the use of more workers than profitably low wage rates would attract. As a result some nonmarket mechanism is required in order for the planters to be sure of a sufficient supply of workers to carry out profitable production. In turn, those nonmarket mechanisms help to define the class relations of the society. The culture which emerges reinforces these class relations.[8]

What distinguishes the plantation mode of production is that, unlike feudalism, labor power is supplied by slaves or semislaves who have no claims to the land and, unlike capitalism, workers are not free to enter into and leave contractual relationships with employers. Rather, "the choice of where and for whom to work is largely dictated to the workers under a system of force and sanction designed to implement the planters' will."[9] The plantation mode of production, then, is primarily defined not in terms of territory or of agricultural production but rather in terms of the authority of the planter, whose most important task was to bind the workers to the estate. Each plantation was as much as authoritarian political institution as it was a business enterprise. The economic essence of the plantation structure lay in the planters' ability to allocate labor time between market and nonmarket activity.[10]

As wage labor expanded in the Northeast, it affected the structure of poor relief. Instead of performing their previous function of protecting the weak, poor laws increasingly incorporated labor-control mechanisms that secondarily affected the economic security of the aged as well as the able-bodied poor. In contrast, in both the pre– and post–Civil War periods, southern planters preferred to keep control over all benefits, mistrusting government intervention in local affairs. Further, the South's orientation toward the international cotton market made the southern elite less interested than their northern counterparts in local development of any kind. Thus, the plantation mode of production created attitudes that left government in the South undeveloped. Even when relief was legislated, the lack of any sort of state relief offices made it difficult, if not impossible, to implement.

THE POOR LAW LEGACY
The Poor Law in the Northeast

English settlers in the New England colonies brought with them the concept of the Elizabethan poor laws, but in practice the American version differed in many respects. The economic conditions under which American poor law policies arose were quite different from those of Elizabethan England, where masses of unemployed agricultural laborers created disorder and where landlords manipulated poor law residency requirements to reduce labor mobility and maintain a local labor force. With land abundantly available and no law-and-order reason to reduce mobility, the poor law in the colonies primarily provided protection. In each township the rationale for adopting the poor law rested on the assumption that giving public relief to those who could not support themselves or secure support from relatives, friends, or private philanthropy was a proper function of local government. Potential recipients of relief included the sick, the disabled, widows with children, and the aged. With only one exception, every community in the Plymouth and Massachusetts Bay colonies provided for relief in the initial stages of settlement and subsequently administered relief as a regular town function.[11] As early as 1647, at the first session of its colonial legislature, Rhode Island adopted the poor law principles stressing public responsibility for the poor. This responsibility was buttressed by the other principles of English poor law—local responsibility, family responsibility, and the residency requirement of legal settlement.[12]

Because life was harsh and amenities were scarce, relief often signified a bargain struck between the individual in need and the community. In 1660, for example, the town of Providence considered the case of Mr. Burrowes, who had need of relief through "age and weakness." His property and possessions were turned over to the town treasury, and Mr. Burrowes moved into the home of a fellow townsman.[13] Sometimes citizens took the sense of communal responsibility quite literally, as when the citizens of Hadley, Massachusetts voted to move the widow Baldwin from house to house "to such as are able to receive her" and let her "remain a fortnight in each family."[14]

The old and the disabled were proper objects of relief, but not the able-bodied poor, who received harsher treatment. Under an indenture system, children and unattached adults were farmed out to the cheapest bidder, who would provide food and lodging in exchange for work. Sometimes these contracts went to private residences, but more often they went to workhouses, which increasingly dotted the countryside from 1657 on.[15] Embedded in the poor law system from its inception, then, was the potential to manipulate the labor supply. In this early period, however, when labor was scarce and wage labor almost nonexistent, the poor law remained primarily a means of aiding the weakest members of society.

In the eighteenth century growing numbers of transient refugees from the colonial wars put burdens on towns and villages, which used settlement requirements to refuse relief to the nonresident poor. As a result, colonial governments rather than towns and villages began to grant relief funds. For example, Providence reimbursed cities and towns directly out of its treasury owing to the influx of homeless refugees during King Philip's War. Other colonies passed similar laws throughout the eighteenth century, with some requiring relief in the workhouse and others reimbursing towns directly. Thus the locus of the relief burden shifted away from local government as colonial governments took responsibility for relieving the nonsettled poor.[16]

In the early nineteenth century wage labor, while not unknown, was less common than independent farming, craft and artisan production, household manufacture, trade and commerce, indentured servitude, family work, and petty commodity production. Beginning in the 1820s, the first phalanx of a permanent and sizable class of wage laborers appeared. Native-born white males supplied the largest source of wage labor, working in the expanding iron, printing, foundry, food, lumber, fuel, chemical, and brewing industries. In addition, unmarried females and children, largely employed in the textile mills, and unskilled immigrants made up an increasing proportion of the industrial work force throughout the nineteenth century.[17]

When the indigent aged or widows with young children made up most of the poor, town councils were willing to provide outdoor relief or see to boarding paupers in neighboring homes. But gradually, many New England villages lost their subsistence character and ethnic uniformity as industrialization transformed them into burgeoning manufacturing centers. As the towns changed so did their treatment of the poor. In Danvers, Massachusetts, for example, home of the shoemaking industry, a mass-production "putting out" system replaced small-scale handicraft production between 1817 and 1837. Critical in expanding the shoe industry was the growth of the labor supply. Employment prospects attracted large numbers of foreign-born immigrants to the town. When unable to find work, these unemployed men turned to the overseers of the poor. Between 1841 and 1856 the proportion of foreign-born paupers increased from 59 to 86 percent, while the average age fell from fifty-nine to forty-one.[18] Thus the composition of paupers changed from native-born unemployables to able-bodied foreigners.

The Danvers pattern recurred throughout industrializing New England. Most public welfare recipients in the 1820s in Philadelphia, for example, were blacks, immigrants, and women. Although southern black immigrants represented only 8 percent of the total city population, they made up 15 percent of the almshouse population. One-third of those receiving outdoor relief were foreign-born immigrants, who also constituted 40 percent of the almshouse residents. In Boston, too, it was the foreign-born aged, not the natives, who filled the city's almshouse.[19]

With the creation of a wage labor force, the practice of granting outdoor relief became more threatening to employers. Operating under conditions of labor scarcity, employers feared that any direct cash grants to able-bodied workers could undermine wages and reduce the small reserve army that did exist. As Gratton explains, "It is the encounter of these two classes—the one outnumbered, the other powerless; the one employing, the other intermittently employed—that explains the rise of a punitive welfare system."[20]

Beginning in the 1820s, a campaign began to eliminate outdoor relief and grant relief only in almshouses, which proliferated between 1820 and 1840. In this period 144 new almshouses were erected in

Massachusetts alone. Although outdoor relief was never eliminated and in some areas was not even reduced, the increase in the proportion of paupers relieved in institutions in many urban areas was substantial. The proportion of paupers receiving indoor relief in Boston rose from 21.4 percent in 1832 to 44.5 percent by 1851.[21] In New York 4,500 persons received indoor relief in 1830 as opposed to nearly 10,000 by 1850.[22] Thus the growth of an industrial wage labor force and the increasing number of foreign immigrants applying for poor relief led to greater harshness in administration and to expanded institutional care.

In 1833 a Massachusetts committee toured the state and found grossly inadequate conditions. The almshouse experiment, committee members decided, was a failure. Institutions could never house all the able-bodied poor spawned by industrial unemployment. Almshouses continued to serve a function, however, albeit a different one than intended by early reformers.[23] Instead of being rehabilitative they became custodial, peopled even more than formerly by the aged, particularly aged immigrants.[24] Since immigrants lacked legal residency, they were taken in with no charge to towns, and public disregard for these marginal people helped perpetuate the institution. Thus, by the late nineteenth century poorhouses had discarded the goal of administering punitive relief to the able-bodied poor and become de facto old age institutions. As long as they were peopled largely by immigrants, blacks, and older women, there was little public concern regarding the fate of the aged.

Poor relief had come to play a different role in an industrializing nation. Initially, its primary function was to aid the more vulnerable members of society. As the demand for wage labor grew, new labor control functions were incorporated into poor law regulations. Although older people were sometimes treated more generously, they often were not separated from the able-bodied poor in the administration of relief.

The expansion of wage labor eventually rendered the poor law principle of settlement anachronistic. Industrial capitalism required labor mobility as workers left small farming communities for factory work in northeastern towns and cities. Increased labor mobility made identifying legal residency a problem. As a result, states began abandoning settlement laws and formalizing poor law administration.[25]

Relief in the South

In contrast to New England, eighteenth-century relief in the South was undeveloped. The settlement pattern was one factor impeding the growth of relief, since vagrants sent from England as indentured servants peopled most of the southern colonies. Bound to a master for several years, these servants formed the chief source of labor, just as black slaves did in the next century. With a population of indentured servants, officials has little incentive to pass poor law legislation.[26]

Harsh living conditions also impeded welfare. North Carolina, for example, contained only small, widely scattered settlements with poor roads and high illiteracy rates. When poor law legislation was finally passed in 1755, it contained vagrancy regulations specifying that persons likely to become chargeable were to be removed to the localities where they presumably belonged. Further, when poor laws were passed, they were often not implemented because they made no provisions for funding and delegated no administrative authority.[27]

Administrative weakness also stemmed from the ties between church and state. Unlike New England, where town officials served as overseers of the poor, in many southern colonies the parish functioned as the local government unit and Anglican clergymen served as administrators. Since they had other duties to occupy their time, in many areas the vestry system of relief failed simply because the clergy lacked the incentive to consider relief a priority.[28]

The introduction of slavery and the continued reliance upon an agrarian economy prevented the development of a large free-labor class. In the cotton-producing counties slaves made up as much as 80 percent of the population. Since both slaves and free blacks were ineligible for relief, welfare in the South remained minimal throughout the nineteenth century.[29]

Reformist zeal spread through industrializing New England, leading to the growth of almshouses, but the South resisted innovation. Although local almshouses contained a few paupers, southerners levied few taxes, leaving services of all kinds un-developed. The lack of a tax base made building almshouses or poorhouses infeasible. State relief for the poor occurred only in unusual circumstances. For example, in 1819 the South Carolina legislature appropriated $8,000 to aid the city of Charleston in caring for the transient poor, and $500 went to Georgetown and Beaumont. Similarly, the state of Georgia advanced $10,000 to the city of Savannah after a large fire.[30] But these instances were isolated and did not represent a general trend toward the formalization of relief functions, as occurred in the Northeast.

Around the turn of the century, the first proposals for both state and national old age pensions began appearing on the political agenda. Some reformers viewed old age pensions as protection for all workers, because they would reduce the reserve army of the aged and unemployed, whose presence formed a permanent barrier to bettering the condition of the working class.[31] Any benefit for marginal workers, they reasoned, would protect the wages and security of all workers.

Employers, who feared both the additional taxation burden and the potential for any form of welfare to create pressure for wage increases, formed one source of opposition to public old age benefits, particularly at the state level. But greater resistance to national old age pensions came from a different source, the southern senators and congressmen, whose control over the Democratic party gave them veto power over all social legislation. Southern resistance to national old age pensions was not predicated primarily on fears that a welfare benefit would undermine their control over labor, for by 1900 a coercive system of tenant labor was firmly entrenched.[32] Rather, it stemmed from a broader political agenda—the protection of the cotton market and the inequitable distribution of wealth between North and South.

SECTIONAL CONFLICT AND THE MILITARY PENSION SYSTEM

Much of the cultural or ideological conflict played out politically in the United States is actually a function of sectional stress, that is, "political conflict over significant public decisions in which a nation is divided into two or more regions, each of which is internally cohesive and externally opposed to the other(s)."[33] Sectional stress arises from the incompatible goals of the two dominant sectors: the industrial and commerical-seaport cities of the Northeast and Midwest and the interior distribution centers of the plantation South. The main axis of sectional stress, which has revolved around a constantly changing set of policy issues, has run between the Northeast and the Deep South. Other regions of the country, which share some characteristics typical of the Northeast and some typical of the South, have shifted their loyalties according to the particular policy issue at stake.[34]

Although often associated with ethnic identity and religious rivalry, in the United States sectional stress has been the result of economic competition grounded in an interregional division of labor, which is in turn a product of the relationship of the separate regional economies to the national political economy and the world system. Interregional competition has thus been a struggle for control over the national political economy, the stakes being the preservation of regional social, economic, and political institutions.[35]

The military pension system in the United States expanded in the context of sectional conflict between an industrializing North, oriented toward a home market, and an agrarian South whose economy depended on exporting raw materials, especially cotton, in an increasingly competitive world market. The trade positions of the two sectors were reflected in their positions on the tariff, which funded the military pension system. The industrial core advocated high tariffs to protect infant industries from the technologically advanced economy of Great Britain. In contrast the South, fearful of tariff retaliation from other nations and resentful of its colonial position as consumer of high-priced protected goods, advocated free trade. As the nineteenth century progressed, the fate of the military pension system and the tariff issue became linked.

The Political Economy of the Cotton South

Before the 1780s cotton was of no commercial importance, and the growth of American slavery was linked primarily to the fortunes of tobacco and rice. The expanding British textile industry stimulated the rise of southern cotton beginning in the 1790s, and within a generation the United States became the world's dominant supplier. From that date forward the progress of the British textile market determined the fortune of the southern economy. By the late antebellum period more than three-fourths of the American cotton crop was exported, with American cotton accounting for more than 70 percent of the cotton imports of Great Britain.[36]

Slave property was the dominant form of wealth in the South, and as slavery expanded, so did cotton production. Since cotton determined the value of slaves, the richest, most fertile regions contained the largest cotton plantations and the highest concentration of slaves. In every part of the cotton South, however, one could also find slave-using cotton farms of varying sizes and small slaveless farms that grew little or no cotton. Regional diversity was largely "a matter of varying proportions of fertile soils and large-scale slaveholdings—each region being a stratified sample, as it were, from what is fundamentally the same cross section."[37]

During the antebellum period there was a significant rise in slave values, making the average slaveowner more than five times as wealthy as the average northerner and more than ten times as wealthy as the average nonslaveholding southern farmer. Yet it was not just a tiny elite who controlled this wealth. A substantial minority of southern farmers owned slaves, and an individual who owned two slaves and nothing else was as rich as the average person in the North.[38] The importance of slave wealth gave the South an organic unity that affected the logic of political coalitions. On the issue of the value of slave property, large and small slaveowners agreed completely. Conflict in the South centered on the different economic interests of slaveholders and nonslaveholders, not large and small planters.

What distinguished southern plantations from free family farms was the way each coped with labor scarcity. Farm labor was scarce because farmers preferred farmownership and were able to attain it. Thus they had little incentive to hire themselves out to others part time. In census data most of those listed as farm laborers were actually members of the farmer's own family.[39] As a result large-scale farming in the North was unsuccessful, and most nineteenth-century farms remained family farms, with size determined by the acreage the family could cultivate. The risk of being unable to obtain a reliable labor supply prevented farmers from permanently expanding their scale of operations, except by expanding the use of agricultural equipment.[40]

In contrast to the inelasticity of free labor, slave labor was almost infinitely elastic, constrained only by the number of slaves a planter could afford to buy. As a result slaveholders could expand farm size beyond the labor resources available to those relying on family labor. Southern plantations were neither land intensive nor capital intensive; rather, they relied on labor-intensive cultivation.[41] Thus, while northern farmers searched for mechanical means of increasing acreage and output, planters concentrated on geographical expansion, systems of labor management, and the political security of slave property.

Owing to the structure of cotton production, slaveholders had certain class interests distinguishing them from nonslaveholders. Unlike land and unlike free labor, their property was movable and salable, with its value determined in an efficient regionwide market. Based on a crop oriented toward an international market, slaveholding made planters independent of local crops, local productivity, and local development. Thus the value of slave property became a great unifying factor in the South and focused the attention of southerners on national politics rather than local development.[42]

Pensions and Tariffs

The military pension system began with the English colonists, who provided for the relief and support of soldiers injured in wars with the Indians or with colonists of other nations. Modeled after British military pensions, pension laws provided that relief to disabled soldiers be paid out of the public treasury. The primary purpose of the military pension system was to encourage men to enlist, not to protect soldiers. While most of these laws provided only for the relief of the wounded, a few like Maryland's also paid an allowance to widows and orphans of those slain.[43]

Congress passed the first *national* military pension law in 1776, even before the Declaration of Independence. It promised half-pay for life to every soldier disabled in the Revolutionary War but left the execution of the law to the states. When some states failed to act, in 1790 Congress paid the amount left in arrears by the states.[44] Thus, before the nineteenth century the federal government had assumed responsibility for the colonial military pension system.

During the War of 1812 the government declared an embargo on imports, which stimulated American manufacturing. As New England capitalists began investing in manufactures, their concern with gaining economic independence from Europe increased. Manufacturers, who saw the tariff as the most effective vehicle for establishing independence, put increasing pressure on government for protection. Moderate protection was granted in 1816,[45] and in subsequent years domestic trade displaced foreign trade in importance. In 1810 approximately two tons were shipped abroad for every ton carried on vessels engaged in domestic trade. By 1840 the ratio of 1810 had nearly been reversed.[46] As world trade became less significant in the American economy the home market became more important, except in the South, which continued to rely almost exclusively on cotton export.

The year 1816 was unusually favorable to the expansion of public expenditures. The United States had borrowed more money than necessary to finance the War of 1812 and had levied new internal revenue taxes in 1814. The large credit balance in the Treasury stimulated demands from veterans to use the surplus funds to increase the rates paid to invalid pensioners. In April Congress passed a law raising the pension rates.[47]

The increased pension rates barely tapped the surplus, spurring sentiment in Congress for passage of a service pension rather than one based merely on disability. A liberalized service pension passed the House in 1818, but the Senate added a needs test. Strong opposition to liberalization arose from the South, particularly South Carolina, the state where the planter class was strongest and slavery most concentrated, whose representatives complained that pensions were being liberalized solely for the sake of depleting the Treasury surplus.[48]

Southern opposition to pensions arose from the clear link between tariffs and pensions. Tariffs protected the manufactured goods of northern industry at the expense of the raw materials—cotton, rice, and tobacco—that the South exported. Since southern cotton and tobacco planters did not expect to sell their crops to the home market, tariffs penalized them by shifting national resources from the South to the North. Further, tariff revenues were redistributed back to the states unevenly.[49] Few southerners qualified for pensions because slaves did not serve in the military.

In 1823 Congress was reapportioned, with the South losing overall in terms of representation. The Treasury now reported substantial surpluses each year, but manufacturers continued to press for protection. Although southerners argued that Britain was the primary market for American cotton and that protective policies might cause it to turn elsewhere, in 1824 and then again in 1827 Congress passed stronger protective measures. Expressing the frustration of the South, a South Carolina newspaper editor declared: "Wealth will be transferred to the North, and wealth is power. Every year of submission rivets the chains upon us."[50]

Throughout the 1820s, Congress interpreted the pension law more liberally as the Revolutionary War veterans aged. Because of the increased tariff revenues, however, by 1828 federal income was still nearly double current expenses. With protective policy well established, northern manufacturers were able to defeat all proposals for reducing duties. As an alternative way to reduce the Treasury surplus, President Andrew Jackson proposed additional pensions. Although Jackson did not link pensions to tariffs, southern congressmen had no doubt that the South was paying for increased pension benefits through import duties.[51]

Opposition to extending the pension laws prevailed that year, but in the next session of Congress new pension bills were introduced in the House and the Senate. The House bill was very liberal, proposing to grant pensions on the basis of service alone, with no needs test. Bitterly opposed, southern and western representatives protested that the pension bill would "prevent the reduction of those taxes that pressed heavily on the Southern people," that only a small part of the pension expenditures went to southern citizens, and that for each dollar of revenue to pay poor soldiers, southerners paid two dollars to rich manufacturers.[52] In the reconstructed Congress their arguments were ineffectual, and within the same week in 1832 a new tariff act and a new pension act became law.[53]

Like earlier pension disbursements, only a small portion of total expenditures went to southern claimants. In addition to the factors operating earlier, the South received less than its share because many

eligible southern soldiers failed to become claimants.[54] The failure of
southern soldiers to press for benefits is related to the nature of
southern politics.

Party Politics and the Expansion of Democracy

The Jacksonian era instituted the beginning of full democracy in the
United States, as the Jacksonians extended the franchise and made
government more accessible. The electoral reforms of the Jacksonian
era—white manhood suffrage, the paper ballot, small polling
districts, direct election of governors, presidential electors, heads of
state executive departments, and local government officials, and
short terms of office—undermined the elite-dominated mechanisms
of election management and political recruitment of the pre-
Jacksonian era and gave citizens a wider voice in the affairs of
government.[55]

Both the electoral and the administrative reforms changed how
the political system functioned. The expansion of the number of
public offices subject to popular election as well as the shortening of
terms of public officials increased the importance of politicians, who
organized the enlarged electorates and turned party management
into nearly a full-time profession. Jacksonians seized the opportunity
to expel notables from public office, creating a patronage-based
political system through which rewards could be distributed to the
cadre who staffed the party apparatus.

In the absence of a strong centralized government, political parties
came to play a major role in state operations. Party organizations
bound the national government to each locale and linked discrete
units of government horizontally across the territory, bringing a
measure of cohesion to national politics. Parties also organized
government institutions internally by routinizing administrative
procedures through patronage appointments, spoils rotations, and
external controls over the widely scattered government offices—the
post offices, land offices, and customhouses.[56] Local party organizations staffed these local federal offices and oversaw their operations,
while national representatives of state party machines distributed
federal offices. Thus the federal patronage appointee became the
embodiment of a series of concrete ties between the president and
Congress and between local and national governments.

In contrast to the extensive patronage systems in the North that
fueled party competition, the late and incomplete democratization of
the South led to the absence of patronage politics and the lack of a
competitive party system.[57] By midcentury five southern states—
Alabama, Mississippi, Tennessee, Arkansas, and Texas—had

instituted democratic procedures, including popular election of the governor, universal manhood suffrage, legislative apportionment in both houses based on white population, and democratic county government.[58] Three of these states, however, departed significantly from democratic procedures by counting slaves as well as whites in apportioning seats in the state legislature. The effect was to grant unequal power to representatives from black-belt counties.[59] This remained the procedure for at least some elective offices in all eight of the southern states that instituted few or no democratic procedures in the first half of the nineteenth century. In five of these states—Kentucky, North Carolina, South Carolina, Maryland, and Virginia—there was no movement toward democracy in county government during the first half of the nineteenth century. South Carolina and Virginia, each with a powerful body of eastern planters and a large percentage of slaves, remained particularly resistant to pressures for democratic government. Both states retained property qualifications for officeholding and taxes as the basis of legislative apportionment. Further, the legislature, not the people, selected the governor and other local officials.[60] Even where states had reformed their state constitutions, implementation often proceeded in a manner that continued to deny the franchise to most of the people. In Louisiana, for example, in spite of democratic reforms, there was little majority rule. Under the original constitution, which lasted to 1845:

> the franchise was conferred on all white males who had purchased public land or paid state taxes, and representation was supposedly "equal and uniform" according to the number of registered electors. On the surface, this suggested majority rule. In practice, however, it denied the ballot to two thirds of the adult freemen and permitted the slaveholding planters to dominate the legislature . . . . [I]n the constitutional convention of 1845, . . . all property tests for voter and public officials were abolished and seats in the upper house apportioned on the basis of total population. These moves were definitely in the direction of democracy. Yet in practice the suffrage reform worked little change because the lesser whites failed to vote. The representation changes, moreover, kept a minority of slaveholders and men of property in complete control of the legislature. A slaveholding minority could check any move that threatened its interests.[61]

Exceptions did exist, particularly in the newly settled southern states like Alabama, where poor whites had significant representation in the state legislature and a spoils system thrived.[62] But throughout most of the South, politicians had little need to appeal to the people.

Civil War Pensions in Postbellum America

Between 1830 and 1860 the link between pensions and tariffs became stronger. Both tariffs and pensions redistributed income from North to South and fueled sectional rivalry. As Baack and Ray note, "from 1830 to 1846 the effect of the tariff was to encourage the expansion of domestic production of textiles and nontraded agricultural goods at the expense of raw cotton production by redistributing income and profits from cotton growers to textile manufacturers and producers of nontraded agricultural goods." By 1858 the tariff was a major grievance of the South, and it was one of the issues that precipitated the Civil War.[63]

Following the Civil War the United States created the industrial infrastructure that was to allow the nation to emerge as a mature and powerful member of the international community. A major stimulus of change was the tariff. Even more crucial politically for the industrializing Northeast than it had been earlier, the tariff allowed the United States to temporarily withdraw from the world economy so that home industries could compete with European products.[64] During this period sectional conflict coincided with the party system as it had emerged from the Civil War, with Democrats the party of the South and Republicans the party of the North.

During the Civil War northern Democrats had to work without the support of their southern wing, as the South defected from the party in 1860. After its defeat in the Civil War the South was under military government. Yet within a few years the southern states returned to Congress, and southern politicians reestablished positions of prominence within Congress through their control of key commit-tees and Democratic party caucuses.

Beginning in 1874, when Democrats gained control of the House, the tariff became the main issue through which Democrats and Republicans attempted to break the political equipoise that had been created by the competitive party system. As Republicans and Democrats rotated in and out of the presidency, with Democrats generally controlling the House and Republicans the Senate, the tariff debates heated up.[65] Northeastern protectionists attempted to contain the move for tariff reduction by recruiting allies among midwestern farmers. Although midwestern farmers might have favored free trade as wheat and grain exports increased along with railroad expansion, they were brought into the protectionist camp through the Civil War pension program. By extending liberal benefits to the numerous veterans in the midwestern states, Republicans realigned the agrarian Midwest with the northern core, solidifying support for a protective tariff. Republicans also tried to convince industrial workers that high tariffs meant big profits for industry and thus higher wages for workers.

Civil War pension legislation began in 1861 with an act of Congress guaranteeing all volunteers the same benefits accruing to members of the regular army—that is, pensions to the disabled or to the widows or heirs of those killed in battle. As heavy losses on the Union side increased pension claims, the commissioner of pensions suspended all payments to agencies in southern states and struck from the rolls any person who had taken up arms against the government or who had encouraged or assisted the rebels.[66] At the close of the war pension offices were reopened in the South, but only those with proven loyalty to the Union were eligible. Thus many southern survivors of earlier wars lost all their pension rights.

An act of 1862 formalized the basic system, grading payments by rank and level of disability. Soldiers were required to apply formally for pension benefits, providing evidence of military service and disability. If a veteran filed an application within one year of discharge, benefits started with the discharge date. Otherwise the pension was paid as of the date of application.[67]

Republican support for increased pension benefits was closely linked to the party's position on tariffs. During the Civil War the output of woolen mills increased so dramatically that dividends in the industry tripled; cotton mills, though they reduced their output, made high profits on what they sold, and railroads carried record quantities of freight. The higher wages of skilled workers, whose numbers increased after the war, also enlarged the home market for manufactured goods. When the war ended, northern manufacturers embarked on a campaign to increase protection for the expanding home industries, a feat readily accomplished now that southern lawmakers had temporarily left Washington. In 1864 Congress raised tariffs generously, and by the end of the war tariff rates averaged 47 percent, more than double the rates of 1857.[68]

Customs receipts not only repaid the war debt but also created a politically significant budget surplus. In subsequent years Congress further liberalized pension regulations to include benefits for dependent widows, mothers, fathers, and orphans, including orphaned siblings, and to allow attorneys who helped disabled veterans in processing pension claims to collect larger fees.[69] Further politicization of the system occurred in 1866 when Congress granted the president the right to appoint pension claims agents in all pension offices throughout the country.[70] Thus pensions served two functions for Republicans: they significantly reduced the politically troubling Treasury surplus, and they became a part of the party's patronage system.

Three years after the war's end, Congress was bombarded with private pension claims from those who had missed the filing deadline. As a result it extended the filing period to permit back claims. Although the bill's aim was to ensure that aid went to all eligible veterans, it unintentionally created substantial variations in individual benefits. When concerned veterans challenged the inequities in payments, Congress considered an arrears bill to provide full back payments (based on the date of discharge) for all new and existing pension claims. Although southern congressmen opposed the Arrears of Pension Act, they did not have a majority, and in 1878 the measure passed in the House. Veterans and claims agents, who had built enormous practices in Washington, D.C., lobbied heavily, circulating letters and petitions directed at senators up for reelection the following winter. In 1879 the Senate passed the arrears bill with little debate. All the negative votes came from the South.[71]

Passage of the Arrears of Pension Act further politicized the pension issue. New claims flooded the Pension Bureau, stimulated largely by the Grand Army of the Republic (GAR), an organization of Civil War veterans, which grew from 45,000 members in 1879 to 215,000 by 1885.[72]

By 1881 southern Democrats had regained control of the Democratic party.[73] The Treasury surplus was the major issue on the agenda of the first session of the forty-seventh Congress. Senator John Williams (D-Ky.) presented an extensive argument for tariff reduction, which he followed with a motion to repeal the Arrears of Pension Act. Although other southerns senators argued that Congress has passed the original arrears bill under duress because of pressure from veterans' organizations and that the act had stimulated thousands of claims, many fraudulent, Republicans countered that "this most sacred of all our national obligations" could easily be paid out of the overflowing Treasury.[74] In the Republican-dominated Senate, the Democratic challenge was easily overridden.

When the GAR next held its annual encampment, it established a permanent standing committee on pensions and adopted an aggressive lobbying strategy for improved benefits. Petitions poured into Washington by the hundreds, not only from individuals and from Grand Army posts, but also from the legislatures of those states with large numbers of Civil War veterans—Iowa, New York, and Ohio.[75]

Although the interests of the pensioners and the high-tariff advocates did not fully merge until a few years later, at this time the GAR recognized that any reduction of the budget surplus threatened pension appropriations. Consequently the organization urged veterans to support high-tariff legislation. As GAR officials warned members:

> In the midst of their discussions as to the merits of the various pension and bounty measures now pending before Congress, there is one thing that our veterans should keep constantly in mind, namely, the danger that the present revenues of the Government will be so reduced by legislative action as to leave no surplus in the Treasury out of which the amount required for the carrying out of any of these new pension and bounty measures can be appropriated. . . . It matters not what their politics may be, or whether they are believers in the doctrine of free trade or protection, [our former soldiers] have a common interest in preventing this reduction, since it would afford an excuse, if not a justification for a refusal by Congress to further consider our claims upon it.[76]

Thus, although the midwestern farm states were part of the agrarian periphery in terms of their world trade position, the northeastern core "purchased" support for protection from this region by redistributing the income derived from the high tariff to Union veterans. As Bensel explains: "This massive tariff-pension engine of economic development fused the interests of industrializing urban centers with rural native populations which had a high percentage of Union veterans. The sections that clearly 'paid' for these development policies were the cash-crop exporting South and, unique among major industrial areas of the North, New York City."[77] New York City joined the tariff foes because of the high proportion of immigrants who were ineligible for Civil War pensions.

In the presidential campaign of 1884, the Democrats pledged to reduce the Treasury surplus. The only reference to pensions was a vague promise to use internal revenue taxes to pay existing pension commitments. By contrast, the Republicans made a clear appeal to the veterans, pledging that pensions for invalid soldiers "shall begin with the date of disability or discharge, and not with the date of application."[78]

During the campaign the Pension Bureau, which had already become a graft-ridden Republican political machine, stepped up its political activities. W. W. Dudley, commissioner of pensions, left his office in Washington to campaign on behalf of the Republican ticket.

He worked extensively in Ohio and Indiana, where he instructed clerks to reject no pension applications until after the election and to take the claims from Ohio and Indiana over other outstanding claims. He also doubled the number of examiners in Ohio in the months preceding the election, using them as organizers in the Republican campaign.[79]

Despite extensive lobbying by veterans' organizations, Grover Cleveland defeated the Republican presidential candidate. Cleveland forced Dudley to resign and reorganized the divisions of the Pension Bureau.[80] To counter Cleveland's actions, Republicans began sponsoring numerous private pension bills to compensate veterans for the loss of readily obtainable benefits through the Pension Bureau. Cleveland, in turn, examined every private bill passed by Congress and vetoed those he believed were based on fraudulent evidence or doubtful constructions of the law. In all he rejected 233 private pension bills during his first term. Attempts to override Cleveland's vetoes produced a clear sectional split. Southern congressmen unanimously voted against overriding the vetoes, whereas northern representatives, regardless of party, voted consistently in favor of the claimant.[81]

The Republicans controlled the Senate, and in 1886 they passed a dependent pension bill, granting a pension to all disabled or dependent soldiers regardless of the origin of their disability. Although the measure also passed the House, Cleveland vetoed it, justifying his action on the grounds that it would "have the effect of disappointing the expectation of the people and their desire and hope for relief from war taxation in time of peace."[82] An attempt to override the veto failed, with support for the veto coming from southern Democrats.

Cleveland's veto unleashed a storm of protest from the GAR, which berated him as a "mere tool of the South." At its annual encampment, the GAR split between advocates of a disability pension like the dependent pension bill vetoed by Cleveland and those who argued for an even more liberal measure, a universal service pension payable to all veterans whether or not they were disabled.[83] The latter was in essence a plea for a straight old age pension, since many of the veterans were now aging and in need of relief, but the final proposal put forth was similar to the one vetoed.

The veterans also continued to resist tariff reform. When a soldier objected to the GAR-sponsored *National Tribune*'s advocacy of a protective tariff, an editorial explained: "Our only motive for doing it is because, for the present, a Protective Tariff and pension legislation are closely connected. The Free Traders are opposed to pension legislation because that will make a use for the money derived from duties on imports."[84]

On 12 December 1887, Republicans introduced the GAR bill into the Senate. Senator James Beck, (D-Ky.) injected a new element into the debate, objecting on the grounds that it would drain the surplus in the Treasury while protecting monopolies:

> [This bill] has been drawn in the interest of the great trust companies and pooling combinations of the country, in the interest of the protected monopolists, who have been robbing the tax-payers for years . . . when every man can be clamored down as an enemy of the country and an enemy of the soldier who does not move up and vote away all the money demanded . . . the protected barons who are now perfecting trusts . . . devised under tariff protection to plunder the country by all sorts of illegal schemes, could not invent a better way to do it than to have the propositions made by this bill carried out.[85]

In a nation growing apprehensive of the monopolistic trusts formed by large corporations, the Democrats had found one more weapon in the tariff battle with the northeastern core. The highly partisan bill passed the Senate and was reported in the Democratic House, but it was never acted upon.

The 1888 election became the "great tariff debate." Cleveland opened his campaign with a strong antitariff stance, while the Republicans boldly identified themselves with protectionism.[86] To ensure veterans' continued support, the Republicans also linked their party platform even more closely to pension benefits, nominating a former soldier, Benjamin Harrison, as their candidate. The GAR rewarded their efforts by endorsing Harrison in the *National Tribune*.

Republicans renewed their appeal to wage laborers, arguing that industrial profits from tariffs would be passed on to workers in the form of higher wages. Although the American Federation of Labor refused to place a pro-tariff plank in its platform, many segments of labor were convinced that high tariffs would protect workers. In the late 1880s the National Amalgamated Association of Iron, Steel and Tin Workers sent delegates to Congress to plead for protection and marched as a body for the Republican party. Even though Democrats countered that high tariffs increased prices to consumers, that the taxes fell more heavily upon the poor than upon the wealthy, and that independent small businesses were destroyed as tariffs supported large manufacturers, their arguments largely fell on deaf ears.[87]

Thus Republicans succeeded in creating a pro-tariff coalition out of diverse groups whose interests might otherwise have led them into the free-trade camp.

While the Republicans unified protectionists, veterans, and northern wageworkers, growing dissension within the Democratic party over the tariff issue cost Cleveland critical support. Pockets of protectionist sentiment existed in the South in Louisiana, where sugar tariffs made a substantial contribution to the Treasury surplus, in Alabama, site of thriving new coal and iron industries, and in West Virginia, where mining interests existed, as well as in several northern states with strong Democratic factions. Militant tariff reductionists within the Democratic party refused to compromise, and several key supporters deserted Cleveland.[88]

Harrison won the election, and his ability to carry Indiana and New York, with 38,000 and 45,000 pensioners, respectively, was a large factor in his victory.[89] In the 1888 election the Republicans also gained control of both branches of Congress, although in the House the Republicans held a majority of only twenty. Thus, southern congressmen still had substantial obstructionist power, even if they could not push legislation through.

Republicans took their victory as a mandate for protection as well as an indication of the veterans' political strength, and the Harrison administration came to power strongly committed to further pension legislation and to maintaining protective tariffs. The McKinley tariff reform bill, reported out of the House Ways and Means Committee on 16 April 1890, passed the House one month later on a strict party vote. Passed by the Senate on 10 September, the bill became law on 1 October 1890. What made it possible to pass a bill granting increased protection to manufacturers was its provision for midwestern farmers, which gave midwestern agricultural products almost complete protection against foreign competition. In contrast, Congress defeated attempts by southern senators to get cotton bagging and other cotton-related products on the duty-free list.[90] Thus a complex tariff proposal strengthened the alliance between northern manufacturers and midwestern farmers at the expense of the cotton-producing South.

Immediately after his inauguration, Harrison also reorganized the Pension Bureau. His new commissioner of pensions, James Tanner, was a former GAR pension committee member who had lobbied for more liberal pension legislation. To eliminate the Treasury surplus, Tanner used the practice of "rerating" to increase pension benefits, even rerating some pensioners who had made no application and sending them checks for thousands of dollars in back pensions. When an Interior Department investigation found substantial evidence of the misuse of funds, Tanner was forced to resign, but his replacement, Green Raum, continued to engage in questionable practices in dispensing pension funds.[91]

At its annual 1889 encampment, the GAR again proposed two bills, one a disability bill with no requirement that the disability be service connected and with no dependency clause, the other a service-pension bill, granting a pension to each honorably discharged veteran.[92] Harrison recommended the more moderate disability bill, which included a means test in its eligibility requirements. In the House many congressmen supported service-pension legislation, while the Senate supported a modified disability measure. The GAR-backed Kansas senator attempted to liberalize the Senate bill by adding a service pension for those who had served at least ninety days in the Civil War and were sixty-two years of age. By this measure the military pension system would have been converted into a de facto old age pension for most white, native-born northern and midwestern citizens.

Sectional conflict characterized the Senate debate over the dependent pension bill. Southern senators, who submitted a minority report to the Committee on Invalid Pensions, particularly objected to a section of the bill removing the limitations on the arrears law, which had ceased operating in 1880. The new provisions extended eligibility to those who had never before applied for a pension, thus potentially raising costs enormously. New Hampshire Senator Henry Blair defended the extension, declaring that patriotic men who had never made a claim upon the government "at last with age and infirmity increasing upon them" had the right to establish their claims. The time had come, he argued, for "the American people to think of something besides the tariff and material wealth."[93]

By 1889 pension expenditures, at $92,309,688, consumed 27 percent of total federal expenditures, and southerners found an unexpected ally in their opposition to the high costs among northern manufacturers.[94] Several factors influenced the growth of a free-trade faction within the business community. One was the desire of iron-consuming northern manufacturers to reduce duties on this product, as their goods grew less competitive with those produced in the thriving iron mills of the newly industrializing South. Another factor was the expansion of big business into foreign markets. As the limited home market forced large corporations to direct their energies toward foreign markets, exports grew substantially.

American business's more favorable attitude toward exports reduced tariff support in some sectors and divided the previously united front of the manufacturing community.[95]

By the late nineteenth century, big business exerted considerable impact on national policy decisions through its increased organizational capacity. Business leaders originally formed the National Association of Manufacturers (NAM) to extend foreign trade, and the tactics the organization chose to pursue this objective, lobbying through politicians and working from within the Republican party, made it visible and effective in national politics. Although divisions within the NAM on tariff reform moved the organization to redirect its energies to supporting the open shop and working against protective labor legislation, other business organizations continued to support trade expansion.[96]

Business pressure against the costly pension program arose during the dependent pension bill debate, in which Blair (R-N.H.) argued: "I say to Senators who are pressing this measure that they are imperiling the truest interests of the soldiers when they undertake to enact it into a law, and they will create a prejudice against pensions amongst the business interests of this country which Congress can not overleap and will not dare to." While Blair "would not care to see an old soldier going to the almshouse," he feared the heavy costs of extending the arrears legislation. When the final votes were tallied, this portion of the bill garnered little support, and it failed to pass.[97] Thus, increasing business interest in international trade expansion divided the core sector on tariff reform and intervened indirectly into the pension issue.

The issue of age arose again when Republicans introduced an amendment automatically extending the Civil War pension to all veterans and dependents over sixty-two. Basing eligibility on age rather than military service would have radically altered the definition of a pension. If passed, the measure would have extended support to most older northerners. Northern senators argued that an age-based pension would preserve the veterans from the stigma of the poorhouse, but a bipartisan coalition, fearful of the potential costs, defeated the measure. In the final vote the dependent pension bill passed in the Senate with the support of only one southern senator.[98]

At this critical point in American history a national old age pension proposal suffered defeat. Moderate opposition came from some manufacturers exporting American goods in an expanding world economy, who saw disadvantages in protectionist policies. Southern congressmen had no incentive to support welfare legislation for the aged of the Northeast and Midwest when funding for this measure would exacerbate existing inequalities between North and South.

A conference committee labored for weeks over the legislation, withdrawing both the service-and-age feature and the dependency clause. The final bill extended pension eligibility to any veteran with ninety days of service who was incapacitated from performing manual labor. Any woman who had married a veteran before 27 June 1890 was eligible for widow's benefits. In heated House debate over the compromise legislation, John Sawyer (R-N.Y.) attacked the southern congressman, charging that "the majority of the Democratic party here today who vote at all will vote against this measure as they have voted against every measure of a general character that has been brought in on pensions." The roll call vote confirmed Sawyer's suspicions: not one southern congressman voted yes.[99] The act of 1890 was a Republican compromise, which satisfied the veterans' organizations without going to the extreme of a simple service pension bill.[100]

The Dependent Pension Act of 1890 caused an immediate and substantial increase in the amount of pension expenditures. In 1889 Congress budgeted $80,500,000 for pensions. By 1893 the cost of pensions had risen to $165,000,000, the largest single appropriation ever made for a government expenditure, and by 1894 pensions consumed more than 37 percent of the entire federal budget.[101]

Southerners had good reason to complain, for within months abuses of the pension system multiplied.[102] Unscrupulous pension attorneys and claim agents, who received substantial processing fees, pushed through thousands of fradulent claims. Further, the program expansion also expanded the size of the Pension Bureau, creating the single largest source of patronage appointments for the Republican party. By 1898 the Pension Bureau consisted of a commissioner, two deputy commissioners, and 1,740 subordinate officials, clerks, and messengers. It also included a field force of 300 special examiners and 4,663 examining physicians, whose fees in one year alone came to $950,000.[103]

Because of preferences granted under civil service legislation, most Pension Bureau staff members were Civil War veterans. As late as 1919, when many of the veterans were dead, the commissioner of pensions claimed that 90 of his 878 employees had served in the Civil War.[104] As one critic bitterly complained, "The position of examining surgeon for pensions became a reward for political activity in the interest of the party in power."[105]

In spite of some Pension Bureau efforts to economize, inequities in the regional distribution of wealth continued within the military

pension system. In 1901, for example, the entire South received
$9,996,674 in federal pension funds, or $300,000 less than the
disbursements for Indiana alone and $5,200,000 less than the funds
received by Ohio alone for that same year. One southern college
professor, who had extensively analyzed the pension system, argued:

> In a scheme for distributing public money, raised by uniform
> taxation throughout the country, no one will claim that this is
> fair apportionment. If the act of 1890 were well guarded and
> sound in principle, the South might well regard her disadvan-
> tage as the necessary result of an unsuccessful war, and hence
> refrain from complaint. But, since this part of the pension
> system involved an inequitable and oppressive disposition of
> the public funds, it is the right and duty of the South to
> protest.[106]

Another observer estimated that since the war the South had
indirectly paid $350,000,000 to pension Union soldiers. As late as
1910, fifty years after the Civil War pension program began, the
average per capita amount received in Ohio was $3.36, in New York,
$1.49, and in Indiana $3.90. In contrast, Georgia, Alabama,
Mississippi, North Carolina, South Carolina, and Louisiana all had a
per capita average of less than 50¢. In South Carolina it was only
19¢.[107]

Although the United States had the financial capacity to implement national old age pensions, as indicated by its support of a vast
and expensive military pension system, no such measure was
forthcoming. While logic predicts that political support for a national
pension should have come from the South, where relief was most
inadequate, no mass movement arose from this quarter.

There are a number of reasons why pressure for a federal old age
pension did not arise in the South. One was that citizens lacked input
into the political system. By the turn of the century most southerners
had been disfranchised, and southern politicians did not have to
worry much about constituents demanding benefits. Another factor
was southerners' suspicion of any expansion of authority that had
previously been used to intervene in the political and economic
structure of the South. Further, the South's experience with the
military pension system had left it mistrustful of government
bureaucratic agencies, which at this time were a source of Republican
patronage jobs for Civil War veterans. Even if southern congressmen
had chosen to press for a national old age pension to relieve the
regional inequities in the distribution of federal funds caused by the
Civil War pension system, their efforts would have been unsuccessful.

During the late nineteenth and early twentieth centuries, the Democrats were not the controlling party. The South's chief source of power was its negative ability to impede legislation, not a positive ability to legislate new programs.

After a 1906 amendment defined age sixty-two as a permanent disability, the Civil War pension system provided economic support for about 60 percent of the dependent elderly. The number of Civil War pensioners peaked in 1901 at 997,735 and then gradually declined as the aged veterans and their dependents died. By 1917, 673,111 pensioners were left.[108] Thus, as native-born Americans found either the almshouses or harshly administered systems of outrelief the only source of public support in old age, the need for state old age pensions grew.

Conclusion

In comparing the poor law tradition of the Northeast and Midwest with that of the South, this chapter has demonstrated that changes in poor law policy reflected broader patterns of economic change. As capitalist expansion in the nineteenth century proletarianized the labor force and made wage labor the prevalent way of organizing production in the North, the poor law responded by shifting from a minimal system of relief for the more helpless members of society to a harshly administered program of labor control for unemployed wage workers. In the South, by contrast, under the feudalistic plantation mode of production, responsibility for slaves and later for tenants rested with the planter. External sources of relief were absent, because any regularized input of funds into a plantation economy would have undermined planter control over a subservient black labor force. Thus, while relief came under the jurisdiction of more centralized government units elsewhere in the nation, the resistance of the South to even the most minimal consolidation at the local level made consolidation at the national level impossible.

The evolution of the poor laws in the North provides support for, though not absolute proof of, the central thesis delineated in chapter 1—that welfare systems respond to changes in the social relations of production. In this broad scenario the South is a historical anomaly. In contrast to other agrarian societies requiring a permanent labor supply, the plantation mode of production provided a substitute for the labor-control mechanism embedded in traditional poor laws. Thus, what we find in the South is not an anachronistic relief system— that is, anachronistic by the standards of an industrializing nation— but virtually no public welfare at all.

Sectional conflict between North and South, stemming from the regions' different trade positions in the world economy, had a major impact on the development of the military pension system and thus on political support for a national old age pension. The military pension system evolved in the context of an increasingly heated battle between northeastern manufacturers and cotton-exporting southern planters over the value of a protective tariff. Tariffs were linked to pensions because they were the sole funding source for the system throughout the nineteenth century. Southern congressmen, whose disadvantageous position increased after the Civil War when southern claimants were excluded from pension benefits, were convinced that tariff relief could occur only by containing the growth of military pensions.

A number of conclusions can be drawn about how the state functions in the development of welfare programs. The military pension system in the United States operated as a de facto national old age pension, at one point supporting a greater proportion of older people than those who received support under old age insurance in the twentieth century. As a precursor to a national welfare state that most likely dampened demand for a federal pension, the Civil War pension system and the politics that accompanied it address many broader theoretical issues.

One of the more important lessons relates to our understanding of the alignment of class factions in the state. Class conflict over benefits was not between capital and labor but placed northern manufacturers in opposition to southern cotton planters; organized labor had no influence within the state. To the extent that working-class interests were represented, they were mobilized through a cross-class coalition between northern manufacturers and Civil War veterans. What impeded proposals for a national pension in this period was a political agenda that had little to do with benefits per se. Rather, the core issue was the tariff, the source of funding for pensions, which favored home manufacturers at the expense of cotton exporters. Throughout the tariff debates, the matrix of social power continually shifted as southerners first lost, then regained, power in the state hierarchy. As the matrix of power changed, so did the fate of the pension.

When changes in the power matrix within the state altered the environment of decision making, the tariff-pension issue lost its sectional character. Incipient industrialization in the South had created a class of entrepreneurs who supported some protection, while trade expansion in the world economy increased the market for American goods and lessened the interest of monopoly capitalists in tariffs. Further, the natural attrition of Civil War veterans and their dependents and the extension of eligibility to include Spanish-American War veterans and World War I veterans nationalized the distribution of pension benefits. This fact, combined with the passage of income tax legislation in 1913, loosened the link between tariff revenues and pension expenditures and paved the way for a national old age pension.

Yet none was forthcoming. Although sectional conflict between North and South served as a drag on the American welfare state, the struggle for old age pensions took place in a different arena. The next two chapters examine how the growth of industrial capitalism shaped the position of labor and capital on national welfare benefits. Chapter 3 focuses on the pattern of unionization, analyzing how the self-protective philosophy of craft workers and the delayed unionization of an industrial protelariat affected the orientation of the working class toward state benefits. Chapter 4 examines the impact of private-sector initiatives on employers' orientations toward public welfare.

Make Him Smell It.

Fig. 3 *The Eagle Magazine,* May 1924, p. 10.

3

Organized Labor and State Old Age Pensions

Throughout the first two decades of the twentieth century, the deaths of the aging Civil War veterans and their dependents reduced the number of older people eligible for military pensions. At the same time public poor relief became less generous, as cities reacted to the depressions of the 1880s and 1890s by eliminating outdoor aid entirely. The impact on older people was decidedly negative, with surveys indicating that the decrease in public aid had increased need among the elderly. For example, the New York Commission on Old Age Security found that between 38 percent and 75 percent of aged individuals and between 10 percent and 48 percent of aged couples fell below the basic income level necessary for survival.[1] Other surveys found similar patterns of old age dependency.

According to the "logic of industrialism" thesis, welfare programs are predicated on need. Since need was apparently greater at the beginning of the twentieth century than in precious decades, a national old age pension should have been legislated at this time. Why then was no such measure forthcoming? One explanation, derived from the social democratic model, locates the failure of the United States to enact social benefits in the weakness of the American labor movement. Organized labor was absent from the national political scene and thus lacked the ability to influence social policy. But to fairly assess labor's political participation in American politics before 1935, it is necessary to examine the state rather than the national level, since the state was the locus of nearly all social legislation until the 1930s.

During the 1920s several states passed old age pension laws. What was the extent of labor's involvement? On the one hand, substantial evidence exists that organized labor was ineffectual at the state level. According to Ann Orloff, the ten states in which pension laws were enacted in the 1920s were not "the relatively well-organized states of America's industrial heartland" but those with relatively low levels of unionization.[2] On the other hand, a study of the proceedings of eighteen state labor federations concludes that "even before the 1920s, labor consistently and aggressively supported state welfare, and during that decade, it was labor organizations and their constituencies which formed the popular foundation of the campaign for old age pensions. . . . Their support was not displayed in the banners of national labor organizations, but it was likely the bedrock of local political strength."[3]

How can these apparently contradictory results be explained? According to Gosta Esping-Anderson's findings from his comparative study of Norway, Sweden, and Denmark, labor does not consist of a single class faction. Rather, industrial workers are more inclined than craft workers to support broad social benefits.[4] The success or failure of the American labor movement in obtaining welfare benefits may depend on which faction of labor is examined. Since skilled craft workers exhibited different patterns of unionization than industrial workers, resulting from their orientation to the social process of production, they should show different orientations to welfare programs.

PENSIONS FOR CRAFT WORKERS

In the earliest phase of capitalist development, craft workers maintained control over the productive process. Their autonomy rested upon their skills, which made them self-directing at their tasks. As large firms expanded in the late nineteenth century, the control and ownership of capital came to reside in fewer hands.[5] To resolve problems of labor productivity employers implemented the "drive" system, which involved increased mechanization, more intense supervision, and decreasing reliance on skilled workers.[6] The result was a loss of autonomy for many craft workers and the homogenization of the work force, which reduced mass-production jobs to a common, semiskilled denominator.

Confronted with changes in the labor process that threatened to remove the protective features of craft work, including the freedom to practice one's craft into old age, skilled workers united early into craft-based unions. Two factors made craft unions uninterested in the state as a vehicle for protecting labor. First, by the early twentieth century, giant industrial firms had gained political ascendancy, resulting in government policies about labor relations that were mainly concerned with the circumstances of large-scale industry. Government policies contributed little to relationships between workers and employers in craft-based industries.[7] Second, the negative experience of craft unions with the legislatures and courts, which had consistently favored employers on labor issues, made unions suspicious of state intervention. To maintain the prerogatives of craft autonomy, they chose self-protection.

By contrast, the emerging class of semiskilled and unskilled workers did not find self-protection a viable mechanism for old age security. Less committed to voluntarism, these workers believed the state could be an instrument of organized collective action. It is from their ranks that a movement for state old age pensions arose. This chapter will explore these two directions taken by organized labor as it attempted to resolve the dilemma of old age dependency.

Self-Protection through Labor Unions

Although employers succeeded in destroying much of the craft autonomy that had characterized nineteenth-century production, in some occupations workers were able to resist the intrusions of homogenization. Craft structures persisted in industries with a sufficiently low division of labor to require skill in a large number of jobs. Even when mechanization changed the labor process in such industries as construction and printing, the demand for skilled workers encouraged the growth of strong unions. Through strike actions and negotiations, these unions prevented employers from replacing skilled labor with standardized production.[8] By limiting the division of labor, craft workers won a collective monopoly over access to jobs in local labor markets. As a result, skilled workers in certain industries were able to maintain viable national unions.

A central goal of early twentieth-century unions was to preserve autonomy, the "culture of control" built around craft traditions.[9] Worker self-protection through union benefit programs was one mechanism for preserving autonomy and winning the loyalty of workers to unions rather than to employers or the state. American Federation of Labor (AFL) president Samuel Gompers recognized the potential contribution of old age pensions to union growth and stability quite early, noting that union pensions were invaluable in "holding and binding the membership together in a bond of human sympathy, winning the admiration and respect of even those who are opposed to union organization," and preventing government intervention.[10] Initially, however, unions were not interested in initiating benefit programs, because such issues as raising wages, reducing hours, and restoring autonomy through the enforcement of union work rules were of more immediate concern.[11]

In 1891 four railroad brotherhoods established the first institution to care for old and disabled union members. Its purpose was "to provide a home for worthy, aged, helpless, and destitute railroad men

who are no longer able to provide for themselves."[12] In the same year
the International Typographical Union also opened a home for its
aged members. Thus, those unions with strong craft traditions and
national organizational capacity were first to initiate programs for the
aged.

It soon became apparent, however, that old age homes could not
cope with the needs of aged members. Many more members were
disabled because of age and infirmity than could be accommodated in
the homes, and others eligible for admittance refused to go because of
family and community ties.[13] Clearly, a different type of benefit was
needed. The Granite Cutters' International Association became the
pension pioneer, establishing an old age pension in 1905. The
International Typographical Union followed suit in 1907 and began
paying out pensions in 1909.[14]

Before World War I two other internationals adopted pension
schemes, but a number of impediments prevented the move for
union pensions from gaining momentum.[15] One was the erosion of
craft work, which not only weakened the craft unions but also
changed the nature of unionism. The AFL had originally adopted the
principle of craft autonomy to further its belief that workers in each
distinct occupational group should form their own union. As early as
1901 the United Mine Workers (UMW), the one strong union
representing the unskilled and skilled workers, resisted the craft
structure, claiming jurisdiction over all jobs in and around mines
regardless of craft or occupation. In succeeding years other craft
unions began to redefine their boundaries beyond the original crafts.
In 1911 the AFL formally abandoned craft autonomy as the central
structural principle of the organization, and by 1915 only 28 of 133
affiliates could still be described as pure craft organizations.[16] Thus
structural changes in craft unionism eroded the principle of self-
protection.

World War I strengthened labor's position. Between 1916 and
1919 AFL membership increased from 2,072,702 to 3,260,168.
Membership peaked in 1920 at 5,047,800, almost 20 percent of the
nonagricultural work force.[17] With membership increasing, organized labor had no trouble maintaining pension funds out of union
dues. Between 1910 and 1920 seven more unions initiated pension
plans, most during the war years.[18]

The wartime gains were short-lived. Unions that had prospered
under the government's protection lost membership in succeeding
years. In fact the unions that best maintained their membership
strength were those that had received no government aid during the
war. In the next decade union membership dropped precipitously.

By 1929 it had declined to 3,622,000, barely 10 percent of the nation's employees.[19]

Several factors eroded the unions' wartime gains. One primary factor was the consolidation of corporate power. In each of the major industries, the centralization of capital had transformed the market, with competition among the many replaced by collusion among the few.[20] Large corporations used their expanded power to intensify the suppression of labor unions. Supported by the courts, employers engaged in direct union-busting activities, using injunctions and "yellow dog" contracts to break strikes and eliminate unions from firms. They also attempted to woo workers by experimenting with welfare capitalist programs and by establishing formal grievance procedures through company unions.[21]

Other factors inhibiting unionism included the emergence of new industries—automobile, utilities, chemicals, and rubber—that were bitterly antagonistic to unions and the migration of older industrial enterprises to the South, where unionization was almost nonexistent. The business cycle also neutralized the prospect for union growth. The increase in real wages allowed workers to raise their standard of living, while unemployment prevented a labor shortage that could have enhanced labor's bargaining power.[22]

The decline of craft unionism spelled the demise of workers' self-protection. As fewer new members contributed dues to union coffers, pension funds shrank. To cope with financial insolvency, unions that had been paying pensions regularly were forced to take increasingly harsh measures. A number of unions discontinued benefits entirely.[23] Others discontinued provisions for widows or imposed increasingly stringent eligibility requirements.[24] By 1930 only eleven out of more than one hundred national and international labor organizations were paying pension benefits to approximately 13,000 pensioners.[25]

The homogenization of labor had undermined the capacity of craft unions to recruit new members, while direct attacks on unions had further decimated membership. These factors, combined with an economic crisis, made organized labor clearly aware that paying pensions by cash disbursement, that is, out of funds generated each year, created a fragile system readily subject to collapse. In contrast to its earlier advocacy of union pensions, by 1929 the AFL warned its members, "Old age pension plans should be undertaken with the greatest caution. Plans developed without adequate knowledge of the particular circumstances to be met may involve the union in serious financial difficulties.[26] The result was an increasing willingness on the part of union leaders to support state old age pensions.

One of the oldest and strongest of the craft unions, the International Typographical Union illustrates the difficulties faced by all craft unions in maintaining solvent pension programs under the onslaught of homogenization.

THE INTERNATIONAL TYPOGRAPHICAL UNION: A CASE STUDY IN WORKER SELF-PROTECTION

Of all the internationals associated with the AFL, the most successful was the International Typographical Union (ITU). Using conservative tactics, the union garnered a virtual monopoly over jobs in the newspaper branch of the printing industry. According to labor historians Selig Perlman and Philip Taft:

> The International Typographical Union boasts of the longest continuous history of any labor organization in the United States. Conservative in its methods and hesitant to precipitate an open break, the Typographical Union has exhibited throughout its history a patient and dogged determination to improve the conditions of its members, and has succeeded in gaining the most complete control over job conditions of any union in the world.[27]

In 1907 the ITU established one of the first trade union pensions for the relief of aged and indigent printers. The union initiated the pension fund during a tumultuous period in its history, as it fought for the eight-hour day. Although the union emerged victorious from the strike, many union members lost their jobs. Older men, who found it impossible to find work, began to press the union for relief. At its 1907 international convention, union officials argued that the organization had a moral obligation to support the older men's claims. As a result, the membership voted to finance a pension out of the assessment made during the struggle for a shorter day.[28] To qualify for a pension, a member had to be at least sixty years of age and to have had continuous membership for twenty years.

The pension fund helped stabilize union membership and served as a useful organizing tool. As union membership grew, the dues of newly recruited members maintained the fund's solvency. The relative youth of the membership and the gradual increase in the assessment, which was based on a percentage of wages, balanced claims against the pension fund. During its first five years of operation, the fund maintained a large balance of receipts over expenditures, because there were few claims. Further, an increasing membership and rising earnings combined to swell the dues. In 1910 and then again in 1911 the union liberalized eligibility requirements for pensions and increased the benefit from four dollars a week to five. By 1916, however, payments exceeded receipts, and in 1917 the liberalized eligibility clauses were repealed.[29]

During the war the ITU, like many other unions, experienced rapid growth, and average wages rose sharply. The pension fund again accumulated a surplus, and an aging membership vociferously demanded a benefit increase.[30] At the annual convention in 1920 the membership voted to increase benefits to eight dollars a week.

By 1925 the pension fund had been operating for sixteen years. Although ITU president James Lynch declared proudly that "ethically and economically the plan has been found right and sound," conditions were changing rapidly.[31] In just one year the number of pensioners had increased by 236, the greatest increase since the funds' establishment, and assets were declining. Although officers noted that the average age at death had increased from 41.25 in 1900 to 57.68 in 1925, still members continued to agitate for an increase in the pension. In 1925 the union was as yet unready to heed the officers' dire warning: "The figures clearly show that an increase in the pension is impossible and indicate that the organization, in its zeal to provide for the declining years of its aged and incapacitated members, has gone much further than the revenue of the pension fund warrants and a more conservative policy should have been followed."[32]

To protect the retirement security of the younger members, the officers recommended either reducing pension benefits to the amount the reserve could bear or increasing the pension assessment. Other suggestions from the officers included increasing the eligibility age from sixty to sixty-five, requiring sick and unemployed union members to continue paying dues, forcing those who joined the union after age forty-five to waive the right to a pension, and discontinuing the practice of allowing retired members to work two days a week and still receive a pension. Union officials were especially concerned about this last policy, because it was not carefully monitored, and pensioners sometimes worked full time at wages below union scale while continuing to receive a pension. Pensions thus subsidized older workers while undermining union wage scales.[33]

The membership, which refused either to raise assessments or to reduce pension benefits, finally reached a compromise after a heated floor battle. The new policies raised the age of eligibility and discontinued the policy of allowing members to work two days a week. The solution left the fiscal problem virtually untouched, except that a portion of mortuary fund earnings was transferred to the pension fund. The struggle left such a residue of bitterness, however, that Lynch, who had been president since 1902, was defeated in the next election.[34]

A 1927 report by a special committee appointed to study the pension question noted that although raising the eligibility age had temporarily stabilized the pension fund, the rule change was harmful to many older men. Since the mean retirement age was much higher than the eligibility age, raising the eligibility age had unfairly penalized a few disabled men nearing sixty who had counted on receiving a pension. Most older men did not seize upon the pension as an excuse to retire.[35]

After perusing these figures, the membership voted to reduce the pension age back to sixty, but only for those who had had a continuous union membership of twenty-five years and were unemployed because of age or disability. The commission's report closed with the hope that public pensions would one day allow unions to liquidate their pension funds.[36] The typographers had already learned that even in relatively prosperous times an aging membership placed union funds in fiscal difficulty and that state support for welfare activities was an eventual necessity.

In the following years the number of pensioners on the rolls increased again. The new slate of officers, elected on a promise not to reduce pension benefits, now endorsed state pensions wholeheartedly. The executive council was given the task of drafting a model old age pension bill for use by state federations and city central bodies in the struggle to get pension legislation enacted. In the same year, the union voted down motions to increase the pension and to extend pension benefits to widows and dependents.[37]

On the eve of the Great Depression, the ITU found its reserve fund greatly depleted owing to an increase of almost $20,000 in pension expenditures over the previous year. Wage rates had dropped, decreasing revenues, while unemployment increased the demand for pensions from older members. Yet the membership remained firmly opposed to any raise in dues or to any increase in the eligibility age. The one possibility for stabilizing the pension fund permanently, a proposal to consider group insurance, was rejected for fear of being "subject to state or federal laws now in force or which may be enacted."[38] Although the union regarded state funding for pensions as an acceptable alternative to a union pension fund, business or state control over union funds was not acceptable.

With few alternatives left, the union was forced to implement eligibility criteria for pensions with increasing stringency. Members who did not meet the criteria in every respect were denied pensions. Joseph G. Brown, for example, who had accumulated thirty years of union membership and nineteen years of continuous service, was eighty-five years old and had been the first president of the Cripple Creek Typographical Union. Yet his pension request was denied on the grounds that he did not meet the criteria of continuous membership.[39] Similar grounds were used to deny a pension to a member who had broken his continuous service record when he was placed in a mental hospital for a year.

Between October 1929 and January 1930, joblessness increased from 492,000 to 4,065,000.[40] As wages dropped, gross aggregate earnings in the printing industry declined by 5.5 percent. Pension revenues decreased by $79,247, and a deficit in the fund was avoided only because of the interest earned from securities on reserve. Between 1930 and 1931 the number of pensioners on the rolls increased by nearly 350 to 3,343, and this comprised only 40 percent of those potentially eligible.[41]

In 1932 the combination of an aging membership, increasing life expectancy, decreased average wages, high unemployment, and a fund running on a nonreserve basis led to the inevitable crisis; for the first time the amount coming into the pension fund was eclipsed by the amount being paid out. The pension fund was running a deficit, and no relief was in sight. As the officers reported, "It is not now a question of whether something must be done as regards the pension fund. It is simply a matter of choice as to what is to be done."[42]

A vigorous floor debate about how to resolve the pension crisis ensued. Pro-pension delegates proposed increasing the pension, while fiscal conservatives suggested implementing a means test for eligibility. The membership finally agreed that "at no time shall the balance in the old age pension fund be permitted to fall below $2,000,000" and charged the executive council "to limit expenditures each fiscal year to accomplish this result."[43] The executive council fulfilled its charge by tightening eligibility requirements and increasing the assessment collected on earnings.

The increased assessment resolved the fiscal crisis but generated intergenerational conflict. The very existence of the union seemed threatened by the higher dues and by the fact that so much of the union's energy and resources went toward resolving the pension fund crisis. Officers pointed out, for example, that one George F. Tucker, who was placed on the pension roll in August 1908 after paying $101 in assessments, had collected $7,914 in benefits before his death in July 1932.[44] In contrast, it seemed likely that younger members would not get a full return on their assessments and might have no pension at all if present policy continued. Even more serious an issue was the impact the increased assessment had on recruitment. After lending the pension fund money from a special defense fund and increasing the assessment again in 1934, the officers reported that "the cost of membership in the International Union has become of such importance that the exemption of certain classes constituting large numbers of the members is becoming a menace. The control of the union should be in the hands of those whose principal interest is in wages, hours and working conditions."[45]

Union pension funds faced an almost unresolvable dilemma. Any action to keep the funds solvent meant increasing membership dues. Increased dues decreased membership and so decreased income into the pension fund. Further, attempts to resolve the pension crisis deflected union energies from the primary goal of collective bargaining for wage increases and job security. Organized craft workers had learned that pensions placed an insupportable burden on unions and that the problem of old age security could be resolved only by relying upon the taxing power of the state.

The Growth of Mass Production and the Erosion of Volunteerism

The AFL was not always opposed to political action. In its early years the leadership supported efforts to obtain labor legislation protecting the status of skilled workers, and the AFL maintained lobbies in Washington and in the state legislatures to carry out these political objectives.[46] Rather than affiliating with any political party, the AFL adopted a nonpartisan stance, hoping to play off competing parties in a bid to win the labor vote. Since many workers already had strong party affiliations, nonpartisanship seemed a more logical strategy than attempting to woo workers away from existing party loyalties.[47]

Owing to intensive lobbying, several state legislatures did pass important labor measures.[48] But labor's successes generated a counterresponse from employers, who began a mass offensive to defeat labor legislation and destroy unions. The National Association of Manufacturers, for example, took the open-shop drive as its trademark and became deeply involved in national politics, opposing labor legislation. Nationally, where large corporations were entrenched within the Republican party, the Sherman Antitrust Act became a strong anti-labor weapon, as courts used the act to interpret strikes as conspiracies in constraint of trade.[49]

Smaller businesses used the decentralized state structure to organize into special antistrike and antiunion leagues expressly to defeat unionism, and these associations provided a stepping-stone from local to national politics.[50] The American Anti-Boycott Association, for example, pressed court cases against boycotts and sympathy strikes, successfully establishing judicial precedents for injunctions and the assessment of damages against unions. At the local government level, police and magistrates liberally interpreted laws against trespass, traffic obstruction, disorderly conduct, and riot to break strikes.[51] Thus employers from both large and small companies not only worked within the marketplace to destroy the power of unions, they also took the battle to the state, using state power as a vehicle to supress unions.

As craft workers demobilized, industrial workers, centered in the Socialist movement, advocated the philosophy that the state could be a vehicle of organized collective action. Founded in 1901 on the heels of a defeated Socialist challange within the AFL, the Socialist party appealed to a different constituency, largely the masses of immigrants who filled the unskilled and semiskilled slots in the expanding industries of northeastern and midwestern cities.[52] By 1912 it had 118,000 members, and in that year's presidential election Eugene Debs, the party's presidential candidate, polled 6 percent of the total popular vote. In some states in the West the party garnered over 16 percent of the total vote.[53]

The Socialists had always viewed the state as the locus of working-class activity, and part of the Socialist agenda was social insurance. As socialist reformer Max Rubinow explained: "Social insurance is a powerful object lesson of the reality of the new concept of the state as the instrument of organized collective action, rather than of class oppression, the concept of the future state in the making rather than of the state of the past."[54]

In 1909 former United Mine Workers secretary William B. Wilson introduced a pension proposal into Congress. Borrowing from the symbolism of military pensions, the proposal called for the creation of an "Old Home Guard" in which all lower-income older Americans would be invited to enlist. In return for reporting to the War Department on the state of patriotism in their communities, they would be paid $120 per year.[55]

Although the AFL did endorse that bill and in subsequent years (1908, 1911, 1912, and 1913) passed resolutions supporting noncontributory old age pensions, it was vehemently opposed to old age insurance. It voted down a proposal for compulsory social insurance in 1904, and the national leadership continued to adhere to this view for another twenty years.[56] A 1916 proposal sponsored by Socialist congressman Meyer London to establish a commission to study social insurance met with heated opposition from Samuel Gompers, who argued that an "attempt has been made in the name of the Socialist Party of America to aim a death blow at the trades union movement," just as unemployment insurance in England took "much of the virility out of the British trade unions."[57] According to Gompers,

> Governmental power grows by what it feeds upon. Give an agency any political power and it at once tries to reach out after more. . . . Compulsory social insurance can not be administered without exercising some control over wage-earners. . . . Industrial freedom exists only when wage-earners have complete control over their labor power. To delegate control over their labor power to an outside agency takes away from the economic power of those wage-earners and creates another agency for power.[58]

No issues were more important to the working class than wages, hours, and conditions of employment, and any attempt by government to provide compulsory social insurance would "result in every government agent going into the homes and the lives of the workers as a spy."[59] Preserving the prerogatives of crafts formed the main AFL agenda, which the national leadership viewed as incompatible with state action for workers' benefits.

It was not only Socialists, however, who challenged the national leadership on the issue of political action in general and social benefits in particular. Another source of opposition came from the state federations of labor. City and state central labor bodies had performed a seminal role in the early years of the labor movement. When the national AFL was organized its leaders, who believed these central bodies were too politically oriented and too easily influenced by radical elements, severely limited their economic power. State federations could not force the affiliation of local unions in their jurisdiction, call strikes, negotiate agreements, discipline constituent locals, or even organize locals without the permission of affected national or international unions.[60] Despite this restricted constitutional role, state federations found an important function in the American labor movement, increasingly devoting their time to the political interests of labor and often, contrary to the wishes of the national leadership, leading the campaign for reform.

In 1911 the Arkansas state federation of labor, dominated by the only strong noncraft union, the United Mine Workers, became one of the first to adopt a resolution supporting Socialist congressman Victor Berger's (S-Wis.) proposal to provide "old age pensions for deserving men and women over sixty years old."[61] Although the convention unanimously adopted the measure, it was never brought before the Arkansas House or Senate. As the radical union recognized, Arkansas poll taxes effectively impeded organized labor from electing supportive candidates and from getting pro-labor measures even introduced, let alone passed. Thus, in contrast to a state like California, where labor continually published lists of congressmen's votes on labor measures, in the South the hands of labor organizations were tied.[62] The federalized structure of the state and the disfranchisement of southern citizens made it virtually impossible for southern labor to work within the state, and its weakness consequently weakened the national labor movement.

Although rank-and-file workers struggled to create solidarity and a program for action, this strategy contradicted the national leadership's agenda. Industrial workers readily recognized that self-protection was not feasible, and they chose instead to support the Socialist agenda of state benefits. Their relationship to the social process of production conditioned their stance on how to achieve economic leadership in old age.

As unskilled workers pressured the national leadership for state action, the leadership itself split over the union's proper role. John Lennon, treasurer of the AFL. John O'Connell, vice president of the AFL, and Thomas Garretson, president of the Order of Railway Conductors, all supported London's compulsory social insurance proposal.[63] An even stronger challenge to voluntarism came from William Green, secretary-treasurer of the United Mine Workers and later AFL president. In 1917 Green published an article in the *American Labor Legislation Review* advocating compulsory insurance for health, disability, and old age, with the cost to be borne jointly by the employee, the employer, and the state. Why, asked Green, "should the working people themselves bear this financial burden? . . . Industry and society at large should be required to bear their share of the burden."[64] Within the labor movement, then, the interests of the unskilled industrial mass pushed the craft unions toward state action on old age pensions.

It was not only internal dissension that shifted the position of the AFL toward government action. Employers' successes within the state in impeding trade unions necessitated counter action on labor's part. In 1907 all the internationals sent representatives to Washington to prepare a bill of grievances to present to Congress and the president.[65] When this initiative failed, Gompers presented labor's demands to both party conventions in 1908. Rudely treated by the business-dominated Republicans, he found greater sympathy from the Democratic party, which introduced several pro-labor pledges into its platform.

In 1912 the AFL dropped its nonpartisan stance entirely, openly supporting the Democrats. This strategy paid dividends during the Wilson administration as numerous pro-labor measures were

enacted. Among them were the Clayton Act of 1914, which granted
labor relief from antitrust legislation, an independent Department of
Labor, and statutes governing industrial safety, providing workers'
compensation, and creating a minimum wage.[66]

Labor's experiences with the government during World War I
further eroded its voluntaristic philosophy and its opposition to
government intervention. As the United States entered the war,
maintaining labor stability became a paramount issue, and the war
industries, spurred by wartime profits, staged a reckless competition
for labor. The AFL willingly came to the government's assistance. In
1916 Samuel Gompers accepted a position on the Council of National
Defense, and in 1917 a conference of unionists and government
officials met. Labor voted unqualified support to the government in
the event of war, pressing its advantages as numerous industries
under pressure from government agencies agreed to substantial
wage increases and liberalization of practices toward unions in
exchange for industrial peace.[67]

In the postwar years, organized labor was at peak capacity. Loyalty,
as measured by the breadth of members' commitments to deliver
resources, was high, because there was less opposition to state action
within the national leadership. Loyalty was also high because the
extent of repression was low; threats from employers had been
minimized as a result of the wartime labor shortage and government
cooperation with unions.[68] Given these conditions and the prewar
commitment of industrial workers to the old age pension issue, it is
not surprising that a pension movement arose from the rank-and-file
local and state bodies of the AFL[69] and the UMW, the sole industrial
union with the potential capacity to mobilize a successful social
movement.

State Pensions and the United Mine Workers

One of the largest and most powerful unions in America, the UMW
reached maximum strength during the war years. The war had
produced a tremendous labor shortage in coal mining, which was
third on the nation's priority list of industries, and the government
struggled for ways to meet the demand for labor. In 1918 retired
miners were asked to demonstrate their patriotism by returning to
work. Coal miners and other mine workers were no longer accepted
for army enlistment, and inducements were offered to former miners
working in other industries to return to the coal fields. By the end of
the war membership in the UMW had increased by 40 percent, many
previously nonunion fields had been organized, wages had increased
throughout the country, and the eight-hour day was firmly

established.[70] Thus the UMW entered the post war era at peak mobilizing potential.

Not organized primarily for political action, historically the UMW had worked toward improving conditions in the mines. Its prior solidarities, however, made it possible to mobilize support for the pension issue. To enhance its chances of selecting a successful pension strategy, the union joined forces with Abraham Epstein, a member of the American Association for Labor Legislation and a longtime old age pension advocate.

In 1918 the union's legislative committee met with Epstein and James Maurer, president of the Pennsylvania State Federation of Labor, to begin planning a state pension campaign. The organizers sketched out a tentative pension bill, which they planned to bring before state legislatures. Thus two organizations, one committed primarily to improving conditions in the marketplace and the other working primarily for protective state legislation, joined forces on a common goal.[71]

The end of the war altered the favorable conditions for the union, and by early 1919 leaders were warning of an oversupply of mine labor. Nonetheless, union strength had not declined greatly, and the Committee on Old Age Pensions put forth its report to a divided 1919 convention. Although the delegates agreed that "something be done to alleviate the suffering and distress of the disabled workman, no matter whether the disability is caused by sickness, injury or old age," they were unable to reach consensus on how to achieve this goal. Instead they formed a new committee to make further recommendations and prepare statistics and arguments to present to legislatures.[72]

Commitment to old age pensions was strong, and within a few months the union presented a bill before the Kentucky state legislature urging support for a state pension. Simultaneously, letters went out to all locals, giving explicit instructions on how to garner support for the pension bill. Members were urged to have their locals endorse the bill, send copies to their senators and representatives, call editors of local newspapers, and attempt to enlist citizen support. Legislators in Illinois and Indiana received similar proposals.[73] Unionists also sent letters to all candidates up for election to state offices, polling their responses to a series of questions regarding proposed legislative measures, including old age pensions. They then published the candidates' responses in the miners' journal.[74] Thus the UMW geared up for a political fight for pension legislation, using tactics that organized labor had found successful since 1907.

An overproduction crisis in the mining industry destroyed the

UMW's agenda for social legislation. During the war high prices had spurred the opening of many new mines, often in the South. The new producers, employing cheap, nonunionized black labor using more efficient equipment and mining higher-grade coal, quickly seized the markets. Competition from other fuels also reduced the demand for coal just as production was expanding. As a result the price of coal dropped drastically. Mineowners responded to the increasingly competitive climate by reducing wages and lengthening the workday. When the UMW refused to compromise on the wage issue, mine operators set about the systematic destruction of the union by evicting striking miners from company houses, recruiting strikebreakers, and using armed guards. In the struggle for survival, the union depleted its resources, and the number of union members declined significantly.[75] By 1930 the union lay in ruins.

The UMW pension movement failed because of the decline of union strength. Repressive measures by employers and the courts were not directed specifically against the old age pension movement, but rather were part of a broader thrust to eliminate unions entirely. The UMW's defeat in the marketplace spelled the demise of the organization's capacity to work for social legislation as well.

Although state federations and central labor bodies continued to work for state pension legislation throughout the 1920s, these organizations were subject to the same constraints that impeded the UMW. Unions lost membership during this period because of concerted efforts by employers, and internal dissension over goals deflected energy toward more basic issues of union survival. As an alternative, many state AFL federations and state branches of the UMW joined forces with a fraternal organization, the Eagles. This odd coalition proved enormously effective in getting state old age pension legislation enacted.

The Eagles and State Pensions

In the first two decades of the twentieth century, fraternal societies played an important role in providing insurance benefits for members. Between 1910 and 1920 they wrote about one-third of all life insurance in the United States.[76] Unlike ordinary life insurance companies, however, they were under no compulsion to maintain a reserve or to proceed on a sound actuarial basis. As membership aged, most societies found their rates inadequate to cover the promised benefits. Many disappeared, while others raised rates to compensate for membership losses, resulting in further declines.[77]

Like many other fraternal organizations, the Eagles encountered a membership crisis in the second decade of the twentieth century.

Between 1917 and 1918 they lost eight thousand members, another ten thousand dropped out the following year, and the order appeared to be in imminent danger of collapse. Recognizing the value of ideological incentives from their earlier campaign for Mothers' Pensions, the Eagles adopted the old age pension issue as a mechanism for increasing membership.[78]

Like most fraternal orders, the Eagles were a cross-class organization that tied workers to the middle class. Their members included politicians, small businessmen, skilled craft workers, and industrial workers. As the organization gained membership and respectability through its pension drive, politicians and professionals also joined the ranks. But in its initial recruitment drive, the group established a coalition with state federations of labor and with the United Mine Workers in states where labor had already been working for state pensions. For example, in Illinois the UMW had been working for state pensions since 1913.[99] Upon learning that the Eagles had appropriated funds for a campaign to educate the public, UMW officials wrote the Eagles' grand secretary pledging support and suggesting they "work together in an effort to secure such legislation." Like those measures supported previously by the UMW, the AFL, and the state federations, the Eagles' pension bill was noncontributory, and in fact, throughout the pension campaign a continuous attack on the concept of contributory pensions appeared in articles in the *Eagle Magazine*.[80]

Ohio had launched its old age pension movement in 1916 with the formation of the Ohio Old Age Pension League. With the strong backing of organized labor, particularly the Miners' Legislative Committee, a commission was formed to investigate old age poverty in the state, and a bill was proposed but not passed. The Eagles joined forces with the Ohio State Federation of Labor and the UMW, continuing to petition to present bills before the state legislature.[81] In Pennsylvania, Abraham Epstein had worked with the Pennsylvania Federation of Labor endorsing pro-pension candidates since 1920. Here too the Eagles used the momentum created by the existing pension movement to form a coalition. As the UMW legislative committee wrote to the editor of the *Eagle Magazine*,

> The United Mine Workers of America, which we have the honor to represent, has been for some time engaged in the work of forwarding this movement. . . . We would be glad to secure your cooperation and especially [that] of the officers and members in the various States where bills will be presented for that purpose. We would also be glad to confer with your

committee . . . with the carrying into effect of your views on the matter, to the end that we may work together in an effort to secure such legislation.[82]

As labor's value as an ally became increasingly apparent, the Eagles set about courting labor organizations in each state, city, and county where they had not already made contact. First targets were labor organizations working independently for pensions, such as in San Antonio, where the Central Trades Council had passed a resolution endorsing the old age pension movement. In other instances labor union members who were also Eagles spread the word through their labor councils. Frank Bernhardt, for example, president of the New York State Aerie and a UMW member, ordered the Eagles booklet "The Times Demand Old Age Pensions" for the use of the labor union members of Buffalo Aerie 46. This scenario was repeated in aerie after aerie throughout the nation, as labor unions and trades councils affiliated with the Eagles and as the Eagles independently sought their support. Although no tally is presented, it seems clear that by seeking an alliance with labor the Eagles recruited many union members, who clearly recognized that their "efforts and motives, coming from a labor organization, [were] sometimes impugned and that the best they [could] do is to get behind our movement and help us."[83] Thus, a leading editorial explained in the March 1923 issue of the *Eagle Magazine:*

> It needs to be emphatically impressed on the public mind that the Old Age Pensions Bill supported by the Fraternal order of Eagles . . . had its genesis in our profound sympathy for workers who by the hundreds of thousands in this country are coming to the economic deadline of 70 years without having been able to lay by from their hard-earned wages enough to live on in their old age, when industry finds them no longer useful. . . . In the face of these facts, is it to be wondered that the Fraternal Order of Eagles, whose membership is so closely aligned with the working groups and so deeply concerned in their welfare, should have been inspired to take the lead and bring this old pension movement to fruition?[84]

According to Charles Tilly, a central ingredient in the success of a social movement is its ability to enter the polity by forging alliances with polity members.[85] This strategy had failed organized labor because employers' organizations had greater strength within the state. As a result, they were able to mobilize counteralliances, which undermined workers in the marketplace and deflected their energies for political goals. The Eagles, by contrast, were able to forge more successful alliances with politicians because they were not vulnerable to counterattacks in the market.

Eagles already holding political positions came out publicly in support of old age pensions, and the organization began to actively solicit the support of candidates during their campaigns. Using the same tactics the UMW had attempted earlier, the Eagles supported pro-pension advocates, publishing their names in publicity material and in the *Eagle Magazine*. As Otto Fey of Everett Aerie 13 reported, "everything in his section was working 'smooth as silk' with candidates asking the privilege of addressing the o.a.p. meetings."[86]

The first victory occurred in Montana, where the Democrats used economy in government as their campaign theme while the Republicans stressed equalizing the tax burden. The Eagles presented the pension bill to the legislature at the last moment, so the opposition had little opportunity to mobilize. Although the farm bloc and the insurance companies almost smothered the bill, charging that it would overburden those already tax-laden, the Eagle supporters, with the state federation of labor, quickly redrafted it. They eliminated a provision for an old age pension board and a superintendent, left administration in the hands of county commissioners, and raised the eligibility age from sixty-five to seventy. Although only 349 individuals received pensions in the following year and many counties paid out no pensions, the Eagles treated the act as a major victory, and the pension drive gained new momentum.[87]

As the pension bill began appearing before state legislatures, opposition organized against it. In state after state, industrial and business interests confronted the labor-Eagle coalition with an equally vociferous attack. In Massachusetts the State Grange and United Industries recorded opposition to the bill, and the Chamber of Commerce declared it un-American; in Nevada the mining interests and old corporations lobbied against it;[88] in Ohio merchants trade associations attempted to "kill the proposition, [particularly] the Retail Merchants, because they know if this bill goes through, it will take away a great source of cheap labor from employers."[89]

Pennsylvania recorded a temporary defeat when the state Supreme Court declared the Old Age Assistance Act—proposed by the UMW and endorsed by the Pennsylvania State Federation of Labor and the Eagles—unconstitutional on the grounds that the legislature was prohibited from making appropriations for charitable, benevolent, and educational purposes. The state chamber of commerce and the Pennsylvania Manufacturers' Association then jointly defeated a 1927 amendment to the state constitution to legalize the pension, describing it as a "costly and vicious scheme" that would "make necessary a Manufacturer's Tax, or an Income Tax, or both."[90] As Abraham Epstein later explained to the House Committee on Labor when it investigated the possibility of a national pension, "In every State in the Union where this legislation has been presented, the manufacturer's associations have been fighting this legislation and are trying to stop the states from doing it."[91]

Employers had two fears about state pensions: that the added tax burden would make their products less competitive with those from companies in other states, and that any social benefit would subsidize labor, thus reducing the labor supply or rendering it more costly. As the labor-Eagles coalition began to mobilize for state pensions, employers recognized the costs to capital of implementing a welfare program.

In the first three states to pass pension laws under the labor-Eagles coalition (Montanna, Pennsylvania, and Nevada), all were county-option plans—that is, each county could determine whether to raise funds and provide a pension to eligible citizens. By 1925 only thirty-one of the fifty-five counties in Montanna were paying pensions. In Nevada the law remained largely inoperative; as late as 1932 only two counties were paying pensions. The Pennsylvania act was declared unconstitutional, as noted above, and it was not until 1934 that a new law was passed.[92]

In 1925 Wisconsin passed a pension law containing a new provision. Pensions were still based on the county option, but the state agreed to reimburse the counties for one-third of their pension costs. Other states continued to pass county-option laws or to have their laws declared unconstitutional or vetoed. By 1929, in six states with operative pension laws, only 53 of the 264 counties eligible to adopt a pension had actually done so.[93]

Dissatisfied with the legislation, some Eagles supporters became suspicious of the group's motivations and ended their collaboration. Epstein, who had initially worked with the Eagles in Pennsylvania, became disillusioned with the "flimsy character of the type of legislation advocated by that group" and dissociated himself from their efforts. Max Rubinow, long-term social insurance advocate, also became disillusioned with the organization, declaring that "the Eagles certainly were successful in putting the legislation through and came very near destroying the entire value of the old-age pension movement."[94]

Some state federations of labor also became concerned about the taxation implications of state-funded pensions, which placed the pension burden disproportionately on the working class. For example, in 1923 the Illinois State Federation of Labor had argued "It is well known that the cost of maintaining an aged person in a public institution is far in excess of the amount it is proposed to pay such person in the form of a pension."[95] Just a few years later the union reevaluated its previously unqualified pension advocacy. As President John Walker explained:

> I confess, I am somewhat doubtful that we shall be able to get a pension law enacted in Illinois until there is a complete readjustment of a state system of taxation. Our present tax law is antiquated and unfair. Under this system the farms and modest homes which present some 20 percent of the value of property in the states, pay 85 percent. . . . Until we get a new tax law which will require people to pay taxes on the basis of their ability to pay, it will be extremely difficult to get a satisfactory old age pension law in the state of Illinois.[96]

At the 1929 AFL convention Walker unconditionally supported a resolution for a national pension.[97]

The Eagles-labor coalition broke down because different goals inspired their intitial participation in the movement. The Eagles succeeded in increasing membership far beyond their initial expectations by using the pension issue as an ideological justification. Their concern with the adequacy of the laws once enacted was minimal, causing their labor allies to reevaluate their support. In contrast, rank-and-file union members turned their attention toward strengthening state pension laws, and in such states as Massachusetts, Ohio, Wisconsin, and New York they were successful.

The national leadership's position on government began to change in 1924 after Samuel Gompers's death, when the AFL elected William Green president. As a man who had always seen a viable role for government in protecting workers, Green supported the more radical state federations, Still, it took a number of years before the AFL officially reversed its position, as numerous proposals got pigeonholed in the Resolutions Committee.[98]

In 1928 a bitter floor fight ensued over the pension issue. In the preceding year the radical San Francisco Labor Council had sponsored a resolution called "for the establishment of an American system of invalidity and old age pensions . . . and to promote its enactment."[99] In the same year President James Lynch of the International Typographical Union, who had served on the New York State Commission on Old Age Security, sponsored a bill requiring the AFL to draft a model state pension bill. Although the pension issue renewed the divisions that had splintered the labor movement for decades, in 1929 the AFL, which had not endorsed a pension bill since 1913, approved the ITU–San Francisco Labor Council proposal to promote the enactment of a model bill.[100] Other labor organizations reached the same conclusion.

Although momentum had swung toward support of national pensions, the AFL endorsement was notoriously weak, and the union remained ambivalent even as its membership pressured for a more radical stance. It was not until 1931 that two powerful AFL leaders well schooled in the Gompers tradition, Daniel Tobin, former treasurer of the federation and veteran president of the International Brotherhood of Teamsters, and W. D. Mahon, president of the Amalgamated Association of Street and Electric Railway Employees, reversed their traditional opposition to government welfare measures. As columnist Louis Stark explained: "Mr. Mahon confessed that after forty years of conferring with employers on matters such as old-age pensions he had been forced to the conclusion that relief of this sort and unemployment insurance could come only through government influence and direction."[101]

By 1932 seventeen states had old age pension laws. None were in the South, where organized labor was particularly weak and where few Eagles aeries existed. Most of the laws passed after 1929 were mandatory on the counties and provided for a substantial state contribution. In spite of the apparent progress, however, the actual field of operation contracted owing to the increasingly limited funds available to states as the depression spread. Although there was an overall net gain between 1931 and 1932 in the number of counties paying pensions, many discontinued their pension plans and others decreased the average monthly grant. Further, about 73 percent of the pensioners and 87 percent of the total expenditures occurred in three states—California, Massachusetts, and New York.[102] The depression only exacerbated the inadequacy of the state pension system, and as the financial woes of the states deepened, attention was increasingly drawn toward a national pension system. The sole labor movement for a national pension was not predicated on the rights of all workers to old age security; it issued from the railroad workers, whose agenda was limited to protection for one industry.

FEDERAL PENSIONS FOR RAILROAD WORKERS

In the nineteenth century railroad workers organized into strong unions based on craft lines. Some of the more than twenty railroad brotherhoods were affiliated with the AFL, but not all. Even those that were affiliated stayed independent of the central body, feeling it was to their benefit to remain free to pursue measures for their membership. When the railroad unions wished to take joint action, their course was followed through the Railway Labor Executive Association, an organization composed of the presidents of the member unions. They rarely joined forces with other AFL affiliates.[103]

Employers on the railroads were among the first to establish private pensions for workers, initiating them during the massive strikes that paralyzed the economy in the nineteenth century. Workers resented the coercive uses to which these pensions were put, since employers commissioned pensioners as strikebreakers and threatened all workers engaged in misconduct with the loss of pension rights.[104] As early as 1928 trainmen began advocating federal pensions as an escape from "the gratuities handed out by the railroads [which were] used to tie the employees to their jobs and hamper them in fighting for their rights."[105] Because of its commitment to collective bargaining, however, the national leadership exhibited no interest in state pensions, and the pension issue did not become a part of the union's formal agenda.

In 1929 a grass-roots movement arose in support of federal pension legislation for railroad workers. Composed largely of older workers, the Railway Employees National Pension Association (RENPA) claimed to represent 95 percent of the rank and file of railroad workers.[106] RENPA formed clubs throughout the United States and in 1932 exerted pressure on Senator Henry Hatfield to introduce the bill in Congress. Because of the workers' negative experiences with the noncontributory company pensions, which gave them no legal claims on benefits, the RENPA proposal called for joint employer-worker contributory pensions. Unions were also dissatisfied with the amount granted retirees under private pensions, and the legislation proposed more generous payments. As pension agitation mounted, labor leaders began to recognize that their indifference to the pension issue was alienating them from the rank and file, and in the same year they succeeded in inducing Senator Robert Wagner to introduce an alternative proposal. Over the opposition of the Association of Railway Executives and other employers' organizations, a revised Wagner-Hatfield bill, which contained most of the RENPA objectives, was passed by Congress in 1934.[107]

Although the bill was subsequently declared unconstitutional by the Supreme Court following a challenge by the Association of Railway Executives, the opposition of railway employers declined. A major factor in reversing the antagonism of the roads to a federal pension was the extreme financial difficulties faced by the railroads' own pension systems. By 1931 railroads were operating at a deficit. Pension payments totaled more than 24 percent of net income, and the aging population of workers indicated that expenses were likely to continue to increase. During the depression, most roads reduced pensions from 10 to 40 percent and rejected numerous applications for retirement.[108] The private pension system had lost its economic viability, and roads were in need of an immediate solution. Employers also became less opposed to federal pensions because of legal decisions limiting the discretionary uses to which pensions could be put. In 1930 the Interstate Commerce Commission had ruled that the roads had to be under contract to pay pensions if they were to charge to operating expenses the appropriations for trust funds. In other words, they were now forced to guarantee pension payments and could no longer make them discretionary with the company. Finally, both employers and workers agreed to cooperate in a joint endeavor to regulate competitive transportation facilities and to organize bus and truck drivers.[109] If competing forms of transport could be brought under union jurisdiction, the costs of welfare benefits could be distributed more evenly across industries.

In 1935 a modified Wagner-Hatfield bill was passed in Congress and signed into law by President Roosevelt, shortly after passage of the Social Security Act.[110] The new law included private car lines and freight forwarders among those who would come under its jurisdiction. Railroad workers had won a generous system of federal benefits, but only for that single industry. The Railroad Retirement Act provided benefits up to $120 per month for all employees of railroads (and other carriers) over age sixty-five upon retirement from service, permitted voluntary retirement for workers who had reached the age of fifty-one and had completed thirty years of service, and covered any worker who had completed twenty-five years of service but had to retire because of mental or physical disability. The plan also had provisions for survivors' benefits.[111] By contrast, the old age insurance provisions of the Social Security Act, which covered all other wageworkers, paid a maximum of $85 per month, offered no disability benefits, no optional retirement, and no survivors' benefits, and were not to begin until 1942.

Organized labor did succeed in initiating a major piece of welfare legislation, but because the American labor movement was organized along craft lines, these workers did not advocate a program of universal benefits to ameliorate inequality. Rather, the railroad unions' traditional autonomy from other unions led to the curious creation of a program for only one group of workers.

CONCLUSION

Because of their core premise that welfare programs are the outgrowth of the basic imperatives of capitalism, neo-Marxist theories of the welfare state have failed to account adequately for working-class impact on program formation. Most neo-Marxist accounts neglect any serious analysis of labor history. The social democratic model does take working-class history seriously, but its core assertion, that the welfare state is a victory for organized labor, precludes exploring alternative avenues of labor influence.

In the United States the splintering of the labor movement into craft and mass-production workers shaped the character of the struggle for welfare benefits. Craft workers, who organized first, focused union activities on the preservation of autonomy, which was gradually being eroded by changes in the production process. Autonomy, in turn, meant self-protection, which became the primary goal of the American Federal of Labor and its internationals for more than twenty years. Thus in contrast to Denmark, where craft workers did obtain power within the state, American craft workers for the most part remained either opposed to or ambivalent about state action. Because they never became a force within the state hierarchy, the one potentially strong voice for workers' benefits was muted.

In the sole instance when craft workers did strongly advocate and win a federal pension, their victory was limited to employees in one industry. The tradition of craft autonomy had turned the interests of railroad workers inward, and instead of using their political power to press for benefits for all wageworkers, they chose to direct their energies toward the federalization of the railroad pension system.

Few mass-production workers were organized in this period, but the one vigorous union organized on an industrial rather than a craft basis, the United Mine Workers, recognized the futility of self-protection for the unskilled. Their need to fight battles in the marketplace impeded their political effectiveness, however, and their efforts on behalf of old age pensions succeeded only when they joined forces with a fraternal organization. An industrial proletariat with a conscience that dictated social action for benefits to mitigate market forces did exist, but because this labor faction represented only a small proportion of all unskilled workers, its opportunities for successful social action were minimal.

This chapter highlights the extent to which the struggle for old age pensions was part of a broader process of class struggle, shaped within the marketplace and within the electoral-representative political system. The American labor movement participated actively in the battle, though on different terms than its European counterparts. While it is difficult to prove a negative hypothesis, the evidence suggests that the failure of most mass-production workers to unionize in this period and the antistate stance of craft workers impeded American welfare state development. If American unionism had proceeded in a different fashion, wth early mass-production unionization, the welfare state might have been initiated earlier.

FIG. 4 *American Labor Legislation Review* 19 (December 1929): 350.

4

Pensions in the Marketplace

A common feature of all theories of welfare state development is their lack of attention to private sector programs. For adherents to the "logic of industrialism" argument, state benefits arise automatically from the failure of traditional support systems—the family or the community—to meet the new needs generated by an industrializing economy. But none of the analyses arising from this thesis systematically examine what kinds of traditional support systems were actually operating, nor do they consider how successful they were in meeting the needs of the elderly.[1]

Social democratic theorists locate public pensions in the wage relationship between workers and employers. Private pensions are viewed primarily as an extension of public benefits, a "part of the larger wage package to be negotiated at the bargaining table."[2] Thus they rarely envision private pensions as worthy of separate analysis.

Neo-Marxist theorists view public social programs as a benefit to capital. The problem with most neo-Marxist accounts, however, is their presumption that the functions of welfare programs—maintaining profitability, ensuring social harmony, and legitimating capitalism—can be provided only by the state. As Gough states, "social security . . . has always been essential . . . to maintain an incentive to work and to reinforce the discipline of the factory over the workforce."[3] By its lack of attention to private sector benefits, neo-Marxist theory implies that capital cannot perform these functions without state intervention. In the United States private sector benefits not only were important precursors to state action but also continued to affect the structure of public benefits after the government enacted Social Security. The central argument to be explored here is that changes in the relationship between workers and employers affected the structure of private pension programs and that pension experiments reflected the evolving worker-employer conflicts.

PENSIONS DURING THE GROWTH OF WAGE LABOR

Nineteenth-century production took place in small firms, with managerial control concentrated within the families or the partnerships of the founding entrepreneurs. Because they were small, these businesses tended to have a local outlook and to depend on a limited market area. Although employers needed control over labor to ensure high productivity, worker-employer relationships were informal and unstructured. A single entrepreneur, in concert with a few foremen and managers, ruled the firm, "intervening in the labor process often to exhort workers, bully and threaten them, reward good performance, hire and fire on the spot, favor loyal workers, and generally act as despots."[4] In an informally structured workplace, personal ties between employer and employee obscured class differences and created bonds of loyalty. To the extent that an employer felt obligated to provide for aged employees, the feeling stemmed from a paternalistic sense of duty. Many felt no such obligation and simply fired older workers when they became less productive. In other companies, however, a sense of moral commitment or a desire to maintain the morale of younger workers did lead bosses to provide for aging workers.[5]

In some industries, such as iron and steel, inside contracting predominated. Inside contractors were skilled workers themselves and had complete charge of production, hiring their own employees and supervising the work process. Becoming a contractor was one source of security for older workers. In the Baldwin Locomotive Works, which employed more than thirteen thousand men, "the contractor [was] always an elderly man who [had] spent many years in the shops, and could be entrusted, if need be, with the superintendency of the works."[6]

Another practice was to shift older workers to lighter tasks and reduce their wages: "The ticket-choppers on the elevated roads in New York City are frequently old men who have been 'graduated' from more active employment. In banks the veterans are set to guarding the vaults; on railroads they sit all day long in warehouses reading the paper and smoking their pipes under the delusion that they are watchmen."[7] According to a study by the Pennsylvania Old Age Pension Commission: "Shifting the older workers to lighter tasks and continuing them on the payroll at their regular wages or at reduced rates commensurate with the services rendered is the oldest and in the past, most common method of taking care of the aged employees. This practice, while it may not be described as a 'pension plan,' is widely in vogue in industry in lieu of pensions."[8]

A few manufacturers established formal programs. Alfred Dolge, a builder of pianos and organs, began the first company plan in 1882. The maintenance of labor, in Dolge's view, was a business cost. Just as an employer set aside funds for depreciation costs of machinery and equipment, so should he "provide against the depreciation of his employees."[9] Dolge placed 1 percent of each employee's earnings into a pension fund, adding 6 percent interest per year. Benefits were contingent upon continuous service, with the amount of the pension varying according to the number of years employed. Employees with ten years of service were to receive 50 percent of their wages as a pension, increasing to 100 percent for those with twenty-five years of service.[10] Even among these early experiments, employers perceived industrial pensions as a business expense, part of the price of wage labor. As wage labor became commodified, payments to workers were one of the costs of doing business.

Although other firms adopted the widely publicized Dolge scheme, the pension collapsed when the firm went out of business. Even before the company's demise, Dolge had become convinced of his plan's failure. His meticulous records highlighted the extremely mobile character of labor. Only 40 percent of his work force remained with the firm more than one year, and just 10.8 percent stayed as long as five years.[11] Since few employees worked for the same firm long enough to earn pension rights, the company pension, Dolge concluded, only impeded labor mobility.[12] Not until nearly half a century later did other employers learn the same lesson.

Other companies established informal pension systems where an employer's personal discretion determined whether a worker had earned pension rights. In 1903 the Standard Oil Company, one of the first major manufacturers to initiate employee welfare programs, established an informal plan providing workers with a pension according to managerial discretion.[13] Like the Standard Oil plan, most of the early informal pensions were considered a reward for merit, a gift of the benefactor. The gift concept meant that the employee had no legal rights to the pension, which could be revoked at the employer's whim. As one employer explained: "We have no rigid or definite pension system. We do, however, have a more or less informal pension policy, under which aged workers are taken care of according to their need. I am positively of the opinion that a pension cannot be claimed by an industrial worker as a right."[14] Thus, informal pensions functioned much like poor relief. If an employer decided that an aged worker was both meritorious and in need, a pension might be granted. The reward, however, was entirely at the employer's discretion, and workers had to prove their worthiness.

PENSIONS AND THE OPEN SHOP DRIVE

Following a depression in the 1890s, labor began an extensive organizing campaign that succeeded in increasing union membership substantially. Between 1897 and 1904, total union membership climbed from 447,000 to over 2 million. Stronger unions brought about more strikes, disrupting business activity. Employers began responding to labor's organizing success in the early 1890s, establishing antistrike and antiunion leagues to combat union activity, but until the twentieth century most organizational activity among employers was local or regional.[15]

In 1898 manufacturers began an open-shop drive to eliminate unions. The drive was spearheaded by the National Association of Manufacturers (NAM), which shifted its organizational focus from stimulating foreign trade to the open-shop issue.[16] The employers' groups, now coordinated on a national basis by the NAM, organized Citizens' Alliances all over the country to inculcate antiunion public sentiment, provided their members with strikebreakers, maintained industrial spies, blacklisted union workers, and attempted to pressure businesses not fully comitted to the open shop by imposing sanctions. Under the tutelage of the NAM, the trade associations also coordinated political pressure to defeat candidates and legislation favorable to labor and to work through the court system to obtain injunctions against labor. In 1908 the courts handed employers a further weapon in their antiunion battle when the Supreme Court ruled that trade unions were subject to the Sherman Antitrust Act.[17]

In many industries the open-shop drive succeeded in destroying unionism. In steel, meat-packing, and other heavy manufacturing industries, unions were defeated.[18] But the success of the open-shop drive was not universal. In a brief period between 1909 and 1912, strikes in the garment industry culminated in collective bargaining agreements. And in the printing and building industries, where divisions among employers impeded the creation of powerful trade associations, collective bargaining procedures were also installed.[19] Thus some of the crafts maintained and even furthered their organizational strength, although the open-shop drive successfully defeated unionization among most industrial workers.

During this period, employers used pensions as weapons in their counterattack to the challenge by workers. Nearly all the early pensions were noncontributory, paid out of current company funds. Of seventy-six pension plans begun by 1910, seventy-one were noncontributory.[20] Between 1910 and 1920, 253 new pension plans appeared. As table 1 illustrates, all but twenty were noncontributory.

TABLE 1   TYPE OF PENSION PLAN AND YEAR INITIATED

Year	Noncontributory		Contributory	
	N	%	N	%
1884–99	3	0.7	4	2.6
1900–1904	22	5.7	3	1.9
1905–9	19	4.9	5	3.3
1910–14	110	28.4	10	6.5
1915–19	123	31.7	10	6.5
1920–24	74	19.1	15	9.7
1925–29	34	8.8	48	31.0
1930–32	3	0.7	59	38.1
Total	388	100.0	155	100.0

Source: Calculated from Latimer, *Industrial Pension Systems,* pp. 908–1113.

Why did pension plans increase so rapidly in this period, and why were they primarily noncontributory? Initially, employers implemented pension plans to contain labor militancy and prevent strikes. In the late nineteenth century the railroad brotherhoods, among the most powerful of the early unions, had repeatedly paralyzed the economy. Management initiated railroad pensions in an explicit attempt to pacify workers and stabilize the labor force, beginning with that of the Baltimore and Ohio in 1884.[21] As a report by the Bureau of Labor Statistics explained: "The first railway company to essay a solution of the problem did so by a pension fund of a primitive sort, following a labor strike. Undoubtedly, one purpose was, if possible, to lessen the attractiveness of the labor unions and to make the men loyal to their employer rather than to one another or to any brotherhood."[22] Railroad pensions multiplied, and by 1903 sixteen railroads operated pension plans and two more were being prepared.[23]

With the onset of the open-shop drive pensions spread from railroads to manufacturing. As table 2 indicates, between 1900 and 1904 56 percent of all pension plans were noncontributory pensions in the railroads. In the next decade the percentage of pensions in manufacturing industries increased to one-third of all plans, and this figure remained stable until 1925.

These manufacturing pensions were primarily in heavy industry, where the open-shop drive was working to defeat unions. U.S. Steel initiated a pension plan in 1910 immediately following its successful

TABLE 2   TYPE OF PENSION PLAN AND YEAR INITIATED, BY INDUSTRY

Year	Noncontributory		Contributory	
	N	%	N	%
1884–99				
Railroads	2	28.6	0	0.0
Manufacturing	0	0.0	0	0.0
Banking	0	0.0	4	57.1
Insurance	0	0.0	0	0.0
Other	1	14.3	0	0.0
1900–1904				
Railroads	14	56.0	0	0.0
Manufacturing	5	20.0	0	0.0
Banking	1	4.0	2	8.0
Insurance	0	0.0	0	0.0
Other	2	8.0	1	4.0
1905–9				
Railroads	7	29.2	1	4.2
Manufacturing	8	33.3	0	0.0
Banking	0	0.0	1	4.2
Insurance	0	0.0	1	4.2
Other	4	16.7	2	8.3
1910–14				
Railroads	29	24.0	0	0.0
Manufacturing	43	35.5	0	0.0
Banking	6	5.0	9	7.4
Insurance	2	1.7	1	1.0
Other	30	24.8	1	1.0
1915–19				
Railroads	33	24.3	0	0.0
Manufacturing	43	30.6	3	2.2
Banking	7	5.1	3	2.2
Insurance	7	5.1	1	1.0
Other	36	26.5	3	2.2
1920–24				
Railroads	17	19.1	0	0.0
Manufacturing	36	40.1	7	7.9
Banking	3	33.7	2	2.2
Insurance	4	4.5	1	1.1
Other	14	15.7	5	5.6

TABLE 2   (*Continued*)

Year	Noncontributory		Contributory	
	N	%	*N*	%
1925–29				
Railroads	8	9.7	0	0.0
Manufacturing	13	15.9	25	30.5
Banking	2	2.4	5	6.1
Insurance	2	2.4	5	6.1
Other	9	11.0	13	15.9
1930–32				
Railroads	0	0.0	0	0.0
Manufacturing	2	3.2	35	56.5
Banking	0	0.0	9	14.5
Insurance	0	0.0	6	9.7
Other	1	1.6	9	14.5

Source: Calculated from Latimer, *Industrial Pension Systems*, pp. 908–1113.

campaign to eliminate unions from the steel industry. The company's plan was instituted with the understanding that "pensions might be withheld or terminated in case of misconduct."[24] As table 3 shows, among pensions initiated in manufacturing between 1905 and 1914, most were in the three heavy industries that employed the largest proportion of unskilled and semiskilled industrial workers. Iron and steel, chemicals, and machinery accounted for more than 49 percent of all manufacturing pensions in this period.

Not only the timing but also the structure of the industrial plans indicates that employers implemented them as strategies to contain labor unrest. Most company plans included clauses prohibiting workers from striking on penalty of forfeiting all pension rights. Antistrike clauses took various forms. Some plans stated that employment interrupted by a strike constituted an irrevocable disruption in service. In others good-conduct clauses specified that the board of directors could revoke pension rights for any misconduct.[25]

Some plans also granted employers the right to recall pensioners to active service:

> On request of the company at any time, pensioned employees will be expected to give it the benefit of their knowledge and experience and to act as advisors whenever called upon.

Table 3   Pensions in Manufacturing Industries

Year	Noncontributory		Contributory	
	N	%	N	%
1905–14				
Food	4	7.5	0	0.0
Textiles	4	7.5	0	0.0
Iron and steel	10	18.9	0	0.0
Paper, printing	1	1.9	0	0.0
Chemicals	8	15.1	0	0.0
Metals	5	9.4	0	0.0
Machinery	8	15.1	0	0.0
Other	13	24.5	0	0.0
1915–24				
Food	6	7.0	3	3.5
Textiles	5	5.8	0	0.0
Iron and steel	14	16.3	0	0.0
Paper, printing	9	10.5	1	1.2
Chemicals	21	24.4	1	1.2
Metals	0	0.0	2	2.3
Machinery	13	15.1	1	1.2
Other	8	9.3	2	2.3
1925–32				
Food	2	2.7	7	9.3
Textiles	2	2.7	8	10.7
Iron and steel	1	1.3	7	9.3
Paper, printing	2	2.7	13	17.3
Chemicals	4	5.3	13	17.3
Metals	3	4.0	1	1.3
Machinery	1	1.3	4	5.3
Other	0	0.0	7	9.3

Source: Calculated from Latimer, *Industrial Pension Systems,* pp. 908–1113.

The employing company reserves the right to recall pensioners to the service of the company, in which event pensions cease for the time being, and wages are paid in accordance with the standard wage rates for the occupation for which the pensioner has been recalled. This right of the company terminates when the pensioner shall have reached the age of 70 years.

The acceptance of a pension allowance does not debar a retired employee from engaging in other business, provided it is not prejudicial to the interest of this company, but such person shall hold himself in readiness and be subject to any reasonable call of the company.[26]

Although it is impossible to determine how often employers actually withdrew pension rights from retirees who refused to become strikebreakers, this practice did occur, particularly among the railroads. In 1915, for example, a Canadian railroad called former employees into service during a strike. In 1920 the Denver Tramway Corporation eliminated its pension because of a strike.[27] In 1925 the Western Maryland Railroad commanded its pensioned engineers to return to work during a strike. When the engineers refused they lost their pensions, which were subsequently paid by the Brotherhood of Locomotive Engineers. As the engineers' journal reported:

> Every member of this Brotherhood has a right to feel proud of the white-haired pensioned engineers on the Western Maryland Railroad, who heroically refused to go back to work and act as strikebreakers on their brothers. . . . It is a matter of great pride to us at this Christmas season to be able to tell you that even though the Western Maryland Railroad has shamefully torn from them their pension rights, the Grand Office of the B. of L.E. has seen to it that they are all properly cared for.[28]

Employers also had wide latitude in interpreting misconduct rules, which contained numerous grounds for revoking pension rights. Grounds for pensions revocation included "bankruptcy of the pensioner, conviction of any felony or misdemeanor, [or] if the pensioner engages in conduct inimical to the interests of the company."[29] As E. A. Vanderlip, president of the National City Bank of New York, explained: "When employees realize that unsatisfactory conduct may at any time lose them not only their present position—a loss which in such a labor market as ours might be easily made good—but that it entails further the loss of a very valuable asset, the employee's right to a pension, the incentive to good conduct is greatly increased."[30] Unskilled workers had none of the bargaining power exercised by craft workers, and in the mass-production industries the loss of a job was a serious threat. The potential loss of pension benefits as well was an attempt to maintain a docile labor force.

Although the first contributory pension schemes appeared in banking in the nineteenth century, the railroad and manufacturing pensions were entirely noncontributory until 1920 (see table 2).

Further, they all contained the restrictions on labor mobility inherent in the early poor laws, with eligibility based on a required fifteen to thirty years of continuous service with the company.[31] Given the high rates of labor turnover, these restrictions meant that few workers could ever qualify.

Noncontributory pensions also symbolized the arbitrary authority of employers and the workers' lack of autonomy.[32] Noncontributory plans typically included disclaimers protecting company funds:

> The pension is a purely voluntary provision for the benefit of aged or disabled employees and does not constitute a contract or confer any legal rights of any kind upon any employee.

> All pensions herein provided for are gratuities and remain the exclusive property of the company until actual payment thereof to the pensioner.

> It is expressly understood that every pension hereunder will be granted only in the discretion of the company, will be continued only at its pleasure, and may be revoked at any time.[33]

Two-thirds of all noncontributory pension plans contained disclaimers asserting, in effect, that workers had no pension rights, even when they had fulfilled the service and conduct requirements.[34] In addition, many contained clauses permitting the company to reduce pension allowances if the pension fund was inadequate to pay the amount promised. The Pennsylvania Railroad, for example, provided that "if the basis of pension allowances creates demands in excess of annual appropriations, a new basis may be established involving ratable reduction of pension allowances to a point that will bring the expenditures within limitations."[35] Just as workers under the drive system had no decision-making power on the job, so they had no independent rights to benefits. Employers controlled all aspects of work.

Such disclaimers were also a natural outcome of the growth of monopoly enterprises. As joint-stock companies superseded traditional family and partnership forms of ownership, boards of directors became agents of the stockholder-owners of the corporation. Agents on the board had no legal right to give away the corporation's assets as gifts, since corporate money could be used only for corporate purposes. Thus employers lost the ability to make decisions about pension rights on an individual basis, because broader changes in the organization of production depersonalized labor relations.

Court decisions supported the provisions of disclaimers. In

summarizing a series of court decisions examining pensioners' claims against their employers, University of Illinois professor Frederick Green declared: "There is no *moral obligation* to pension persons retired after long service which will support a pension. Such a pension is merely additional compensation for past services, and the fact that the original compensation may be thought to have been inadequate will not justify it."[36] Discretionary clauses allowed corporations to establish pensions based on criteria that met corporate purposes, while protecting corporate funds if the financial risk seemed too high.[37]

To keep pension rolls down, some employers tightened up personal conduct rules as the worker approached retirement age. As the president of the Brotherhood of Electrical Workers explained: "The usual stipulation in these schemes is that the employee must have worked twenty years with the company to secure a pension. But in seventeen out of every twenty cases, investigation has disclosed, such employees are dismissed for some cause or other between the 15 and 20-year period of employment, and comparatively few ever get on the pension rolls."[38]

Employers also adopted pension programs as a simple means of retiring old, inefficient workers. Some employers believed that the practice of shifting older workers to lighter tasks while continuing to pay them a salary was more costly than pensioning them off, and many employers adopted pensions with this goal in mind.[39] For example, the Pennsylvania Railroad pensioned off all employees at age seventy:

> This rule must be an inflexible one in order that it may accomplish its purpose, and to it no exception is therefore made. With all its trainmen, clerks, workmen and executive officers retiring at seventy, the Pennsylvania can be reasonably sure that the whole property is being managed by men at their greatest period of efficiency. The pension system permits the company to get rid humanely of any drones who encumber the service and to keep the entire staff constantly fresh.[40]

Finally, pensions protected employers from workers' injury claims. Workers' compensation laws enacted in the early twentieth century held employers liable for injuries on the job, a potentially serious loss given the higher accident rates of older workers. As protection against claims of injured workers, many of the roads added clauses stating that "no pension is allowed to any officer or employee who shall make or enforce any claim against the company for damages by reason of any injury or accident occurring within three years prior to the date when such employee shall be retired or leave the service."[41] Thus employers used the early pension plans primarily as a containment device, to control the behavior of workers, reduce labor militancy, and save the costs of older workers' wages. Like public relief, private sector pensions reflected the relationships between workers and employers in the transformation of the social process of production.

PENSIONS UNDER THE AMERICAN PLAN

World War I reduced net immigration from 815,000 in 1913 to 19,000 by 1916, limiting the pool of unskilled workers and creating a high demand for labor. The spread of the eight-hour day and the entrance of several million men into military service intensified the labor shortage.[42] Labor turnover roughly doubled, strikes increased, and union membership grew from 2,716,900 in 1914 to 3,508,400 by war's end.[43]

Although the war temporarily strengthened labor's position, government's wartime encouragement of the coordination of production had created support for corporate collusion. When the war ended, the large corporations emerged with secure positions in most major industries. Rather than creating single-firm monopolistic control, however, they learned to exploit their market power with shared control. Thus, in the monopoly sector competition was reduced to nonprice behavior among established rivals.[44]

Organized labor's wartime gains war were rapidly erased as employers embarked on a massive campaign to destroy the power of unions. Termed the "American plan" by oil industry magnate John D. Rockefeller, Jr., the movement extended the open-shop tactics adopted before the war. The employers' initial offensive focused primarily on such negative tactics as increased use of injunctions and "yellow dog" contracts to break up strikes and exclude unions and the speedup, which forced workers to increase productivity.[45]

In response to the employers' offensive, a massive strike wave broke out across the country. In 1919 more than 4 million workers went on strike, approximately 20 percent of the labor force, and the strikes continued over the next three years. But the employers' organized activity was stronger than that of the workers, who quickly found they could not defeat the massed power of open-shop industry. By 1923 the American plan had checked the growth of unions, with organized labor losing more than 1.5 million members.[46]

The use of force was successful but costly. It increased labor turnover, a growing employer concern since immigration restriction had reduced the supply of cheap labor. One study found that in twelve factories, "72.8 percent of the employees engaged during the year had not been employed in these factories before." Employers also discovered that although the American plan had weakened unions, workers fought back by deliberately restricting output through informal work groups.[47]

Faced with high turnover and reduced productivity, employers shifted their focus to new practices of labor management, designed to create a "homogeneous, contented body."[48] Turnover-reduction policies took the form of an industrial relations movement, which attempted to place labor policy on a rational, organized basis. The industrial relations movement centralized labor administration in industrial relations departments, rationalized recruitment, and buttressed the welfare philosophy of big business. If modern industrial life created insecurity among workers, then management had the responsibility to free workers from anxiety over illness, unemployment, and old age. Secure workers would reduce turnover and induce labor peace. Clarence Hicks, a professional labor relations expert, explained: "The employee who is saving his money becomes a capitalist and is no longer hostile to capitalism."[49]

Employers had long experimented with such corporate welfare measures as shop grievance committees, life insurance plans, and pensions. As organized labor's wartime strength stimulated further employer efforts at peaceful labor relations, more pension plans appeared. In the years immediately following the war, at least 133 new pension plans were initiated, more than in any previous five-year period.[50]

Most of the new pensions appeared in the manufacturing industries. Of the forty-three new manufacturing pensions implemented in that period, seventeen were in the petroleum industry, eleven in either Standard Oil companies or its subsidiaries.[51] Standard Oil's interest in pensions reflected its evolving labor management strategies. Standard Oil was the first giant monopoly in America, a large, vertically integrated, centrally administered concern operating in worldwide markets. The target of the antitrust movement, the Standard Oil trust was dissolved by a 1911 Supreme Court decision. A dissolution in name only, the 1911 decision merely resulted in a rearrangement of stockownership. Although Standard Oil was made temporarily more cautious by the hostile political environment, the individual companies that the trust comprised never became competitors and continued to secretly collude on prices, rates of production, and profit levels.[52]

The war had strengthened the oil industry's position. During the war, oil industry leaders, working together through the National Petroleum War Service Committee chaired by Alfred C. Bedford, chairman of the board of directors of Standard Oil of New Jersey, worked out an agreement with the Federal Trade Commission releasing them from the provisions of the Sherman and Clayton antitrust acts.[53] This agreement granted the industry the official freedom to set prices and limit production.

Although the oil companies emerged from the war with a near monopoly of the industry, they were plagued by labor troubles. In 1915 and 1916 workers struck Standard Oil of New Jersey, the largest and most powerful of the Standard affiliates. In response to outbreaks of violence at the Bayonne refinery, the company used armed guards to break up the strike. In the ensuing battle, many workers were killed and much property was destroyed. As public opinion turned against the company and the press renewed its attack upon Standard Oil, John D. Rockefeller, Jr., decided that a major overhaul of labor policy was needed. He called in labor consultant Clarence Hicks, who recommended a sweeping plan of employee benefits.[54] In 1918, the same year that the AFL attempted to organize the oil fields, all the Standard Oil companies initiated pension programs and other extensive employee benefits.[55] Thus Standard Oil abandoned its motto regarding labor—"Whenever it shows its head, hit it"—and embarked on a more positive agenda for labor relations.[56]

Other companies followed suit. Analyses of pension programs now included discussions of how they might reduce labor turnover.[57] Employers also incorporated more guarantees into their pension plans. The Phelps Dodge Corporation, one of the few mining companies to provide pensions, increased its pension benefits and reduced the length-of-service requirement, explaining that "these measures have been effectual in increasing the stability and efficiency of the working force and keeping the men contented."[58] Thus, corporate philosophy shifted from an emphasis on pensions as a threat to a greater concern with instilling loyalty and inducing goodwill.

While pensions may have induced goodwill among the unorganized, labor strongly opposed even the more liberalized company pension plans on the grounds that they impeded labor mobility, prevented strike action, dissolved worker representation on pension boards, and were merely a gratuity to which workers had no legal right.[59] As the railroad engineers' journal explained,

> Union insurance . . . is incomparably superior to the company brand. Locomotive engineers holding Western Maryland

pensions understand why, as do the Pullman pensioners who lost their old age fund when they refused to scab during the shopmen's strike. Neither will the pensioners of Morris Co., the Chicago packers, soon forget the shameless perfidy shown by that company in dumping overboard its pension obligations when it was gobbled up by Armour & Co.[60]

Labor was right! Studies indicated that fewer than 4 percent of all male industrial workers and fewer than 3 percent of all female industrial workers ever worked for a single company long enough to qualify for a pension.[61] Thus a vice president of the Brotherhood of Locomotive Engineers warned union members: "My advice to our members is to have nothing to do with any of these proposed schemes, for you can get better and cheaper pension protection through your own organization and you will have the satisfaction of controlling it yourselves."[62]

INDUSTRIAL RELATIONS AND CONTRIBUTORY PENSION SCHEMES

The new industrial relations policies reduced labor turnover by increasing job stability. With a more stable labor force, controlled by internal mechanisms rather than external sanctions, employers saw advantages in implementing contributory pension schemes. As table 1 shows, beginning in 1925 there was a major shift in pension strategy, with most of the new plans having a contributory rather than a noncontributory structure. Of the contributory pensions in existence in 1929, 56 percent had been initiated since 1923 and 40 percent in the preceding three years.[63]

What was significant about the shift was that for the first time manufacturing concerns began experimenting with contributory plans. As table 2 shows, 30.5 percent of the contributory plans initiated between 1925 and 1929 and 56.5 percent of the contributory plans initiated between 1930 and 1932 were in manufacturing. The leaders were in the chemical and the printing industries. In chemicals, as table 3 shows, thirteen contributory plans were established between 1925 and 1932, 17.3 percent of all plans. Seven of the contributory plans were in the petroleum industry, which began converting its noncontributory pensions in 1927.

For the most part contributory pensions were implemented in large corporations, monopolies operating in national and international markets. These corporations required a mobile labor force, freed of the restrictions inherent in noncontributory systems that locked a worker to a single company for thirty years. The structure of contributory pensions eliminated the restrictions on labor mobility by granting benefits based on amount of contributions rather than length of service.[64] Under the increasingly common annuity plans, employers and employees jointly purchased annuities from insurance companies. The annuities then became the property of the employee, payable when he reached retirement age, regardless of when his employment terminated. As one labor analyst explained, "Thus, a workman would receive credit for the time he worked during his life, irrespective of the concerns that hired him."[65]

Another advantage of contributory plans, which took a portion of the funds directly out of workers' wages, was that they reduced employers' costs.[66] A study conducted by the New York Building Congress conclusively proved that a noncontributory plan paying $600 per year beginning at age sixty-five would cost a company from 6 to 25 percent of payroll; the same benefits, funded through joint contributions from workers and employers, would cost from 1.5 to 7 percent of payroll. Further, labor turnover, so common among younger employees, now became an asset, since the employer's contributions to an annuity would be returned to his account if a worker left the company.[67]

Courts had already begun to reverse earlier rulings regarding contractual rights to pensions, affirming that workers did have rights to pension funds. For example, the Supreme Court of Virginia determined:

> In the case of the pension fund, the employee has a contractual relationship with the employer from the beginning of the employment. An offer is held out to him from the beginning and continuing throughout the employment of a certain part of the pension fund that he will be entitled to when he has reached a certain status based upon the duration and satisfactoriness of his service. . . . [This offer] is irrevocable to the extent of his pro rata of the funds set apart for the fulfillment of the purpose as to him and others entitled thereto.[68]

These rulings undermined the rationale for the discretionary noncontributory pensions that had so alienated labor.

Employers now concluded that contributory pensions improved labor relations "if a few features on which they lay special stress are embodied. Prominent among these are the return with interest of their deposits in the event of withdrawal, the guaranty of the pension, a stipulation that funds paid into the pension system shall not in any case revert to the employer."[69] Although many unions continued to oppose any type of company pension on the grounds that employer benefits threatened union loyalty, some union leaders saw advantages in plans that formally recognized the worker's share.[70] Since workers' contributions came directly out of wages, they expected some control over fund management. Some employers objected to this feature, but others felt that "the satisfactory results were largely due to the fact that employees directly participated in the administration of the scheme."[71] Not totally convinced that contributory schemes enhanced security, the national leadership of the AFL did note that "other pension plans accept the contributory principle and if on a sound actuarial basis with provisions for the return of contributions upon death, resignation or dismissal places the employer under definite contractual obligations."[72] Although contributory schemes guaranteed workers only the return of their own contribution (not the employer's), nonetheless they were an improvement over the total loss associated with noncontributory pensions.

Without the resources for centralized personnel planning, small firms were unable to pursue the job redivision, labor allocation, and redistribution of production among plants that characterized these initial attempts by large firms.[73] Thus pension schemes tended to mirror the divisions between firms. Large monopoly corporations implemented new industrial relations policies and experimented with contributory pensions; smaller competitive firms maintained the more negative features of the open-shop drive and offered either noncontributory pensions or none at all.

Contributory pensions not only differentiated companies by size and degree of monopolistic control, they also discriminated among workers. These initial attempts at stabilizing the labor force occurred in association with a process of labor segmentation, which systematically allocated different groups of workers to different plant divisions. Female employees were segregated into limited jobs in manufacturing or into clerical work, and blacks were relegated to certain shops in steel plants or to the foundry at Ford and other auto plants. As a result, job segregation became embedded within the job structure.[74]

A consequence of job segregation was that individuals in different sectors of the labor force came under different eligibility requirements for pensions. Most contributory plans were compulsory for salaried employees but optional for wageworkers. In effect, this meant that few wageworkers chose to enter the plan, since contributions would reduce take-home pay.[75] Those most likely to be wageworkers were women and minorities. Women and minorities were also penalized by the classification schemes written into

contributory plans "to eliminate as far as possible the transient
employees or the type of employees that are only engaged for a
short period of time, such as extra help." The "flotsam and jetsam—
those individuals who come and go in industry—have no claim on
the industry itself."[76] Since those with sporadic work records were
again more likely to be women and blacks, the flotsam and jetsam of
industry, corporations felt no need to provide for these marginal
elements of the labor force. The classification schemes eliminated
those employees with irregular work histories from eligibility.[77]
Thus the introduction of contributory pension plans initiated a
pattern of inequality in benefits, favoring white males employed in
stable salaried positions to the disadvantage of women and blacks,
who were more likely to work for wages and to have short job tenure.
The market structure that segregated women and blacks into jobs
paying lower wages and offering less job security was extended into
inequality in old age.

Contributory plans appeared to be more secure, because employers were more likely to place them in trust funds guaranteed through
insurance companies. In 1929 only 21.8 percent of noncontributory
pensions were guaranteed, in contrast to 78 percent of contributory
pensions.[78] As employers' concern with reducing turnover grew,
their willingness to commit funds to trusts increased.

Even before the onset of the Great Depression, instabilities in
corporate pensions appeared. As early as 1920 analysts warned of "a
general breakdown of these well-intentioned schemes upon which
hundreds of thousands of corporation employees are trustfully
depending for support in old age." The problems in the threatened
plans were numerous. None had anticipated the tremendous
expansion of the industrial labor force, the product of deskilling,
which increased 233 percent between 1890 and 1920.[79] As the plan
matured, the increased number of pensioners placed a heavy burden
on corporate funds.[80] Coupled with the numerical increase in
employees was an increase in wage scales, which affected benefit
levels. Companies found that their estimates of future pension costs
based on earlier expenditures left their plans seriously underfunded.
For example, the annual expenditure of the Pennsylvania Railroad in
1903, when pensions began, was less than $300,000; by 1925 that
amount had grown to $3,500,000.[81] An expanding industrial labor
force of increasingly restless semiskilled workers doomed industrial
pension plans.

The result was that many companies were forced to reduce, alter,
or abolish their promised pension disbursements. By 1929 several

had already abandoned their programs completely, as pensions mounted to 30 percent of active payroll.[82] One major study of industrial pensions concluded that "such practice will ultimately result in a level of payments which no one organization can bear if it is competing with companies which do not have such charges."[83] Although no legal obligation to pay pensions existed, employers were more aware now that their business success depended upon "popular good will." The failure of the industrial pension movement might impair "friendly relations with workers," "shake the confidence of labor in the good faith of capital," and "deprive corporate management of an important administrative device for freeing their payrolls of the ruinously expensive burden of aged and under-efficient employees."[84]

The depression quickly terminated any notion that contributory pensions were by nature more reliable. In fact, during the early 1930s the rates of failure were higher on these plans than on noncontributory programs, because many companies were unable to pay the insurance premiums.[85] As we shall see in chapter 7, when the newly organized mass-production workers began demanding pensions through collective bargaining, their goal was noncontributory plans.

CONCLUSION

In chapter 1, I argued that welfare responds to changes in the social process of production. This chapter has examined that thesis empirically by analyzing the development of private sector pensions. In contrast to much of the welfare state literature that views social benefits as a product of the state, this chapter demonstrates that benefits arising within the marketplace perform the same functions as public welfare. In the United States, private sector benefits became the vehicle through which workers and employers waged the initial battle over the commodification of wage labor.

During the initial expansion of wage labor, pensions functioned like poor relief, a discretionary gratuity that aged workers might receive from a benevolent employer. As employers used the open-shop drive to counter the growing strength of labor unions, noncontributory pensions became one of the weapons used to prevent strikes, improve efficiency, and impede labor mobility. Most of the pension plans in this period were instituted in the nonunionized manufacturing industries, which relied on large numbers of unskilled and semiskilled workers. In craft industries, by contrast, where workers had negotiated collective bargaining agreements with employers, no pensions appeared. Thus the presence or absence of pension benefits was predicated largely on the relationship between workers and employers.

With the growth of monopoly capitalism, the need for a mobile labor force made noncontributory industrial pensions an anachronistic form of employee benefits. Noncontributory pensions were more befitting a set of economic relations in which employers governed labor paternalistically and depended upon such impediments to labor mobility as poor laws. But in the emerging industrial order, employers abandoned the more punitive tactics of the open-shop drive and adopted an industrial relations program to improve worker morale. Contributory pensions eliminated the restrictions on labor mobility by basing benefits on contributions rather than on years served. They also reduced labor turnover and enhanced employer-employee relationships. Because of employers' desires to reduce the costs of contributory systems, women, blacks, and other minorities with irregular work histories were excluded from benefit protection. Thus, as the stratification among workers divided the industrial labor force along lines of gender and race, pension benefits came to reflect market inequalities.

If public benefits are part of the wage-setting process negotiated between capital and labor, then private benefits are equally so. This has generally not been recognized in either neo-Marxist or social democratic theories of welfare state development. Yet it is important to examine private sector benefits, particularly when no action is occurring in the public sector, to help interpret the agenda of the relevant class factions. It is this agenda that capital and labor bring to the bargaining table when the option of state action appears. In the United States organized labor remained opposed to contributory pensions until the 1930s, when a few labor leaders unenthusiastically endorsed them. Monopoly corporations, by contrast, had turned toward contributory pensions by the mid-1920s as a means of reducing costs, enhancing labor mobility, and improving labor relations. Contributory pensions were simply more compatible with the needs of an advanced industrial economy.

Fig. 5 *American Labor Legislation Review* 25 (June 1935): 50.

5

Legislating Social Security

For three decades the old age pension battle took place in the market. Labor's efforts at self-protection had failed, and employers' attempts to provide industrial pensions, so clearly linked to labor market objectives, in most instances only exacerbated workers' grievances. The limitations of state-level pensions, visible even during prosperous years, were highlighted during the depression, making the need for federal action seem imperative.

The Social Security Act of 1935 initiated a market-based welfare state that set an agenda for incremental reform in all future efforts. Its core program was contributory social insurance for wageworkers combined with noncontributory old age assistance for those outside the industrial marketplace. The enactment of national pension legislation signified the official beginning of the American welfare state. But why did the United States legislate an old age pension that combined social insurance with a federal-state assistance program?

One argument regarding how that structure originated locates support for the old age insurance component among a group of influential policy reformers associated with the American Association for Labor Legislation (AALL). According to this approach, during the 1920s the AALL pragmatically adopted the Wisconsin model of social insurance. The Wisconsin approach emphasized "competition and the profit motive to achieve collective security" rather than redistribution through government-subsidized welfare programs during a period when public opinion was hostile to labor legislation.[1] Although the AALL had earlier promoted both a preventive philosophy *and* government-run and -subsidized social insurance programs, it shifted toward the preventive approach because "this perspective could mesh well with the New Era's celebration of welfare efforts by private corporations." Welfare capitalism and "Hoover's associative state" had set "the ideological and institutional limits of possible reform," and though the AALL played little direct role in building the New Deal, key individuals did become "master builders of the new edifice."[2]

And what about old age assistance? The federal-state structure of old age assistance arose because of competition from preexisting state pension programs. As Theda Skocpol and Edwin Amenta declare, "The greater and more entrenched the state-level initiatives before Social Security, the fewer the federal controls built into that part of the Act."[3]

The argument that the preventive philosophy of the AALL meshed with welfare capitalism appears valid, given that many large corporations had turned to contributory pension plans in the decade before the Social Security Act was passed and that noncontributory assistance-based state pensions were in existence. But attributing the structure of Social Security to the key figures in the AALL and to ongoing state-level initiatives ignores the matrix of social power within the state, both in terms of the access to power held by various class factions and in terms of the ability of these factions to shape the environment of decision making. As old age security shifted from the private sector to the state, the class forces that had shaped pensions in the marketplace continued to affect their structure. This chapter examines these forces.

THE BUSINESS AGENDA

Throughout the first quarter of the twentieth century, the business community persistently opposed state old age pensions. Objections to pensions centered on employers' fears that they would undermine prevailing wage rates and that industries in states with pensions would experience a competitive disadvantage because of higher tax costs. State intervention in the free operation of the labor market would undermine the capital-accumulation process.

The first challenge to laissez-faire came not from organized labor but from reformers, who argued that the common welfare could be protected only by an aggressive program of government control. For Henry Rogers Seager, author of *Social Insurance: A Program of Reform*, social insurance against disability, unemployment, and old age not only would protect workers against the ravages of industrialization but, more important, would reduce the size of the reserve army of the aged and unemployed, whose presence formed a permanent barrier to bettering working-class life.[4]

In response to pressures for protective legislation, Massachusetts formed a commission in 1907 "to assess the advisability of establishing an old age insurance or pension system."[5] The Massachusetts

Commission on Old Age Pensions rejected state pensions on the grounds that they would have a number of undesirable effects. Pensions would undermine character by breaking down the habit of thrift and would impair family solidarity by removing the filial obligation to support one's aged parents. Further, a pension system would attract workers into the state, overcrowding the market. The overall impact would be to depress wages, since pensioners would outcompete younger workers for jobs.[6]

State pensions were also undesirable, because they would place industries in states that implemented them at a competitive disadvantage with neighboring states "unburdened by a pension system." The commission concluded that "if any general system of old age pensions is to be established in this country, this action should be taken by the national Congress and not through State legislation."[7] Thus in 1910, when the federal government administered no national welfare program, the possibility of a federal pension was not inconceivable to industry, which feared unequal competition between industries in different states more than federal intervention. Couched in the ideology of preserving the traditional family, the commission preserved the interests of manufacturers by not imposing a tax that would reduce their ability to compete and by not guaranteeing welfare benefits that might prove a disincentive to labor.

Over the next two decades, business opposition to state pensions remained strong, as state associations of manufacturers mobilized against attempts to legislate state old age pensions. At hearing after hearing, representatives from both local and national trade associations testified against state support for welfare legislation.[8] But as the private sector waged an increasingly futile battle to fund its own pension programs, a few far-sighted employers recognized that government pensions not only were inevitable but, if properly structured, could be advantageous to industry.

The idea that state intervention might have advantages for industry was first broached in 1925, when the National Industrial Conference Board (NICB) examined industrial pensions. The NICB was founded in 1916, a reincarnation of the open-shop movement organized by the National Association of Manufacturers. The organization was funded by a few powerful industrialists, with the largest donations coming from General Motors, General Electric, Firestone, and Westinghouse—all employers of large numbers of mass-production workers.[9] Its goal was to place backdoor political lobbying above the negative tactics of antiunionism, and in subsequent years the organization embarked on a series of studies of various aspects of labor issues and policies.[10] By the time the NICB held its 1925 meeting, there were already signs that company pension plans might be unworkable, and concerned executives mobilized to seek new answers.[11] Although the board concluded that "the task of correctly estimating and properly funding the cost of a pension plan [was] by no means beyond the ability or resources of industrial management," it suggested that a central fund be established, either under state control, as in accident compensation, or by a designated group of insurance companies.[12] By pooling their premiums, businesses could even out the risks, with the state providing the necessary regulation.

The central fund concept was never implemented, and by the end of the decade, it was clear that business had been unsuccessful in resolving the problem of economic insecurity in old age. The National Civic Federation (NCF), an organization of business magnates, conservative labor unionists, and civic leaders, had endorsed contributory pensions in private industry in 1916. In 1927 the NCF discussed the problems of industrial pensions and the trend toward state legislation. Disturbed by the "extravagant, defective, unsatisfying and demoralizing" effects of the noncontributory state pensions already in operation, the organization recommended compulsory contributory old age insurance for wageworkers, which would fit benefits "to suit the widely varying needs, means, ambitions and temperaments of all the different classes and grades of wageworker." The NCF further concluded that the pension system had to be at the federal rather than the state level, because of the mobility of American labor.[13] Thus, well before either national or contributory pensions were given serious consideration, an association with members from big business advocated an agenda that was to become the core program of the Social Security Act.

Toward the end of the decade articles supporting national pension legislation also began appearing in business journals. These articles recognized that industrial pensions "have not provided, and in all probability will not provide, a satisfactory means of eliminating destitution due to old age." Because of the private sector's inability to meet these needs, "governmental agencies are very likely to assume the burden of care for worn-out workers." As long as the tax burden was "universal and proportionate," industry had no need to concern itself with the problem.[14]

Some employers still remained firm in the belief that industry could provide for its own workers, but even these came to recognize that the state was the only solution for individuals not employed by industry. As welfare capitalist Owen D. Young of General Electric explained to Bishop Francis J. McConnell, president of the American Association for Old Age Security, in 1928:

> I am not yet ready to commit myself to the principle of Government appropriation for old age pensions. It may be necessary, and probably will be, to do something along this line, but my feeling is that it should be only for the last fringe of people who cannot otherwise be provided for. I am deeply interested in seeing that the industries themselves establish programs by which at least industrial workers will never become a charge on the taxing power of the state, but will be taken care of through the economic machinery of the industries themselves.[15]

This agenda was not merely an ideological outgrowth of welfare capitalism but was established by businessmen from large corporations who recognized the inability of the private sector to meet an advanced industrial economy's needs for efficiency and labor mobility.

The industrial relations movement, which attempted to place labor policy on a rational, organized basis, arose out of welfare capitalism. One supporting organization was Industrial Relations Counselors, which supplied the experts in policy analysis for business decision making.[16] A 1929 study by Industrial Relations Counselors found that only 329 industrial programs existed and that these were not evenly distributed throughout the occupational structure. Eighty percent of covered employees were in railroads, public utilities, metal trades, oil, banking and insurance, electrical apparatus, and supply industries. In contrast, among the highly competitive and largely unregulated manufacturing companies, only one-eighth of all employees were potentially covered by a pension plan, and these were in the larger manufacturing establishments.[17] For small manufacturers who relied on less working capital beyond payrolls, whose ratio of payroll costs to value of manufacturing output was often higher than in larger companies, and who in many cases functioned seasonally, with a high degree of labor turnover in the off-season, the disadvantages of pension costs outweighed any potential advantages.[18].

If contributory state pensions emerged as the agenda of large corporations, this vision was not shared throughout the business community. Small companies and those operating in local product markets had higher labor costs, and they feared the tax consequences of any public welfare measures more than labor turnover.

The inadequacies of industrial pensions were exacerbated by the depression. In prosperous periods when demands for labor were high, the opportunity to earn better wages often delayed retirement among employees who might otherwise have chosen to leave the labor force. During downturns in the business cycle, however, many who had delayed retirement entered the pension rolls, while employers pensioned off others as a means of reducing the active labor force.[19] Thus recessions placed tremendous pressure on pension funds.

Between 1929 and 1932 employers discontinued pension programs at a rapid rate. Almost 10 percent of the programs operating in 1929 were discontinued, closed to new employees, or suspended.[20] Termination occurred most frequently in smaller companies. By contrast, larger corporations were more likely to keep their programs operating, compensating for economic difficulties by reducing the scale of benefits for pensioners or otherwise deliberalizing their plans.[21] Although many new plans were established in the same period, overall fewer employees were eligible for pensions in 1932 than in 1929. Thus, within the private sector the instability of private pension programs made contributory state pensions an increasingly viable alternative.

STABILIZING THE ECONOMY

The large corporations that arose during the first decades of the twentieth century represented one solution to the problem of microeconomic regulation faced by every business. To stabilize fluctuations in product demand, producers initially formed pools— that is, agreements among producers to fix prices or limit output. When these failed, they turned to horizontal mergers. These mergers shifted power to central management, which then moved to consolidate the corporation by closing down the weaker branches and organizing the market to stabilize production.[22]

Corporations used two strategies as they attempted to stabilize product markets. One approach was segmentation, in which the market was divided, with the base level of demand retained for the corporations' mass-production products and the rest left for smaller producers. As an alternative to market segmentation, corporations met demand fluctuations by varying inventory. Concern with stabilization also extended to the input markets, including labor. Thus corporations attacked labor organizations in order to maintain tight control over their own internal operations.[23]

The corporation was only a partial solution to maintaining stability of production, for markets ultimately depended not only on the corporation's control over the market for its products and for its immediate supply of resource inputs, but also on the stability of the national economy. As industry recognized that national economic stabilization was beyond its control, it turned to the federal government for assistance. Industry hoped to stabilize aggregate demand for mass-production products concentrated in consumer durables through government spending.[24]

The first plans for industrial stabilization revived the central fund concept through joint government and industry plans for economic stabilization. The two most influential were those of Henry Harriman, of the New England Power Company and the United States Chamber of Commerce, and Gerard Swope, president of General Electric, who also held memberships in the Chamber of Commerce, the NCF, and AALL.[25] Both encompassed welfare provisions under broader programs for economic recovery through the stabilization of industry. According to these plans, economic stabilization could be achieved most effectively through trade associations of all commercial and industrial companies with fifty or more employees. In Swope's vision these associations would outline trade practices and exchange information on prices under the supervision of the Federal Trade Commission or the Department of Commerce. The plans also called for social benefits paid through a reserve fund to "care for unemployment, old age, sickness and accidents"[26]

Swope's pension plan, to be adopted by all trade association members and approved by the federal supervisory body, called for joint employer-employee contributions of 1 percent of employee wages into a trade association trust fund. If a worker changed jobs, the accumulated funds would be transferred. Any employee leaving an occupation covered by a trade association plan could withdraw his or her contributions plus interest (but not the employer's contribution).[27] Thus Swope's plan would have stabilized contributory private pensions by pooling funds across companies.

In stressing how his plan would contribute to industrial stabilization, Swope noted that "this plan seeks to place the same social burdens on companies competing in various parts of the United States."[28] Industry had learned that if it had to pay the costs of pension programs, it needed to reduce competition by equalizing costs across industries. If one company found certain labor market advantages in pension plans, it did not want to be at a competitive disadvantage. Forced compliance through government-regulated trade associations was the solution. For Harriman and Swope, the term "stabilization of industry" was a euphemism for reducing competition through regulation.

Although the National Association of Manufacturers was in a

period of transition in terms of membership, at this time it still primarily comprised small manufacturers. The organization expressed doubts about Swope's plan for industrial regulation, and President Hoover vigorously denounced it: "There is no stabilization of price without price fixing. . . . It is the most gigantic proposal of monopoly ever made in history." Yet big business reaction was on the whole favorable, with many industrial capitalists like Owen Young and Walter C. Teagle of Standard Oil of New Jersey favoring "curtailment of production to reasonable demand" through trade associations.[29]

Roosevelt's election signified a new agenda for national politics. Early in 1933 Roosevelt asked one of his chief advisors, Raymond Moley, to approach key business groups and work out a plan for industrial regulation. The AFL was also interested in recovery legislation and lobbied hard for the inclusion of promises of employee organization. To create mechanisms to facilitate a planned adjustment based on the rationalization of competitive conditions, the National Industrial Recovery Act (NIRA) established the National Recovery Administration (NRA), under which "employers would be permitted to combine in trade associations and construct codes of fair competition which would fix production quotas and prices." Section 7(a) of the NIRA also made concessions to labor, guaranteeing employees the right of organization and collective bargaining.[30]

To ensure limitations on the federal government's role, a Business Advisory Council (BAC) was formed within the Department of Commerce to represent management interests within the NRA structure during the period of code setting. BAC members, the honor guard of welfare capitalists, included both Gerard Swope and Walter Teagle as well as fifty-eight other big-business leaders.[31] The BAC advised top NRA administrators concerning overall agency policy and assisted in drafting and presenting code proposals for minimum wage scales and maximum work hours.

In this context it is not surprising that the biggest firms within each industry were able to define the codes that emerged. For instance, under Swope's leadership, General Electric had stabilized employment by reducing the average workweek at its plants to thirty hours.[32] By reducing the maximum workweek for all electrical companies through the NRA, Swope's plan kept smaller companies from increasing production by lengthening the workweek. Because of the NRA, many small businesses were injured, and American industry became more heavily concentrated.[33] A source of growing controversy, the NRA came under increasing attack as an instrument of monopolies. It also lacked enforcement power to guarantee labor's rights to organize. In 1935 the Supreme Court declared it unconstitutional.[34]

Although some of the NRA's price-setting proposals succeeded, its attempt to extend welfare programs throughout industry did not. The NRA experiment had revealed the limits of voluntary business organization for solving the nation's problem, and welfare capitalists now clearly understood that their company programs required substantial federal underpinning to be effective. As the public lost faith in the ability of business to solve the problems of the depression, pressure for government action increased.

In 1930 the House Committee on Labor began considering a national noncontributory old age pension.[35] NAM representatives and other small business organizations argued against it, reversing their opposition to state pensions under the threat of federal intrusion into welfare legislation. As one NAM representative asserted, "Now we have Congress considering the matter of engaging in helping the people by a Federal old-age pension, while not a State has been here saying it is necessary to have Federal aid care for such problems as may exist."[36]

In response to small business opposition to a national program, Senator Clarence Dill proposed a modified plan. The federal government would pay states one-third of their pension costs if they enacted statewide, compulsory laws.[37] Both proposals brought further heated opposition from manufacturers' associations, whose representatives argued that "employers . . . can not be expected to favor new taxes, which will simply increase production costs, add to the difficulties of competition, and restrict employment and the welfare of industrial workers."[38] These taxes, they charged, particularly penalized those companies operating in highly competitive markets, whereas a monopoly could readily meet any new charge. After three more years of debate, a modified Dill-Connery bill, authorizing a federal appropriation of $10,000,000 per year to pay one-third of states' old age assistance costs (H.R. 8461 and S. 493), passed the House Committee on Labor in 1934 and almost passed the Senate.

CREATING THE SOCIAL SECURITY ACT
The Terms of the Debate

As the country moved toward national old age pensions, competing factions attempted to set the terms of the debate. Organizations such as the NICB and the NCF, dominated by large corporations, agreed

that if federal pension legislation became necessary, it should be
based on the contributory model that welfare capitalism had adopted.
Organized labor, as represented by the craft-based AFL, had also
come to terms with a contributory pension. Yet neither of these class
factions was sufficiently interested in old age pensions to exert a
powerful influence on the state to act. The source of pressure that
moved the nation most rapidly toward national legislation was a
reform movement of the aged. This movement, led by retired
physician, Francis Townsend, proposed a proto-Keynesian measure
to solve both the nation's woes and the problem of old age insecurity.

Townsend demanded that the federal treasury pay all citizens over
sixty a flat pension of $200 a month on the single condition that the
entire amount be spent immediately.[39] The initial Townsend bill
(H.R. 3977) called for financing through a 2 percent transaction tax
on business. In response to criticisms that arose during congressional
hearings, Townsend drafted a modified version, which would raise
additional revenues through income taxes, inheritance taxes, and gift
taxes.[40] In contrast to existing state pensions and the Dill-Connery
bill, the Townsend plan carried no poor law assumptions in its
distribution plan. *All* older people were to receive this income,
regardless of residency, number of living relatives, or income level—
thus the term "flat plan." Hundreds of thousands of elderly people
supported Townsend, and members of Congress felt increasing
pressure for a pension as elderly constituents bombarded them with
petitions.[41]

In the political furor created by the Townsend plan, a critical
Roosevelt administration launched an investigation through the
Committee on Old Age Security.[42] The committee described the plan
as unworkable and financially unsound, a point on which both
business and labor agreed. But the labor movement split over viable
alternatives.

The radical labor proposal, introduced by Minnesota representative Earnest Lundeen, had the support of socialists, dissident union
chiefs within the AFL, numerous local unions, and communist-
dominated unemployment councils, many of whom testified in its
favor.[43] The Lundeen bill advocated compensation equal to average
local wages for all unemployed workers, supplementary benefits for
part-time workers unable to secure full-time employment, and
payments to all workers unable to work because of sickness or old age.
Funding was to come from the general treasury, with supplementary
income to be provided by taxes levied on inheritances, gifts, and
individual and corporate incomes of $5,000 a year or over.[44]

Ideologically, the Lundeen bill challenged existing welfare policy.

Supporters argued that it would maintain a basic standard of living, that it would protect strikers from being disqualified from benefits, that it provided for union participation in benefit administration, and that it put the financial burden on those most able to pay.[45]

Lundeen supporters rejected the Townsend plan, because its advocates "direct various kinds of verbal attacks against capitalists even while they bend all their effort to the task of saving the capitalist system." Further, it provided insurance only for those who reached the age of sixty, not for all in need.[46] But critics linked the Lundeen bill with the Townsend plan, portraying both as fantastic and unworkable schemes. The opposition of the AFL's national leadership to the Lundeen bill also contributed to its defeat. Although representatives from several locals testified before the House committee, the conservative AFL national leadership was notably absent and took no position on this bill. The AFL's reluctant support for any state old age pensions, won just a few years earlier, did not extend to such radical measures.[47]

By 1934 Roosevelt had three welfare measures before him: the Lundeen bill, the Dill-Connery bill, and a Wagner-Lewis bill for unemployment. As governor of New York, Roosevelt had sponsored an unsuccessful contributory pension bill, so the contributory philosophy was not unfamiliar to him.[48] On 8 March 1934 Roosevelt lunched with Gerard Swope, author of the Swope plan, to get his views on unemployment insurance and old age pensions. Swope described General Electric's own joint contributory pension plan, in which both employer and employee had a vested interest.[49] Before the luncheon was completed Roosevelt, his political imagination triggered by Swope's proposal for a federal system that provided cradle-to-grave coverage, asked Swope to summarize his ideas. Two weeks later Swope presented the president with the completed proposal, a detailed statistical document that included plans for unemployment, disability, and old age pensions. Roosevelt immediately began pushing for a comprehensive social security measure incorporating both unemployment and pensions.[50] As a Social Security official later recalled: "The President . . . insisted from the very beginning that there should be one omnibus bill, because his idea was old age assistance, aid for dependent children, aid for the blind were very popular and would carry the other two." Thus Roosevelt did not push for Wagner-Lewis because "he had a bigger fish to fry."[51]

In 1934, when national welfare legislation was under consideration, most workers had no voice in the state. The AFL opposed the one piece of legislation that might have created an egalitarian welfare state, and mass-production workers, whose interests were represented by that bill, were still unorganized. The one exception was the railroad workers, whose successful campaign for the federalization of company pensions had been overturned by the Supreme Court. State representatives thus learned that the taxing authority had to be separated from the disbursement of benefits if any federal pension was to pass the test of constitutionality. Although organized labor had little impact on the Social Security Act, the precedent established by the railroad unions did supply a model for subsequent legislation to benefit a broader range of citizens.

The business community was split, with some organizations representing the large corporations recognizing the necessity of, if not explicitly supporting, contributory national old age pensions. The business agenda was supported by the AALL, and it is from the ranks of this organization that Roosevelt drew the committee members to form a legislative proposal.

The Creation of the Committee on Economic Security

In a speech on 8 June Roosevelt clearly discarded income redistribution as a goal of social security and committed himself to a contributory plan: "I believe that the funds necessary to provide this insurance should be raised by contribution rather than by an increase in general taxation."[52] To implement this program, Roosevelt excluded from the legislative planning committee—the Committee on Economic Security (CES)—all advocates of a more radical, redistributory social welfare policy. The CES was composed entirely of Wisconsin-approach supporters, who held a preventive, business-centered philosophy.[53] Prevention, according to AALL member and Princeton economist J. Douglas Brown, could be achieved through the individualization of benefit rights, which related the prevention of old age poverty "to the individual's customary way of life and the normal costs of sustaining that way of life."[54] In Brown's view, as in the earlier National Civic Federation proposal, benefit levels should reflect income variations between individuals. Whether the concept emerged from the Wisconsin-schooled advisory committee or from the business community, it was compatible with earlier proposals from the liberal segment of the business community.

Roosevelt gave to Secretary of Labor Frances Perkins, Harry Hopkins, director of the Federal Emergency Relief Administration, and Secretary of Agriculture Henry Wallace the task of selecting the CES membership. Perkins had previously worked with Arthur Altmeyer, former secretary of the Wisconsin Industrial Commission, which administered Wisconsin's unemployment relief. In 1933 she had appointed him director of the Labor Compliance Division of the National Recovery Administration.[55] Thus Altmeyer not only was well schooled in the Wisconsin philosophy but had also worked closely with businessmen in the NRA, who approved his selection. As Eastman Kodak executive Marion Folsom later recalled, "I naturally liked Altmeyer's approach because he came from Wisconsin . . . and they were on an individual reserve basis."[56]

Altmeyer's first choice of a CES chair was Bryce Stewart, director of research for Industrial Relations Counselors. Stewart was willing to act only in an advisory capacity but later did agree to head the study of unemployment insurance.[57] Altmeyer then appointed Edwin Witte, secretary of the Wisconsin Industrial Commission, to select other staff members. At Roosevelt's request, he made a special trip to consult with industrialists Gerard Swope, John Raskob of General Motors, and Walter Teagle of Standard Oil, all members of the Business Advisory Council, to "get from them their ideas on what ought to be done, which they had previously presented to the President."[58] Witte recalled:

> I had several conferences with Mr. Harriman [president of the United States Chamber of Commerce] during the fall and again immediately preceding his testimony before the Senate Finance Committee. Mr. Harriman's general attitude was that some legislation on social security was inevitable and that business should not put itself in the position of attempting to block this legislation, but should concentrate its efforts upon getting it into acceptable form.[59]

Altmeyer also appointed Murray Latimer, Barbara Armstrong, and J. Douglas Brown to design an old age pension plan. Latimer was employed by Industrial Relations Counselors, compiled that organization's study of industrial pensions, and was involved in hammering out the details of the Railroad Retirement Act. He was also a member of the AALL and had served as an advisor on annuities and pension plans to Standard Oil of New Jersey, California, and Ohio. Armstrong's book *Insuring the Essentials* advocated contributory federal old age pensions.[60]

In addition to the technical board, an Advisory Council on Economic Security, which included labor, citizen, and employer representatives, was created to assist the CES. The employers selected were a group of moderate welfare capitalists, including Swope, Folsom, and Teagle, along with Morris Leeds, president of Leeds and Northrup and a member of the NICB and the AALL, and Sam Lewison, vice president of Miami Copper Company and AALL president from 1927 to 1928.[61] Roosevelt wanted Swope or Young, as businessmen who recognized the inevitability of social security legislation, to chair the council, but Perkins advised him that this would be politically unwise.[62] Instead a southerner, Frank Graham, president of the University of North Carolina, was selected, to avert some of the opposition expected from the South.

Business Reaction

In its official capacity the Advisory Council had little impact, but the employer members exerted considerable unofficial influence. A major employer concern was to obtain as much federal control over the legislation as possible so as to regulate competition from companies who might otherwise circumvent the proposed taxes. The benefit of the employer contribution, according to Brown, was that "it makes uniform throughout industry a minimum cost of providing old-age security and protects the more liberal employer now providing pensions from the competition of the employer who otherwise fires the old person without a pension when superannuated. It levels up the cost of old-age protection on both the progressive employer and the unprogressive employer."[63]

Employer members of the Advisory Council shared Brown's advocacy of a national pension. From their own experiences with company pensions, they had learned that labor mobility in an advanced corporate economy impeded both state pensions and individual corporation plans. Folsom's own experience with Eastman Kodak's pension had brought home the need for a national old age pension:

> I was very critical of government getting into this thing. At that time a few states had old age assistance, but that's about all. . . . But when the depression came along, I realized that employers could not generally inaugurate plans voluntarily, although I went around everywhere trying to urge employers to adopt a pension plan themselves. But as far as states are concerned, you couldn't possibly have it by state because people go from one state to the other so frequently. . . . You just had to have a federal system because a lot of people don't live in the same state all their lives. It would be impossible to transfer reserves for pensions from one state to another. . . . So I just came around to the conclusion that you just couldn't do it by individual companies or by states and the only thing to do was to have the federal government.[64]

Folsom, whose company operated internationally, saw other benefits to a national pension scheme. European businessmen had convinced him that welfare benefits would contain labor's desires for more radical change. One London banker explained: "Now, we've had it over here over the years and we think it's a good thing, because we feel that with this contributory system of old age insurance and unemployment insurance that the worker feels he's got a stake in our system and he's not interested in changing the system. We think it ties him into our whole system rather than the other way around."[65]

Business leaders were thus quite satisfied with national old age insurance (OAI), for it involved complete federal control over the imposition of employer and employee contributions. In fact, when this plan ran into opposition from CES members because it was national in scope, "help came from an unexpected source, the industrial executives on the Committee's Advisory Council . . . their practical understanding of the need for contributory old age annuities on a broad, national basis carried great weight with those in authority."[66]

The OAI provisions thus represented an approch to social welfare created by private businessmen. They retained the joint contributory format of private pension plans and did little to redistribute income. Only wage earners received benefits, ensuring that America's social welfare system would to be tied to the private labor market. The contributory structure, which maintained a relationship between benefits and wages, guaranteed that OAI would not undermine existing wage levels. Further, by tying benefits to wages, OAI retained regional variations within the bounds of a universal program.

As the proposed legislation moved toward passage, small manufacturers, who had fought for years against all forms of federal welfare taxation, unleashed a storm of criticism against it. Representatives from the National Metal Trades Association, the Illinois Manufacturing Association, the Connecticut Manufacturers Association, and the National Association of Manufacturers all testified against the bill in the Senate Finance Committee. Fearful that the tax levied on their payrolls would reduce their competitive advantage, they vainly argued that the bill was unfair. James Emery of the NAM testified:

> The tax is inequitable between employers because it often occurs that two companies with the same payroll, paying the same tax, have obviously different annual business, according to the nature of the product, the rapidity of the turn-over, and the risk in the particular industry as to either profit or loss. . . . It

is said that the method of taxation proposed, as it meets with
response by the States, will secure uniformity in costs of
production. . . . It is a serious question as to whether the
equalization of the costs of operation among the States is a
sound policy, because, on the contrary, we are not only due to
respect the differences in economic conditions, the advantages
in lower living costs, access to raw materials and the various
natural advantages enjoyed by the States, but throughout the
life of the NRA, the claim for labor differentials, based on the
recognition of these inequalities, has been a continuing issue
requiring recognition and adjustment.[67]

Thus smaller manufacturers argued that equalizing welfare costs
would not equalize other costs, which varied according to prevailing
wage rates and access to raw materials. Further, while a greater
percentage of working capital beyond payroll costs buffered the large
companies against the proposed tax costs, the smaller manufacturers
were unlikely to have cash working capital greater than 10 percent of
their total annual payroll. According to Illinois Manufacturing
Association representative John Harrington, "50 percent of the
manufacturers in Illinois are today reduced to a hand-to-mouth basis
as regards cash-working capital."[68] Smaller companies were also less
able to pass the taxes on to consumers, since the financing for cost
shifting, which involved a period of adjustment, would have to come
out of immediate working capital.

    Although a core of House Republicans—John Taber, James
Wadsworth, and Daniel Reed—faithfully reflected the small-
business position by vehemently opposing the impending legislation,
fears of reprisal at the polls made their opposition collapse. On 19
April Social Security legislation passed the House by a resounding
371 to 33 margin.[69]

    In shaping the old age insurance program the business agenda,
first formulated in the 1920s, dominated. Business leaders from the
monopoly sector did not have to intervene directly, although a few
farsighted welfare capitalists did. Rather, government leaders had
already accepted the business approach to social insurance, and only
those with compatible views were appointed to key policy-formation
committees. Labor's input was minimal, because dissension within
the labor movement prevented workers from advocating a unified
proposal and because labor had not yet formed a coalition with the
Democratic party, which was to pay future dividends. Although small
manufacturers had the support of their state congressmen, their
agenda was essentially a negative one, that of holding back legislation.
Thus their only input was to delay, not to shape, the impending bill.

Southern congressmen also had a negative agenda, but as we shall see, their position of strength within the state hierarchy gave them the power to insert their demands.

The Influence of the South

In its first reports the CES recommended including agricultural labor and domestic servants, as well as industrial wage earners, under OAI. Some historical accounts attribute the eventual exclusion of these workers from the program to the intervention of Secretary of the Treasury Henry Morgenthau, who purportedly felt that keeping track of their work records posed an insurmountable problem. In fact excluding agricultural labor was just one of several Treasury Department recommendations, but southerners, who packed the House Ways and Means Committee, seized upon it.[70] Although Witte presented evidence during the Senate hearings describing how European nations successfully administered pension programs for agricultural workers, the southern agenda prevailed.

Southern congressmen also influenced the structure of old age assistance, a jointly funded and administered federal-state program. Originally the OAA titled specified that states had to furnish assistance sufficient to provide "a reasonable subsistence compatible with decency and health." Another clause required the state to designate "a single state authority to administer or supervise the administration of the plan and insure methods of administration which are approved by the Administrator."[71] Southern congressmen objected to both clauses on the grounds that the federal government was undermining states' rights. As Virginia Senator Harry Byrd argued:

> Do I understand . . . that this Administrator has supreme power to deny a sovereign State of this Union any benefits of this pension system at all unless that State complies with the regulations that he makes and he thinks are proper. . . . The statutes do not go into details as to what is a standard of decent living. He [the administrator] can say what a standard of decent living is, as to how much each pensioner should obtain if the State does not provide that additional money, and then, as I understand it, the entire appropriation is denied to the particular state.[72]

What was the southern agenda? Most basically, southerners feared that federal benefits would undermine planters' paternalistic control over tenant labor, particularly black labor. In 1935 three-fifths of all black workers, most of whom resided in the South, were employed in agriculture or domestic service.[73] Southern congressmen had no intention of letting federal funds go directly to black workers. Further, southern industrial wage scales, which were in fact considerably lower than northern wage scales, could also be undermined. For example, the ratio of payrolls to the value of output was 33.9 percent in Massachusetts, but only about 25 percent in Georgia, North Carolina, and South Carolina in cotton manufacturing.[74]

Roosevelt needed southern support to get his programs through Congress, and in response to southern objections, OAA was left under local control. The "decency and health" provision was eliminated, leaving the states free to pay pensions of any amount and still recover 50 percent of the costs from the federal government. States were also granted the right to arbitrarily set eligibility criteria more stringent than those stipulated in the bill. Finally, states were given the right to select anyone they chose to administer old age assistance through a clause qualifying the original stipulation that the methods of administration satisfy the federal government. The combined effect of the two programs was to exclude blacks from OAI almost entirely, leaving the matter of old age security for southern blacks in the hands of local authorities.

Black leaders argued for greater federal control of standards, explaining that "in many communities there is a prevailing idea that Negro persons can have such a reasonable subsistence on less income than a white person" and that local standards would become the rationale "to give less assistance to aged Negroes than to aged whites."[75] Further, the residence requirements for OAA were likely to be particularly unfair to blacks engaged in migratory labor, since they could be used to deny benefits. These objections were raised before a silent Senate Finance Committee and never discussed.

THE IMPACT ON BUSINESS AND LABOR

A 1939 *Fortune* magazine poll asked businessmen to evaluate the New Deal. Overall, business reaction to the Social Security Act was moderate. Only 17.3 percent felt it should be repealed, 24.3 percent were satisfied with its present form, and 57.9 percent wanted some modifications. In contrast, over 19 percent wanted the Federal Housing Authority repealed, 21.4 percent the Wages and Hours Law, 44.4 percent the Works Progress Administration, 40.9 percent the Wagner Act, and 66.2 percent the undistributed profits tax. The *Fortune* survey also classified manufacturers on the basis of company size and found that "not one big manufacturer wishes its repeal."[76]

Big business had good reason to feel positive. When the Social Security Board faced its first major task of establishing 26 million accounts for individuals, its members consulted with the Business Advisory Council. In July the board, assisted by the BAC, hired the director of the Industrial Bureau of the Philadelphia Chamber of Commerce to serve as head registrar, and the BAC insisted on starting registration as soon as possible. At the suggestion of Gerard Swope, J. Douglas Brown was appointed chair of the new Advisory Council.[77] Thus, businessmen helped select the personnel for a major federal welfare program.

Businessmen also found decided benefits to the legislation, as companies with existing pensions simply transferred part of their costs to the government with no benefit loss to retiring employees. Folsom explained how he integrated the Eastman Kodak pension plan with Social Security: "We adjusted our plan so that the cost to the company remained practically the same as before and the employee received the same benefits from the company contribution he previously received, part coming from the Government and part from the insurance company. We have since 1936 adopted supplementary plans for several subsidiary companies." Pensions, according to Folsom, were good business.[78] They allowed employers to eliminate the hidden pension costs of keeping on older employees, and the help afforded by the Social Security Act let Eastman Kodak extend its coverage to its subsidiaries, secure in the knowledge that competing companies had the same costs.

Folsom took on the task of explaining Social Security to employers and, in cooperation with the Social Security Board's Informational Service, launched an educational program for various business associations. Not only would Social Security help a company meet the needs of its younger, low-wage employees, it would also "be of assistance to companies who have not yet established pension plans because the benefits which would be paid to the present older workers are greater than could be obtained for the same contribution made to an insurance company." Further, since employees paid half the cost of the contributory government plan, companies should find it easier to adopt contributory plans.[79]

The period between 1932 and 1938 was one of rapid private pension growth. At the end of 1938 a total of 515 industrial pension plans were operating, nearly 75 percent contributory. A study conducted after passage of the Social Security Act demonstrated that, whereas previous revisions in industrial pension plans were attempts to resolve financial problems, recent revisions primarily reflected efforts to coordinate plans with Social Security. Those most likely to reduce their pension benefits directly by the amount the employee was eligible to receive under OAI were the largest companies. Although this group represented only a small percentage of all plans, large numbers of workers were affected by this strategy. Overall, more than one-third of all pension benefits were reduced, with calculations based on anticipated rather than actual OAI benefits.[80]

Employers also benefited from Social Security through tax laws, which recognized employers' Social Security contributions as a nontaxable business expense.[81] In subsequent years further amendments in the Internal Revenue Code provided tax advantages both on money paid into pension funds and on interest generated by those funds.[82] According to some estimates, nearly half of the employers' welfare costs were made up in tax savings.[83]

Organized labor, by contrast, was more ambivalent. Workers rightly feared that employers' costs would be passed on to consumers, meaning they would pay twice. Further, the old age assistance regulations had the potential to undermine union pension benefits. The officers of the International Typographical Union reported in 1935:

> In view of the fact that the contribution of the employers is a direct payroll tax, it will require effective organization on the part of workers to prevent maintaining wages at a low point where the workers will be compelled to make contributions of the entire 6 per cent. In other words, it will require effective organization to compel the employer to take from profits his contribution to the old age pension fund. The plan further provides for a contribution of $15 per month where the state adopts a law providing for payment of a like sum as a minimum. While age and other qualifications differ in the states which have adopted or are considering old age pension laws there is one provision in which our members are directly interested. Laws thus far adopted disqualify any person from the federal-state pension if the person has an income from any source equal to $30 per month. Under this condition it is apparent members will have 3 per cent withheld from their pay envelopes as their contribution to the government-state pension fund. They will be confronted with the necessity of establishing and maintaining wages at a level that will prevent the employer from placing the entire tax burden on them. At the same time they will continue to pay a percentage of their earnings to support the old age pension activity of the International Union. If and when they apply for the federal-state pension they will be disqualified

for the reason that they are receiving the pension provided by their organization.[84]

Thus workers feared that all Social Security costs would fall upon their shoulders. Employers might keep wages low to make up for their share of the payroll tax, while workers still had to make their contribution. Yet the benefits they received from their employer or the union could disqualify them from eligibility for old age assistance.

Gradually, labor's fears were quieted as the Social Security Board actively sought AFL cooperation. From the beginning, Social Security administrators recognized that the cooperation of both business and labor was necessary for OAI to succeed, and they recruited AFL president William Green as a liaison with state and local federations of labor. Green saw cooperation with the bureaucracy as a dual opportunity for organized labor to participate in shaping social policy and to demonstrate the value of union membership by providing liaison services.[85] Working with the Informational Service, the AFL began an educational campaign intended to elicit union members' compliance in signing up for social security numbers and, it hoped, to reduce resistance to the taxes.[86] The newly formed Congress of Industrial Organizations (CIO), in contrast, was more antagonistic. CIO officers challenged employers' right to keep track of workers' wage records, fearing that striking workers might be penalized, and requested forms on which workers could keep their own records.[87] Thus, while craft workers were drawn into a relationship of active cooperation with the state, mass-production workers feared state intervention in the affairs of organized labor. Although labor now had a greater opportunity to shape social policy, the split between craft and industrial workers reduced its potential effectiveness.

THE 1939 AMENDMENTS

Almost immediately after the Social Security Act passed in Congress, criticism arose. The most negative reactions came from those who had advocated more radical measures. Abraham Epstein, of the American Association for Social Security, charged that old age assistance in many states had become a sink of corruption and that the residency requirements had to be changed "to permit pensioners to migrate freely from state to state without loss of pension privileges." Epstein also attacked OAI on the grounds that the inadequate benefit structure did not include pensioners' wives and that it was "socially unfair and economically dangerous for the government to shift its responsibility for the accumulated burden of old age dependency to the workers."[88] To resolve the inequalities in OAI, Epstein advocated increasing the minimum benefit and adding protection for wives and widows. The funds, Epstein suggested, should come from the vast reserve that was expected to accumulate between the time payroll taxes were collected and the time benefits began.[89]

Labor organizations also recommended changes so that Social Security would more adequately meet older workers' needs. The CIO advocated coverage for the entire population, increased benefits, representation of organized labor in the administration of the system, and payment of benefits from general taxation rather than payroll taxes.[90] Similar demands were made by the International Ladies Garment Workers, the United Automobile Workers of America, and numerous AFL affiliates.[91]

Business leaders expressed even greater concern, particularly insurance company executives, who feared that the accumulation of a large reserve would divert funds from consumer purchasing power. A large reserve fund could adversely affect the capital market, encourage demands for increased benefits, and necessitate the reduction of other federal taxes.[92] In January 1937, at the urging of sixty presidents of leading life insurance companies, Senator Arthur Vandenberg (R-Mich.) introduced a resolution that called for abandoning the full reserve, "which needlessly creates a fiscal and economic menace."[93]

Arthur Altmeyer, Social Security Board chairman, initially defended a full reserve, arguing that the alternative—pay-as-you-go financing—would eventually require a federal subsidy out of general revenues. Vandenberg then reminded him of the importance of business opinion:

> And when you build your reserves on a full reserve basis you are doing something that is absolutely unnecessary and desperately burdensome. Now, I cannot dismiss the testimony of men like President Buckner of the New York Life Insurance Co., President Duffield of the Prudential Mutual Life Insurance Co., President Brainard of the Aetna, and President Cleary of Northwestern Mutual, and all the rest of them. Here is a file of the unanimous opinion of the great insurance executives of the United States who are a body with a century of experience behind it saying to us that we are on the wrong basis.[94]

The problem of a large reserve had been anticipated by business executives on the Advisory Council. Although the original CES recommendations had favored pay-as-you-go financing, Treasury

Secretary Morgenthau suggested changing the tax structure to build up a big reserve so that the system would be self-supporting. Although Folsom argued against the Morganthau recommendation, Roosevelt, convinced that a reserve would protect the general treasury from future claims against it, supported the changes. Business leaders let the legislation pass, intending to bring up the issue of reducing the reserve as soon as the system began operating.[95]

Immediately after the close of the Senate Finance Committee hearings on the reserve, the Social Security Board met to discuss OAI amendments. Folsom presented the BAC views on the reserve issue, noting that "the chief criticism of the Act centers around this big reserve being built up in the future and you get it from all sides. . . . In talking with business men and organizations of all sorts in the last few months (and I have spoken to quite a few of them) that is the one point they all talk about—the reserve."[96] In the face of such concerted opposition, Altmeyer reversed his earlier position.[97] The 1939 amendments liberalized old age insurance somewhat by including dependents, beginning benefits earlier, revising the benefit formula, and holding the contribution rate for employers and employees at 1 percent. These measures reduced the size of the reserve in a manner that mollified social insurance advocates and organized labor.

In mediating between various factions demanding modification of the Social Security Act, the state apparently responded evenhandedly, balancing the concerns of all the groups and reaching a satisfactory compromise. A closer evaluation of the demands of business and labor, however, indicates that only the business community got what it wanted—the abandonment of the full reserve. This could be accomplished most readily by expanding coverage and paying out benefits immediately. Labor and social insurance advocates did win extended coverage for dependents and more generous benefits—both goals that were compatible with the business agenda—but they won no improvements in old age assistance, and the basic structure of OAI remained unchanged.

CONCLUSION

The primary goal of large corporations in the pre–New Deal era was macroeconomic stabilization. When attempts at self-regulation failed, farsighted business leaders recognized that state intervention would become necessary. A major impediment to economic stabilization was the threat posed by small companies, which could escape the welfare costs that monopoly corporations found increasingly necessary to maintain a tractable labor supply. The

Social Security Act of 1935 performed a service for corporations with existing pension programs by leveling out their costs through taxation. It was not that large corporations came to dominate government, but rather that state representatives were sensitive to the business agenda. When it came time to enact legislation, the business community had no need to direct policy, because those granted the planning capacity were already attuned to how welfare programs could regulate competition. Rather, the most significant impact of big business was its ability to shape the environment of decision making through the commitment of influential organizations to contributory pensions.

The national representatives of craft workers begrudgingly supported the legislation, though unionists had serious concerns about its structure. An entirely different agenda came from the masses of as yet mostly unorganized mass-production workers, who advocated a noncontributory pension paid out of general taxation. Because these workers had yet to find a voice in the polity, their impact on the state was negligible.

In the United States, public sector benefits were thoroughly integrated with those in the private sector. The Social Security Act did not move pensions from the private sector to the state; rather, it entangled capital and wage labor in a complex relationship with the state that became the core of future pension policy. The implications of this joint public-private benefit structure will be examined further in chapter 6.

Theda Skocpol and Edwin Amenta have argued that "the greater and more entrenched the state-level initiatives, the fewer the federal controls built into that part of the act." Yet there is no evidence that representatives from those states with existing pension programs were opposed to national old age assistance. Nor did any state with an old age pension in operation resist the idea of transferring state pension costs to the federal government. Most state pension programs were in serious financial difficulty because the depression had depleted their treasuries, and the possibility of federal relief was welcomed.

Yet old age assistance did become a federal-state program with most administrative control entirely in the hands of individual states. Where did the pressure for state control originate? The opposition to federal control over old age assistance came solely from southern states, which had no welfare programs of any kind. In legislating Social Security, then, the state was not a unified body but a coalition of regional and class interests. No legislation could pass with taking into account the interests of the South, and although southern congressmen did not set the agenda, they were able to maintain a controlling negative influence. The next chapter will examine in more detail how and why southern representatives chose to impede national welfare legislation.

FIG. 6 *American Labor Legislation Review* 25 (June 1935): 98.

6

The Politics of Old Age Assistance

Social policy is created not only in its formulation but also in its implementation. Claus Offe explains:

> The real social effects (impact) of a law or institutional service are not determined by the wording of laws and statutes (policy output), but instead are generated primarily as a consequence of social disputes and conflicts, for which state social policy merely establishes the location and timing of the contest, its subject matter and the "rules of the games." . . . the developments and innovations of state social policy can be conceived not as the *cause* of concrete social conditions or changes, but only as the initiator of conflictual interactions, the outcome of which is open and ambivalent precisely because it is determined by the structural relationship of power and the constellation of interests. From this observation we draw the conclusion that the task of any specifically sociological investigation of social policy cannot be the prescriptive development of "policy designs" and "policy outputs," but is pre-eminently that of offering an explanatory description of the conditions of socially implementing policy regulations.[1]

The Social Security Act reshaped the matrix of social power, as the development of old age insurance brought the struggle between labor and capital more directly under the jurisdiction of the state apparatus. It was not only workers and employers who had a vested interest in federal social benefits, however, for southern congressmen heavily influenced the structure of the old age assistance program. This chapter further explores the connection between welfare and the social relations of production by analyzing the transformation of old age assistance (OAA), a program jointly funded and administered by the states and the federal government, into Supplemental Security Income (SSI), the first permanent federal welfare program providing relief to the aged, blind, and disabled (P.L. 92-603).

What processes determined this transformation? The most compelling argument postulated thus far has been presented by Jerry Cates, who advocates a "tool view," in which an organization—in this case the Social Security Board—becomes "an instrument in the hands of its leaders, an instrument through which leaders can at times marshall resources to dominate the environment rather than simply responding to and adapting to the environment."[2] Cates argues that program administrators within the Social Security Administration sought to contain the expansion of OAA lest it supersede and eventually replace the nascent old age insurance (OAI) program that was enacted simultaneously as part of the Social Security Act of 1935. Pressures for the expansion of OAA came from "flat plan" advocates who wanted a universal national pension for the aged. According to Cates, Social Security Board members launched a campaign to control growth in the OAA program as they sought to expand the wage-related insurance program. In the process old age assistance was relegated to being a residual program of relief.

The problem with this argument is not that it is wrong but rather that the interpretation of factors that shape social policy is narrowed almost exclusively to the activities of officials within the state bureaucracy. Thus, other aspects of government action as well as fundamental political and economic factors external to the state are ignored. This chapter locates the Social Security Act and the implementation of its old age assistance program in the context of a broader political economy.

THE NEW DEAL DEMOCRATIC COALITION

Until Franklin Roosevelt was elected president, southerners had dominated the Democratic party, maintaining a controlling influence on national legislation in spite of their minority position through the organizational and procedural structure of Congress. At the core of southern congressional power was a committee system through which legislation had to pass. Since a bill could not be brought to the floor of the full House without favorable committee action, committees had enormous powers to obstruct legislation. Coupled with the committee system was a procedure, established in the middle of the nineteenth century, that used seniority as the criterion for selecting committee chairmen. Democratic congressmen, who often ran for office unopposed, gained seniority and thus control of key congressional committees throughout most of the period from the end of Reconstruction in 1877 until 1963.[3]

Roosevelt's landslide victory brought many nonsouthern states into the Democratic party, eroding southern dominance and creating an uneasy coalition between northern and southern democrats. Organized labor, represented by northern Democrats, favored permanent national programs operated through a centralized bureaucracy beyond the reach of potentially unsympathetic state governments, whereas southern congressmen consistently opposed any expansion of central government authority. The solution to maintaining a working coalition between two sectors with such different policy goals was to strengthen the committee system. Early in the New Deal, committees became dominated by the interests that fell within the regulatory or distributive scopes of their respective jurisdictions, developing strong norms of reciprocity between them. In practice this meant that members of committee majorities supported the position of other committee majorities during floor consideration. The committee, in essence, determined the position of any given piece of legislation for the entire party. Exceptions occurred largely on issues where there was such a clear divergence between the interests of northern labor and southern representatives—as with the wage and hour bill—that sectionalism rather than committee reciprocity dominated.[4]

As chapter 5 demonstrated, southern congressmen used their committee-based power to obstruct social security legislation. Their response to old age assistance was typical of their response to all programs of federal relief. Ravaged by the depression, the southern states desperately needed an infusion of funds, and their congressmen supported vast relief programs. They consistently argued, however, for these programs to be temporary or to constitute a decentralized system that worked through state and local organizations, so that "a central state would [not] destabilize the social caste system upon which the economic and political hegemony of the plantation elite was founded."[5] The insistence of southern Democrats on local control for setting standards and administering relief is related to the economic structure of the southern cotton region and the political character of the southern racial state.

THE POLITICAL ECONOMY OF THE COTTON BELT

The abolition of slavery after the Civil War created a severe labor problem for the southern cotton-growing region. Although thousands of black slaves were available for agricultural labor, many refused to work in gangs under the conditions that had existed during slavery, creating a need for new forms of labor control. After experimenting with a wage system, planters inaugurated the crop lien or sharecropping system, through which most southern farmers, black and white, were converted into debtors.[6] Wage labor did not disappear entirely, but the number of wageworkers on plantations gradually decreased as the share system grew in importance.

Sharecropping consisted of a contract betwen a laborer and a landlord in which the former sold his labor and often that of his entire family in return for half the crop at the end of the season. Although the share contract was made with the male head of household, planters viewed the entire family as the working unit. Every able-bodied person, including women, children, and the elderly, worked to increase the crop, and if an older male headed a household with enough able-bodied laborers, he could continue to sharecrop.[7]

Tenants worked under similar arrangements except that a tenant contributed a mule and a plow as well as his own labor in return for two-thirds of the crop. Both classes depended on the landlord to advance food and clothing until the crops were harvested, and the cost of this "furnish" plus heavy interest charges was deducted from the cropper's share at the end of the year. Sometimes there was a money balance due; often there was none, and it was not uncommon for a sharecropper or tenant to find himself continuously in debt to his landlord.

Although the indebtedness of a cropper sometimes forced him to stay with a planter through successive seasons, paternalism was also an important component of planter-cropper relationships. By providing in-kind benefits to workers, planters profited by a more loyal and stable labor force.[8]

By 1930 three-fourths of all southern cotton farms were operated by tenants, and a high proportion of all tenants were black. As table 4 shows, in 1930 28.2 percent of all black agricultural workers in the South were croppers, another 15 percent were tenants, and 36.7 percent were wage laborers. By contrast, 42.4 percent of all whites were owners or managers.[9]

Unevenly dispersed throughout the South, cotton plantations were heavily concentrated in the "black belt" counties of six states—South Carolina, Georgia, Alabama, Mississippi, Arkansas, and Louisiana—which also held 80 percent of the plantation acreage in the United States.[10] Plantations also developed in portions of Texas and Oklahoma. In all of the cotton counties at least 50 percent of the population was black, and in many the proportion of blacks was 80 percent or more. As figure 7 illustrates, the plantation system, dominated by a mule-powered economy and a high dependence on black labor for cotton production, was transformed nearly intact from a system of slavery to one of tenancy.

TABLE 4   BLACK AND WHITE AGRICULTURAL WORKERS IN THE
SOUTH, BY TENURE, 1930

Tenure	Black		White	
	N	%	N	%
Owners and managers	183,000	13.1	1,250,000	42.4
Cash tenants	98,000	7.0	140,000	4.8
Other tenants, except croppers	208,000	15.0	569,000	19.3
Croppers	393,000	28.2	383,000	13.9
Wage laborers	511,000	36.7	603,000	20.5
Totals[a]	1,393,000	100.0	2,945,000	100.0

Source: Data on owners, tenants, and croppers are from U.S. Bureau of the Census, *Fifteenth Census of the United States, 1930, Agriculture,* vol. 2, part 2, county table 1. Data on wage laborers are from the *Fifteenth Census of the United States, 1930, Population,* vol. 4, state table 11.
[a]Exclusive of unpaid family workers.

The economic system of sharecropping was supported by a legal system guaranteeing white planters domination of black tenants. Laws such as the lien laws and the black codes, which restricted the mobility of labor and enforced the tenant system, were accompanied by the disfranchisement of blacks. Disfranchisement was completed between 1875 and 1908 when all the southern states enacted legislation restricting the voting rights of blacks and, as a secondary consequence, those of poorer whites as well.[11]

Disfranchisement reduced the electorate to less than 20 percent and in some cases as low as 12 percent of the adult population in all southern states.[12] It also established the planter-dominated Democratic party as the sole vehicle for political expression, thus eliminating opportunities for the mobilization of discontent and ensuring that for the next half-century southern politics were conducted by amorphous factions within the Democratic party.[13]

Since candidates for political office often ran unopposed in the main election, primaries became the main point at which political choices were made. In some instances the winner of the primary could become governor or senator by receiving votes from less than 7 percent of the electorate.[14] Once in office, politicians had visible advantages over opponents who had no party machine around which to organize a campaign. Thus southern politicians tended to remain in office for decades, gaining power in Congress through the seniority system.[15] At the local level, planter power was consolidated by constitutional revisions that further reduced the influence of the

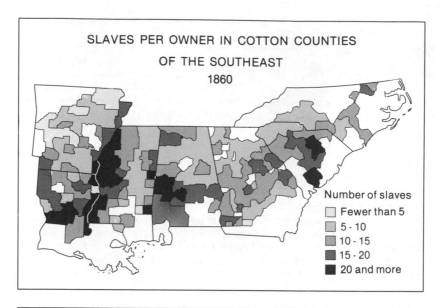

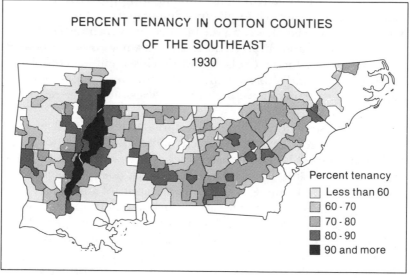

FIG. 7 Slavery and tenancy in the cotton counties of the Southeast, 1860 and 1930. From *Eighth Census of the United States, 1860,* and *Fifteenth Census of the United States, 1930.*

electorate by favoring the executive over the legislative branch, by increasing the appointive power of the executive, by expanding the number of appointive over elective offices, and by removing the judiciary from popular influence.[16]

THE SOUTH IN THE GREAT DEPRESSION

At the onset of the Great Depression relief in the South was almost nonexistent, and what public welfare did exist was entirely under local control.[17] Only two southern states had public welfare boards or any centralized authority, a system that led to corruption and inefficiency.[18] Local autonomy in the administration of relief supported the sharecropping system by helping planters maintain a docile and immobile black labor force. Until the depression, planters had maintained tenants through advances against the crop, resulting in an almost noncash economy. Clearly, any direct flow of cash into this system would have lessened the dependence of the sharecropper on the planter.

With the onset of the depression, many landlords found themselves unable to continue financing all their tenants. Forced to cut down on expenditures, they could not advance subsistence and production credit to as many families. Local and state governments, faced with depleted treasuries and decreasing revenues, were unable or unwilling to provide relief to the needy, and when the Federal Emergency Relief Administration was established southern families went on relief by the hundreds of thousands.[19]

Many planters helped to get their tenants on relief. A study of farm families on relief in Alabama in 1933 revealed that approximately 30 percent of the tenants receiving assistance had been helped by their landlords to get on relief rolls.[20] Yet landlords also feared that direct cash payments might undermine their control over the labor force. The Department of Labor estimated that perhaps as many as half of the landlords opposed any change in relief techniques for fear it would cause loss of control over croppers. At landlords' requests, relief offices in many rural cotton counties were closed during the two months of cotton picking.[21] Thus the labor supply for cotton picking was augmented, and standards of relief expenditures were prevented from disturbing the local wage rate for cotton pickers.

Both blacks and whites appeared on relief roles, but levels of relief indicate greater hesitancy to give blacks subsistence-level benefits. As table 5 shows, in the cotton belt counties of the rural South, blacks unilaterally received lower rates of relief than whites. Relief was kept below the subsistence furnished by the landlord so that tenant families would not be subsidized beyond what was minimally adequate. Thus subsistence advances by landlords averaged $12.90 per month, while relief was considerably lower.[22]

Even with the guarantee that relief would be kept below furnished subsistence and that relief offices would be closed during the harvest, planters were still often hesitant to let blacks get relief. In 1933 the

Table 5   Average Amount of Relief Received by Rural
           Households during June 1935, by Usual Occupation
           of the Head, in the Eastern Cotton Area

| Usual Occupation | Median Amount of Relief | | |
of Head	Total	White	Black
Agricultural cases	$ 8.98	$10.05	$7.00
Owners	9.47	9.58	8.88
Tenants	10.19	11.74	5.98
Croppers	10.09	10.49	8.69
Farm laborers	7.75	8.91	6.55
Nonagricultural cases	12.44	13.75	9.92

Source: Thomas J. Woofter, *Landlord and Tenant on the Cotton Plantation*
(Washington, D.C.: Works Progress Administration, 1936), p. 167.

relief rate for blacks was one-half that for whites, even though blacks
constituted more than half of the population in all the cotton belt
counties. In Mississippi blacks represented slightly more than half of
the population, but only 9 percent were receiving relief as opposed to
14 percent of whites.[23] Relief officials, almost invariably representatives of the largest property holders and employers, saw to it that
relief did not interfere with local labor requirements.[24] Using the low
standard of living of the great majority of rural blacks as the basis for
determining budgetary deficiencies ensured that fewer blacks were
ruled eligible for relief, and smaller grants were extended to those
accepted. As one observer explained, "The prevailing policy in some
localities has been that a Negro must be in much more desperate
straits than a white person before he can qualify for relief
assistance."[25]

THE ADMINISTRATION OF OLD AGE ASSISTANCE

The enactment of the Social Security Act released federal funds for
relief to the aged poor. Less than twelve months later, thirty-six states
and the District of Columbia had developed plans and were receiving
grants-in-aid to help finance their programs.[26]

The initial southern response was to resist. None of the southern
states had state pension laws on the books before passage of the Social
Security Act, and they were slowest to pass pension legislation. In fact
some black belt congressmen, presuming that Social Security was a
temporary measure, at first worked to repeal it. When a delegate
from the South Carolina House of Representatives wrote to the Social

Security Board requesting information on "the proportion of white to negro people," which "would be particularly valuable to us at this time in the consideration of old age pension legislation," the board circulated a confidential memo documenting its concern about responding to the South Carolina delegation: "There are strong factors in S.C. trying to kill Social Security already, and a high showing of negroes could make things worse."[27]

As old age assistance laws were passed, all the southern states incorporated more stringent criteria into their eligibility standards than were required, making OAA merely an extension of relief. This was recognized by the Bureau of Research and Statistics of the Social Security Board, which estimated that states with high percentages of OAA recipients drawn from relief rolls stringently interpreted the law, whereas states with low percentages interpreted the law more liberally.[28] With the exception of Texas, all the southern states drew more than 60 percent of their old age assistance recipients directly from relief roles.[29]

As noted above, in shaping the provisions of the Social Security Act southern congressmen insisted that old age assistance remain under local control. When southern plans were approved, they always included measures that kept decisions about benefits in local hands. For example, Mississippi required an applicant for old age assistance to be a resident of the *county* in which the application was made, even though the federal law required only five out of the previous nine years in the *state*.[30]

In Louisiana the administrative unit of relief before 1935 was the local parish. In devising their old age assistance plan, Louisiana relief authorities simply combined parishes into twelve administrative units "to include parishes with similar cultural, agricultural and economic problems."[31] Each local administrator was granted almost total autonomy in determining need. Area supervisors in consultation with the parish director were also granted the right "to approve the removal of an applicant or recipient of public assistance to another parish where he will continue to receive aid."[32] The right of removal of paupers, a traditional poor law mechanism of labor control from the earliest Elizabethan era, allowed local authorities to manipulate manpower according to local labor needs.[33]

In Georgia, which was even more adamant in adhering to the principle of local autonomy, officials refused to establish any administrative units beyond the county level. The result was high administrative costs and fewer funds for assistance. Jane Hooey, director of the Bureau of Public Assistance, explained her frustration with the South's insistence on local administration: "Now you can find a state like Georgia, for example, that had so many counties in that state. Some of them have 200 population, and yet you have the whole plethora of public officials. That would be a waste of money. Yet to get them to join those and have larger limits . . . well, we have no authority."[34]

The labor-control functions of southern welfare programs were not unrecognized. When Senator Harold Knutson (D-Minn.) and Abraham Epstein debated raising the minimum old age assistance grants in order to increase average grants in southern states, Knutson asked, "Suppose you establish an $18.50 minimum in Mississippi, how would they get their cotton picked?" Epstein responded, "That may be a problem. But I believe you can defend a $20 average even for Mississippi better than a $5 or $6 monthly average. Since this money goes to old people, I do not believe it would affect cotton picking."[35]

What Epstein failed to recognize was that cropping was a family affair. In one Alabama county grants were not paid out at all, because local authorities feared they might subsidize whole black families. The labor control functions were explained by Mrs. Frank Pou of Gordo, Alabama, in a letter to Harry Hopkins, director of the Works Progress Administration:

> As I wrote you, unless the Federal government pays the *entire* amount to the old people it will never be paid in this state. Now I shall trust you never to mention what I shall say to anyone except to our President himself. . . . The *main* reason the Old Age Pension fund will *never* be paid from the *state* funds is that they claim it will effect the labor situation. I have heard some say that they opposed, strongly opposed the Old Age Pension because if they paid them, why the negroes getting them, the entire family would live off of the money, and they could not get them to work for us on our farms. They would be worse about working for us than they have been ever since the government started to hand out to them. They would be too independent if they should get a Federal old age pension.[36]

In 1937 in Louisiana during June and July, when black labor was in heavy demand, the governor arbitrarily ordered that payments to black recipients be "cut in half, while payments to white recipients were made on the usual basis."[37] Similar incidents occurred in other southern states.

Owing to local discretion, grants to blacks were low. As table 6 demonstrates, in all the southern states the average grant to blacks was lower than the average grant to whites. Further, the lowest grants were in the cotton-producing counties of the plantation belt. For example, in the cotton counties of Alabama in 1939 the average old

TABLE 6   OLD AGE ASSISTANCE: COMPARISON OF AVERAGE GRANT
TO WHITE AND TO BLACK RECIPIENTS ACCEPTED DURING
THE FISCAL YEAR 1938–39, IN STATES ACCEPTING ONE
HUNDRED OR MORE BLACK RECIPIENTS

	Average Grant per Recipient			Amount by Which Average Grant to Blacks Is More (+) or Less (−) Than Average Grant to White Recipients
State	Total	White	Black	
New York	$21.79	$21.69	$24.30	+$2.61
Michigan	13.94	13.90	16.20	+ 2.30
Pennsylvania	20.33	20.24	22.20	+ 1.96
Indiana	17.17	17.10	18.63	+ 1.53
Iowa	18.25	18.23	19.51	+ 1.28
Illinois	20.38	20.30	21.26	+ .96
Massachusetts	26.52	26.50	27.37	+ .87
Ohio	21.56	21.52	22.09	+ .57
Missouri	18.69	18.66	19.06	+ .40
Oklahoma	17.59	17.62	17.61	− .01
Arkansas	7.49	7.52	7.42	− .10
California	30.54	30.53	30.24	− .29
Kansas	17.33	17.35	17.01	− .34
Kentucky	7.39	7.44	7.10	− .34
West Virginia	13.54	13.60	12.87	− .73
Maryland	15.82	16.05	15.22	− .83
Tennessee	10.22	10.50	9.40	− 1.10
New Jersey	19.27	19.47	17.91	− 1.56
Virginia	9.42	10.01	8.44	− 1.57
Georgia	7.41	8.14	6.40	− 1.74
South Carolina	7.79	9.14	6.94	− 2.20
Delaware	11.33	11.88	9.51	− 2.37
Mississippi	7.06	8.08	5.71	− 2.37
Alabama	15.56	16.77	14.24	− 2.53
Louisiana	10.66	11.84	9.21	− 2.63
North Carolina	10.45	11.27	8.46	− 2.81
Texas	14.27	14.94	11.88	− 3.06
Florida	12.46	14.04	10.04	− 4.00
District of Columbia	24.57	27.08	22.40	− 4.68

Source: Social Security Board, Bureau of Research and Statistics, Division
of Public Assistance Research, National Archives, RG 47, Records of the
Executive Director, box 279, file 632.36.

age assistance grant was $7.16, whereas in the noncotton counties it was $11.42. Similarly, in Mississippi the cotton-county grants averaged $6.92 as opposed to $8.07 in the noncotton counties.[38]

Even though the Social Security Act guaranteed a high degree of local discretion, southern welfare officials still feared that the Social Security Board might intrude on local autonomy. In 1939 the Arkansas commissioner of public welfare invited administrators to meet to confront common problems. The agenda was "to coordinate the economic efforts of the Southern States, or low-income states with reference to public welfare" and "to urge upon the Social Security Board and the Labor Department to minimize supervisory regulations and to leave to the Southern States every possible administrative function, since the states more nearly understand the local problems."[39]

As one mechanism for paying higher benefits to whites than to blacks without violating federal regulations, several southern states used a separate standard for Confederate veterans. Before the Social Security Act, most southern states had paid pensions to Confederate veterans. Beginning with benefits to disabled and diseased veterans of the Civil War, southern states gradually expanded pension systems to widows and, in some states, to servants.[40] In writing their old age assistance plans, these states incorporated special provisions for veterans, requesting that they be allowed to pay the maximum benefit of $30 a month to all veterans.[41] Although the board could not flatly approve a plan that totally disregarded need, it allowed the states to define "need" differently for veterans (all whites) than for nonveterans. In debating how to handle this potentially tricky situation, Hoey suggested that the board

> recognize that a distinctive method of treatment for veterans has been established by Federal and State laws and go as far as possible in making the method of establishing eligibility for veterans and non-veterans the same, but admit that in the treatment of these two groups, there would be a distinction which has been recognized by law, namely, that of giving more adequate assistance to veterans than to non-veterans. A statement could be made that the Federal government, in setting up the $30 in the Social Security Act, did not assume that this was a sufficient amount to meet the basic needs of a needy individual. . . . Therefore, the statement could be made that the State has decided to meet the needs of veterans more adequately than for non-veterans merely because they do not have sufficient funds to equalize these. The States could be asked as

quickly as possible to bring up the average grant of non-veterans to something approximating that of veterans.[42]

The board adopted this policy even though it knew that the grant to Confederate veterans ranged from $30 to $50 a month while the average to nonveterans was only $5 a month in Mississippi and $10 to $11 in other southern states.

Historically the South had feared strong central government, and though bureaucratic agencies proliferated under the New Deal, a policy of "cooperative federalism" allowed national policies to vary widely in response to regional politics.[43] In the case of old age assistance, national authority in program administration was thus circumscribed by the political economy of the South. Cash grants to blacks were carefully monitored so as not to undermine prevailing wage rates and so as to intrude as little as possible on the planter-tenant relationship. Although discrimination was illegal, southern states were allowed to pay blacks lower grants than whites by using different criteria for determining need and by paying Confederate veterans and their dependents the maximum grant.

The lack of concern for racial disparity in spite of legal prohibitions against discrimination reflected both the political clout of southern congressmen and the prevailing view that racial differences in income were natural. According to John Corson, director of the Bureau of Old-Age Insurance, blacks earned less than half of what whites earned, and women earned only slightly more than half of what men earned, because "these variations [were]—a historical, firmly embedded characteristic of the American wage structure."[44] Average lower payments to blacks were not seen as racial discrimination; they simply conformed to the traditional wage structure.

OLD AGE ASSISTANCE AND THE REGIONAL DISTRIBUTION OF WEALTH

Although a planter class dominated the Democratic party until Roosevelt's election, opposition did exist in the South. The center of conservatism was the black belt, but in all southern states there were factions, varying in strength and influence, that reflected the interests of urban workers, farmers from the hill country, and in Louisiana the general voice of Populist protest, filtered through the Huey Long machine.[45] The interests of these factions found expression in the House of Representatives more readily than in the Senate, since congressmen from particular districts were responsive to their constituencies, however limited. It was from these politicians that protests arose around the issue that had long soured North-

South relations—inequities in the regional concentration of wealth arising from the ways federal programs redistributed benefits. Depending on such factors as overall population size, the size of the average grant, the percentage of older people in the state, and the percentage receiving relief, some states were eligible for millions of dollars more than others. As table 7 shows, the amount of federal funds received by the states per year ranged from nearly $17,000,000 in California and over $14,000,000 in New York to only slightly over $421,820 in Mississippi and $157,000 in Virginia.

This disadvantage did not go unrecognized by southern congressman, who perceived that northern states were receiving a disproportionate share of federal funds. Congressman A. Leonard Allen of Louisiana explained the South's dilemma: "This Nation has been suffering from too much concentration of wealth for a long time. Where ever wealth is concentrated, power likewise is concentrated. Some sections of our Nation have been the agricultural sections, and some sections have been manufacturing and banking centers, and everyone knows that the tendency has been for wealth to gravitate to the manufacturing and banking centers."[46]

To reduce this inequity Allen, following the "share the wealth" legacy of Huey Long, introduced a bill paying a federal old age pension of $30 a month financed out of general revenues (H.R. 1816).[47] Congressman William Colmer, a non-black-belt Mississippi Democrat who had protested the OAA financing provisions during the original hearings on the Social Security Act, proposed a similar measure for a flat federal pension of $15 per recipient to each state regardless of the state's ability to match dollar for dollar (H.R. 1814) or, if that was unacceptable, having the federal government increase its proportion of old age assistance to 80 percent.[48]

The Social Security Board also recognized that federal funds exacerbated existing inequities in the concentration of wealth between the states:

> Prior to 1931 Federal grants-in-aid never amounted to more than 8% of combined state revenue receipts. . . . Since 1933 it has never been less than 80%, and in 1936 it exceeded state revenues by 24%. . . . The facts and prospects indicate that the old fifty-fifty matching requirement will have to be abandoned if a generalized Federal aid program is not to render the situation of the poorer states worse than ever.[49]

Of equal concern to board members was the unruly growth of the old age assistance program in several nonsouthern states:

> The percentage grant without any limitation on the amount which the federal government will match (other than the thirty

TABLE 7   GRANTS TO STATES FOR OLD AGE
                   ASSISTANCE, 1938

State	Total Federal Payment
Alabama	$ 832,331
Alaska	145,275
Arizona	759,962
Arkansas	1,086,060
California	16,938,074
Colorado	5,769,225
Connecticut	2,288,037
Delaware	196,277
District of Columbia	464,442
Florida	2,222,413
Georgia	1,496,446
Hawaii	126,660
Idaho	1,183,120
Illinois	12,982,696
Indiana	4,038,216
Iowa	4,870,841
Kansas	1,166,302
Kentucky	2,731,308
Louisiana	1,561,516
Maine	326,031
Maryland	1,755,318
Massachusetts	10,906,455
Michigan	6,845,645
Minnesota	8,113,821
Mississippi	431,820
Missouri	6,046,542
Montana	1,412,945
Nebraska	2,169,879
Nevada	290,571
New Hampshire	527,353
New Jersey	2,628,075
New Mexico	264,955
New York	14,247,070
North Carolina	1,045,451
North Dakota	707,167
Ohio	13,795,148
Oklahoma	6,812,088
Oregon	1,869,710
Pennsylvania	13,202,092
Rhode Island	635,660
South Carolina	588,719

TABLE 7   (*Continued*)

State	Total Federal Payment
South Dakota	1,268,448
Tennessee	949,981
Texas	9,763,265
Utah	1,791,780
Vermont	422,414
Virginia	157,700
Washington	5,162,773
West Virginia	1,811,166
Wisconsin	4,482,796
Wyoming	396,838

Source: National Archives, RG 47, Records of the Executive Director, box 274, file 622.

dollar per case limit) operates to give a tremendous stimulus to old age assistance. The more the state puts up the more it will get. . . . I believe that an investigation would show that in a number of states disproportionate sums are being expended for old age assistance, and that other governmental activities . . . are being unwisely curtailed in order to provide funds for old age assistance.[50]

Instead of the existing fifty-fifty match, the board proposed a system of "variable grants," which would establish a basic minimum to be paid by the federal government ($7.50 per month was the suggested sum) and an additional federal appropriation on a dollar-for-dollar basis for all grants over $10 per month, apportioned between the states according to the number of persons over age sixty-five.[51]

Although the Social Security Board and a few southern congressmen pushed for some type of program to balance the apportionment of federal funds to the states, the House Ways and Means Committee, chaired by Congressman Thomas Cullin of New York, rejected board chairman Arthur Altmeyer's proposal for variable grants. Like many of the wealthier states, New York stood to lose a substantial sum if a truly variable strategy was enacted. The Senate Finance Committee, controlled by southern Democrats, discussed Altmeyer's proposal but eventually rejected it.[52] In 1939 the cotton South was simply not willing to establish a minimum level for welfare grants or to relinquish control of a major welfare program. Although bringing in federal funds was important to noncotton county representatives, the planter class still held a firm grip in most regions of the South.

Pressure from minority factions of southern congressmen

continued to increase, and by 1946 Congress was sufficiently concerned about the inequity of the fifty-fifty matching to attempt to introduce variable grants into the program.[53] The problem was that implementing a truly variable strategy would have meant reducing the percentage already granted to the larger states, which was politically impossible. Instead the federal government agreed to pay 80 percent of the first $25 and 50 percent of any amount above $25 up to a maximum of $35. Under the amendments, federal funds could contribute an additional $5 per recipient but no minimum was established.

The avowed intent of Congress in approving the legislation was for federal funds to increase payments by this amount. Instead most of the southern states used the federal supplement to increase the number of recipients rather than the amount of the average grant. For example, Arkansas increased the number of recipients by nearly 45 percent but raised the average payment by only 94¢. Alabama increased the number of recipients by nearly 40 percent but *reduced* the average payment by $1.16. Louisiana, similarly, increased the number of recipients by approximately 30 percent but *reduced* average payments by $1.71. Most typically this was accomplished by splitting payments to husbands and wives that formerly were jointly given. In contrast, states like Kansas, Rhode Island, California, Wyoming, Texas, New York, New Hampshire, New Jersey, Minnesota, and many others raised their average payments by at least $4.00 while increasing the number of recipients by less than 20 percent.[54]

There are two ways to interpret these findings. One is that the overall need was greater in the South than elsewhere in the nation and that the policies pursued by the southern states represented an attempt to extend relief to as many of the needy aged as possible. The other possible interpretation is that southern states used this strategy to increase the amount of federal funds received without increasing welfare payments and thus undermining control over labor. In all likelihood some truth may be found in both assertions. The widest distribution of relief occurred in Louisiana, where popular sentiment for generous benefits received acknowledgment from Long and his followers. In other states, which had previously provided generous pensions for Confederate veterans, it is more likely that benefits were spread widely but maintained at minimum levels both to control labor and to contain pressure for a real wealth redistribution through tax increases for elites.[55]

In 1958, over the objections of President Dwight Eisenhower, southerners on the House Ways and Means Committee pushed through a controversial bill increasing to 65 percent the federal share of public assistance to the aged, blind, and disabled for those states whose income was less than the national per capita average and increasing to $65 the maximum average benefit payment. Although opposed by Virginia Senator Harry F. Byrd, the bill passed the Senate as well.[56] Thus, without reducing averages to the wealthier states and without setting a minimum payment, this legislation enabled the southern states to increase their share of federal dollars.

POLITICAL AND ECONOMIC CHANGE IN THE SOUTH

Between 1935 and 1970 political and economic change rendered the principle of local control of relief increasingly anachronistic. Before the 1930s cotton production required the year-round labor of stable tenant families, supplemented by day laborers drawn from the nearby cities and towns during harvest. The Agricultural Adjustment Act (AAA) of 1933, strongly supported by the planter-dominated Farm Bureau, encouraged mechanization and subsequent displacement of the tenant population by paying farmers cash subsidies to reduce the amount of acreage planted. Since acreage restriction decisions by landlords were, in effect, acreage restrictions imposed on tenants, thousands of tenants were displaced. Among evicted tenants, blacks outnumbered whites two to one.[57] The AAA set the amount of acreage to be used in cotton production for future years, freezing the number of tenants and croppers at something like the 1932 figure. As long as production was restricted, thousands of families formerly employed as cotton croppers could not get a crop to tend.[58]

The AAA also displaced tenants indirectly by providing the stimulus for planters to mechanize. Since farmers were paid for taking cotton acreage out of production, the only rational way to maintain or increase productivity was to substitute capital for labor. The subsidies provided the capital for planters to purchase machinery. Thus the AAA rewarded the more prosperous farmers by helping them circumvent the problem of obtaining credit and by providing further economic incentive to reduce the number of tenants.[59]

Several factors contributed to the demise of tenancy after the depression. One was the wartime labor shortage, which encouraged mechanization. Between 1940 and 1945 tractors increased by 136 percent in the eastern cotton states.[60] This form of mechanization occurred primarily in land preparation; harvest, chopping, and weeding remained hand operations. The impact was to reduce the need for year-round tenant labor and increase the need for seasonal day labor. The cotton acreage allotments imposed by the United States Department of Agriculture between 1940 and 1943 also reduced the demand for tenant labor by limiting land in cotton production and by encouraging planters to shift to less labor-intensive crops such as rice and soybeans.[61]

In 1943 International Harvester equipment for cotton picking was introduced into the Mississippi Delta area, and the flame cultivator was modified to handle the tasks of chopping and hoeing cotton.[62] Between 1945 and 1948, tractor-drawn plows and movers increased by over 250 percent, and by the late 1940s cotton-picking machinery had spread throughout the cotton belt. Thus all aspects of cotton production became mechanized.

In the early stages of technological change, tenant labor was pushed off the farms to nearby villages and towns, where former tenants provided a conveniently located labor pool that could be inexpensively transported to surrounding plantations and farms. This was the predominant pattern between 1941 and 1949. After 1949 the demand for unskilled farm labor dropped sharply. In the Mississippi Delta, for example, the employment of unskilled agricultural labor fell by 72 percent in the three years between 1949 and 1952.[63] As a result, day laborers became a surplus commodity.

The precipitous drop in unskilled labor demand led to a second migration as agricultural laborers moved from rural areas to southern towns and cities and to the urban North and Midwest.[64] As a result, the South experienced a gradual process of urbanization, with the nonurban population declining from 52.3 percent in 1950 to 35.5 percent by 1970.[65]

Although the number employed in southern agriculture decreased by 69.5 percent during this same period, blacks were still more highly concentrated in agricultural occupations than whites.[66] Blacks were particularly likely to be found in nonmechanized agricultural jobs, and the income gap between black and white farm operators widened in spite of the relative improvement in southern wage levels.[67] Thus the out-migration continued, as limited job opportunities and a decline in relative earnings pushed blacks northward and to cities.

In each decade the young, better-educated people left while the widowed, the old, and the illiterate remained behind.[68] The economic repercussions of tenancy's demise and black out-migration were severe. Rural areas of the cotton belt were left with a smaller labor force, fewer consumers, and in many areas, a smaller tax base.

Political changes accompanied economic change, gradually reducing the power of the southern planter class, both within the region and in its ability to influence national legislation. Until Roosevelt's election, the Democratic party was dominated by the South. After his sweeping victory, southern congressmen for the first time became a minority faction in the majority party. In every election between 1932 and 1944, Roosevelt's election totals were so great that he could have lost every southern state and still won the election. The same was true of every Democractic president until John F. Kennedy, who had to carry some southern states to win.[69]

Although southern Democrats initially supported Roosevelt, many of his policies alienated them, and by 1939 Congress was in full revolt against the president. The rift between northern and southern Democratic factions widened in subsequent years over Truman's civil rights and welfare programs, and in 1948 the split was formalized when the four southern states most invested in plantation farming (and with the highest proportion of blacks) bolted to form the Dixiecrat party. The Dixiecrat revolt, though short-lived, was the beginning of the demise of the solid South. Never again did the South return entirely to the Democratic fold.[70] Republican party growth began in the 1950s and accelerated during the 1960s. By 1972 the Republican party held 31 percent of southern seats in Congress and 17 percent of the legislative seats; only Mississippi, Louisiana, and Alabama remained one-party states.[71]

One factor that hastened Republican party expansion in the South was the increased reluctance of organized labor, represented by the northern faction of the Democratic party, to respect the procedural prerogatives of the committee system. Increasing tension developed around the issues where the two factions of the party differed, and by 1960 the desire of the northern democrats to unify the working class made them unwilling to maintain a cohesive stance with southern Democrats in opposing civil rights legislation.[72]

Other changes, some internal and some externally imposed, modified the balance of power in the South, providing a political voice for opposition to planter dominance. The 1944 Supreme Court decision invalidating the white primary began the enfranchisement of the electorate. This was followed by the repeal of the poll tax in several southern states during the 1940s, as well as a drive by the CIO to help blacks pay poll taxes and to register unionists in southern cities. Between 1940 and 1960 the proportion of southern blacks registered to vote increased from 5 percent to 28 percent.[73] Finally, there was a tremendous expansion in industrial development. By 1952 the South had four-fifths of the cotton textile industry; half of the new plants of the chemical industry were in the South, and in the next decade industrial research laboratories sprouted thoughout the region.[74] All these factors reduced the power of southern planters.

The civil rights movement dealt the final blow to plantation agriculture and the Democratic coalition. Aided by federal intervention, the movement transformed the state structures of the South, making them incompatible with plantation agriculture. The process began with the voter registration drives, as planters evicted hundreds of tenants who attempted to register.[75] The movement culminated in the Voting Rights Act of 1965, which incorporated blacks into the southern electorate and split the Democratic party into two opposing factions.

Black workers benefited in other ways from legislation passed as a result of the civil rights movement. In 1963 the federal government took Alabama to court on the grounds that the state had accepted federal funds in violation of merit system requirements prohibiting racial discrimination in hiring. After five and a half years, in 1968 the Justice Department finally brought suit against the state to force compliance. Gradually blacks gained positions in state and local governments, administering the programs that received federal funding. Among the various federal programs in which non-discrimination regulations applied, welfare programs were the most integrated, implying that citizen pressure on these programs was strongest and most effective.[76]

Although southern congressmen continued to chair key committees until the late 1960s, within Congress changes in the rules and procedures reduced the power of the southern coalition. Party caucuses, which had previously made decisions about the fate of bills privately before they ever reached the floor, became less important because southern congressmen no longer formed a majority within the House. Attempts by southern congressmen to bottle up legislation in the Rules Committee were increasingly overridden by discharge petitions, and in the Senate cloture was imposed to prevent southern senators from using the filibuster.[77] Thus the power of the planter class to impede legislation through negative action gradually declined.

Economic and political change in the South between 1935 and 1970 rendered the principle of local control of relief increasingly anachronistic. The out-migration of younger blacks from rural areas gradually aged the plantation region. By 1970 older citizens living on meager incomes composed a significant proportion of the county population. For example, the cotton county of Bolivar, Mississippi, which had an aged population of only 5 percent in 1940, had more than 11 percent of its population over sixty-five by 1970[78] Thus local governments in declining rural areas, confronted with relatively high per capita overhead and a limited tax base, found the increased welfare burden of an aging population more difficult to manage.[79]

It is within this context of a declining tenancy, a declining population of day laborers, and an increased welfare burden that the changes in Social Security must be placed. Step by step, southern congressmen released welfare for the aged poor from local government, passing control to the federal government as the burden of maintaining aged blacks surpassed their economic value and as the threat that direct cash payments to an older relative would subsidize an entire family became less critical to a changing plantation economy. Changes in the South were accompanied by political and economic changes elsewhere in the country that made Social Security reform more pressing.

Shortly after passage of the Social Security Act, an Advisory Council was formed in response to insurance company executives' concerns that a large OAI reserve would adversely affect the capital market.[80] One solution for reducing the reserve was to expand OAI coverage to uncovered groups, including agricultural workers. The council considered the task of including agricultural workers too onerous administratively and did not recommend coverage.[81]

The newly organized CIO strongly supported covering agricultural workers under OAI.[82] The Social Security Board, however, agreed with the Advisory Council that such coverage was administratively impossible. The southern-dominated House Ways and Means Committee not only continued to exclude agricultural workers but expanded the exclusion to those involved in processing agricultural products.[83] Thus, when the 1939 amendments took effect, old age relief for southern blacks and poor whites remained under the old age assistance program.

Over the next decade Congress made no substantial changes in Social Security, though pressures were building to extend coverage. Organized labor had continued to advocate covering agricultural workers. After a Republican Congress reduced coverage in 1948, President Harry Truman made social insurance expansion a major campaign issue.[84] Members of the Social Security Board, concerned that twice as many persons were receiving old age assistance as were covered by old age insurance, reversed their earlier opposition to including agricultural workers under OAI and began to push for expanded coverage.[85]

After the election Truman followed up his campaign promises by urging the House to act on several pending Social Security bills. The Democratically controlled Ways and Means Committee chaired by Robert Doughton (D-N.C.) brought H.R. 6000, a bill to revise the Social Security Act, to the floor under a gag rule, which meant that no amendments could be added. Although Republicans opposed the gag rule, an attempt to override it was turned down by the Democratic House.[86] H.R. 6000 raised benefits and extended coverage to the nonfarm self-employed, provisions that satisfied organized labor, but it continued to exclude farmers and farm labor.[87] Although farm-state Republicans protested that polls indicated farmers wanted coverage, that they paid Social Security taxes anyway in the increased costs of manufactured goods, that many had periods of nonfarm employment in towns too brief to allow them to qualify for OASI, and that the Advisory Committee had recommended extending coverage to farm workers, southern democrats countered that no farmers came to their hearings to argue for coverage. Northern Democrats supported the committee position, arguing that, while not perfect, the bill represented a significant improvement in Social Security.[88]

When the bill went to the Senate Finance Committee, numerous groups testified in favor of extending coverage, including the National Association for the Advancement of Colored People, representatives from the Food, Tobacco, Agricultural, and Allied Workers Union of America, the National Farm Labor Union, AFL, CIO, and members of the American Public Welfare Association (APWA), an informal partner of the federal government.[89] Southern APWA officials were behind the move to extend social insurance coverage, modifying their former stance on local control when faced with the economic reality of an increased welfare burden. As the public welfare commissioner for Alabama explained, "We have larger and larger numbers of needy old people and correspondingly smaller numbers within the population who can earn and pay taxes. Not only do we have an increasing number of old people, but we are a State with an unusually high proportion of children. . . . Our rate of application for aid also continues to be as high, as there is less and less demand for unskilled and older workers." Thus the increased dependency ratio created by the out-migration of younger workers and the decline in demand for marginal unskilled agricultural labor created funding problems for southern states. These issues did not pass unnoticed by southern state legislatures, which also wanted to know, "When is the load going to stop getting heavier?"[90]

Pressure to extend coverage to agricultural workers came from another source—various coalitions of small businessmen and the Chamber of Commerce who wanted coverage extended to all, so that people would not feel they were getting free pensions. It was the consensus among conservative businesses that paying for pensions out of payroll taxes held costs down while maintaining income maintenance payments to the aged at a basic subsistence level.[91]

The Senate Finance Committee amended the House bill to include agricultural workers, but only those who were regularly employed. Farm operators were still excluded. When the bill as passed by the

Senate was returned to the House, House members could not agree with the changes and sent the bill to a joint House-Senate Conference, in which five of the eleven members were from southern states. After more than a month of debate, regularly employed agricultural workers were finally included.[92] The term "regularly employed" was narrowly defined, however, to include only those who had put in at least three months' steady work for one employer and had then worked at least sixty days and earned at least $50 during the next calendar quarter.[93] Since average agricultural wages in the South were only 40 cents an hours in 1949[94] and since many cotton pickers worked only for a few weeks, few southern farm workers were covered.

In 1952 Republican Dwight Eisenhower was elected to the presidency, and the Chamber of Commerce movement to extend coverage reemerged with renewed vigor. A newly appointed advisory committee, dominated by Chamber of Commerce representatives, recommended mandatory old age insurance coverage of farm operators and currently ineligible farm workers.[95] As the Ways and Means Committee began hearings on new legislative recommendations, proposals to extend benefits to farm operators had the support of small business organizations, the Chamber of Commerce, and all major farm organizations except the planter-dominated Farm Bureau.

The new bill that emerged from the House Ways and Means Committee now included coverage for self-employed farm operators and for farm workers paid at least $200 in a calendar year. The bill passed with only eight negative votes, to the embarrassment of the Democrats, who attempted to take credit for the more liberal social security measure.[96] The now Republican-controlled Senate Finance Committee broadened coverage generally but still attempted to exclude farm operators, largely at the insistence of Senator Walter George of Georgia, former chairman of the committee and its ranking minority member.[97] Also excluded were all those employed in "a service performed in connection with the production or harvesting of any commodity defined as an agricultural commodity." During debate John Stennis (D-Miss.) questioned whether tenants were included under farm workers. Reassured that they were not, he proceeded to suggest an amendment, rejected by voice vote, excluding all farm workers from coverage. The final version of the Senate bill included only "farm workers paid at least $50 in cash wages by one employer in a calendar quarter."[98]

The bill was returned to the House, and a joint conference was appointed to resolve the differences. The final measure extended coverage to farm operators and broadened farm-worker coverage to those paid at least $100 in cash wages in a single year.[99] This bill was passed and signed into law on 20 August 1954, even though Senator George refused to sign the conference report.[100] Although the 1954 amendments did not extend federal coverage to all farm workers and tenants, they did remove substantial numbers from sole reliance on locally administered old age assistance, placing their economic security in old age under a national program.

The inclusion of farm operators and agricultural laborers under old age insurance helped to relieve the South's welfare burden, but it did not eliminate it. Since workers in both categories tended to be in the lowest income group, upon retirement they qualified only for minimum OASDI benefits. Thus all the southern states still had to supplement the income of most old age insurance recipients with OAA. For example, in 1959 Louisiana, Mississippi, and Alabama were ranked first, second, and third in the number per thousand of the aged population receiving OAA and were also highest among those supplementing OASDI payments. In contrast, the industrial states of New York and Pennsylvania were ranked fifty-fifth and forty-seventh in proportion of aged receiving OAA or a combination of both.[101]

WELFARE REFORM AND SUPPLEMENTAL SECURITY INCOME

Concurrent with the civil rights struggle came a precipitous rise in relief rates. The increase in the welfare load was most extensive in the Aid to Families with Dependent Children (AFDC) program,[102] but rising relief rates in one program reduced state funds for other programs. Under increasing pressures for reform, President Richard Nixon introduced a welfare reform bill in 1969 that proposed sweeping changes in the AFDC program as well as in the adult category programs, among them old age assistance. Under Nixon's plan old age assistance, along with aid for the blind and disabled poor, would have been continued and a national minimum standard for benefits set, with the federal government contributing to the minimum payment and sharing the cost of additional state payments above that amount.[103] The bill also would have prescribed nationally uniform eligibility standards.

On 31 October the Family Assistance Act of 1969, embodying the president's proposals, was introduced into the House of Representatives and referred to the Ways and Means Committee. Among its other goals, the bill was meant to remove the tremendous disparity that still existed between states in terms of eligibility requirements and levels of benefits. For example, in 1969 old age assistance payments in Mississippi averaged $39.80 per month as opposed to $139 in Wisconsin. The bill was also intended to provide fiscal relief to the states. The program was structured to disproportionately benefit the southern states and provide a substantial federal supplement for their welfare expenditures. In the adult category programs, Alabama would save an estimated $15.7 million, Arkansas $12.4 million, Georgia $22.3 million, Louisiana $1.4 million, and Mississippi $12.7 million. In contrast, many other states would have their costs increased in this category, even though the overall impact of the entire program was to categorically reduce state welfare expenditures.[104]

Although the family assistance portion of the bill met considerable opposition, southern congressmen strongly supported the adult category programs. An earlier Supreme Court decision had declared residence requirements for public assistance unconstitutional, agricultural workers were now covered by old age insurance, blacks had gained administrative positions in welfare programs, and the rural areas of the South were faced with an aging, dependent population in need of extensive welfare benefits. With all the conditions favoring local administration altered, there was no longer any economic or political rationale for keeping OAA a local program. After several hearings in both the House and the Senate, the bill (H.R. 1) was reintroduced in the ninety-second Congress with the adult category programs 100 percent federally funded and administered.[105] H.R. 1 passed the House with the family assistance plan deleted, and old age assistance became supplemental security income (SSI), an income program for the aged poor that provided a floor of income support with no relative responsibility tests and more generous income exclusions than had been present in many state programs. SSI came into being with little controversy, because it was packaged as part of a broader welfare reform bill that generated all the public attention. An assistant to Senator Abraham Ribicoff of Connecticut explained: "People were so concerned about Title IV [the family provisions] that no one paid any attention to Title III [provisions pertaining to aged, blind, and disabled adults]. If SSI had been on its own it never would have made it. Also, it passed because it looked like peanuts next to the family programs."[106]

CONCLUSION

The old age assistance program was not shaped within the isolated confines of the state bureaucracy, subject primarily to the goals of program administrators. Rather, the political economy of the southern racial state in the cotton plantation areas dictated the structure of OAA, guaranteeing maximum local autonomy so that relief would not undermine landlords' control of black tenant labor. The ability of the southern planter faction to wield a disproportionate share of power in the broader nation-state influenced social policy. Southern planters gained political power through the establishment of a one-party South, which effectively stifled opposition to planter dominance, and through the structure of the committee system in Congress, which allowed southern representatives to exercise a controlling negative influence on national legislation. As long as tenancy dominated the cotton region, planters resisted relief for agricultural laborers, since any direct cash benefits would undermine their paternalistic control over the labor force. After subsidy and allotment programs by the federal government encouraged the mechanization of cotton farming and indirectly contributed to the demise of the tenant system, the benefits of maintaining local control of relief were offset by the loss of federal funds. The initial strategy was to circumvent this dilemma by demanding greater federal contributions for old age assistance and by increasing the number of relief recipients.

The mechanization of cotton gradually replaced tenants with day laborers and then lessened the demand for these workers too, who migrated in massive numbers to the industrial centers of the North and Midwest. Left behind were increasing numbers of older blacks and poor whites whose presence turned OAA into an anachronistic burden. As the South industrialized, the planters' political power was challenged by industrialists who wanted a free and mobile labor force and relief from the burden of welfare expenditures. These demographic and economic changes occurred in conjunction with a decline in the ability of southern congressmen to exercise negative power in Congress, while the civil rights movement provided a political voice for opponents to planter rule. In the process the southern agenda was changed from a demand for local autonomy to a plea for federal relief.

This chapter demonstrates that a major factor impeding welfare state growth in the United States was the coexistence of two distinct economic formations within the boundaries of a single nation-state: an industrialized, democratic North with an active labor movement, and an almost feudal agricultural sector in which there was no democracy and in which a dominant planter class exerted a negative, controlling influence on national legislation until well into the second half of the twentieth century. The formation of the American welfare state was constrained by the political economy of the cotton South, in which the political mechanisms associated with an advanced capitalist economy were manipulated to protect an undeveloped agrarian sector from centralized government authority.

FIG. 8 *American Labor Legislation Review* 26 (March 1936): 8.

7

Depoliticized Labor and the Postwar Agenda

After passage of the 1939 amendments to the Social Security Act, there was an eleven-year lag before Congress legislated any program improvements. Attempts by the Social Security Board to expand social insurance were continually frustrated as Congress rejected all expansionary proposals.[1] Finally, in 1950 Congress passed amendments that liberalized eligibility standards, extended coverage to groups previously not included, increased benefits by 77 percent, and raised the wage base and tax rate.[2] Then for the next twenty years the Social Security Administration maintained a strategy of incrementalism, gradually winning the inclusion of new population groups under Old Age and Survivors Insurance, the lowering of the retirement age for women, early-retirement options, and benefit increases. Until the 1960s, however, Social Security was still basically a poverty program. It was not until a series of amendments were legislated by Congress between 1968 and 1974, which substantially increased benefits, raised the wage base, and implemented automatic adjustments, that Social Security guaranteed older citizens a true retirement wage.[3]

Incrementalism is associated with what Mary Ruggie terms the liberal welfare state model—that is, a welfare state in which the proper sphere of state behavior is circumscribed by market forces. Piecemeal institution building results in a fragmented structure. In the corporatist welfare state, by contrast, an integrated labor policy and a commitment to social equality lead to the blurring of the boundaries between state and society. The key factor in shaping the direction of state policy, toward a liberal or a corporate welfare state, is the status of labor and the extent to which it obtains influence within the state hierarchy.[4]

It is not just the status of labor per se that affects the structure of the welfare state, but rather which faction of labor is in a position to influence social policy. According to Gosta Esping-Anderson, a working-class movement dominated by unskilled workers is better situated to invoke broad class solidarity than one in which skilled workers gain power.[5] During the New Deal thousands of mass-production workers did organize into powerful industrial unions. Yet no expansion of the welfare state occurred. Why mass-production workers did not gain a citizen's wage in the postwar era was a function of their exclusion from the matrix of social power.

This chapter demonstrates that the postwar depoliticization of mass-production workers privatized organized labor's goals and helped shape the subsequent character of Social Security. Blocked from political action for benefit expansion by conservative forces within the state, industrial workers took the battle to the private sector, struggling with employers for workers' pensions. Their victories redefined capital's agenda. Because the strategy of pension integration meant that Social Security increases lowered costs to capital, employers' previous resistance to the expansion of public benefits dissipated. In the long run, however, industrial workers' struggles in the private sector were costly for invoking class solidarity. Although they succeeded in guaranteeing unionized workers a full retirement wage, their emphasis on private sector benefits retarded the development of a generous program of public old age insurance.

THE GROWTH OF INDUSTRIAL UNIONISM

At the beginning of the New Deal, the unionized portion of the non-agricultural labor force was at one-tenth, unchanged from thirty years earlier. The weakness of the labor movement was not only a matter of numbers, however, but one of distribution, for the vast numbers of unskilled and semiskilled workers in the core mass-production industries remained unorganized. After 1935 a major breakthrough occurred, and within a decade most mass-production industries unionized.[6] The forces that expanded industrial unionism came from within the state and from within the labor movement.

The inclusion of organized labor in the corporate political economy was partially a result of a shift in attitudes about the impact of labor on the economy. During the depression policymakers came to believe that the markets of mass-production industry depended on stabilizing the national economy and that the private sector clearly could not reach this goal without help from the state.[7] As a result public policy shifted to emphasize safeguarding the wage earner's income by autonomously expanding private purchasing power at the same rate as national capacity expanded.[8] Unionization in mass-production industry and the establishment of rules and procedures for setting wages were viewed as mechanisms for maintaining consumerism.

The first legislation to alter labor's relationship to the state was section 7(a) of the National Industrial Recovery Act (NIRA) (discussed in chap. 5), which required that each code of fair competition set by trade associations contain provisions quaranteeing employees the right of organization and collective bargaining. The craft-based AFL strongly supported section 7(a), which it believed would legitimate industrial self-regulation based upon employer-employee cooperation.[9] A wave of union organizing followed enactment of the NIRA. The United Mine Workers, which had been decimated by employers' antiunion campaigns, committed its entire treasury to an organizing campaign and fought violent battles to extend unionization to the captive mines of the steel companies. Other previously powerful unions, such as the Amalgamated Clothing Workers and the International Ladies Garment Workers, also invested heavily in organizing and recovered much of their lost membership on the heels of section 7(a).[10]

In those industries that had never been organized—automobiles, rubber, and electrical manufacturing—the AFL made some attempt to unionize the workers, creating "federal labor unions" of locals directly affiliated with the federation to serve as a core for the new internationals.[11] Although the AFL had many successes, organizing over forty-thousand rubber workers, it was never fully committed to the principle of industrial unionism—the inclusion of all workers in an industry within one union—and its lack of interest kept unionization in the mass-production industries minimal. Further, its tactic of pursuing a craft structure by dividing workers among the jurisdictional unions alienated workers and decreased their commitment to unionization. Thus much of the momentum was lost. Equally detrimental to industrial unionism was an AFL executive council decision to exclude specific groups of craft workers in the auto and rubber industries from the union's jurisdiction.[12] Even though the 1934 AFL convention instructed the executive council to charter unions in mass-production industries and to inaugurate a union drive in steel, it continued to put few resources into organizing, and by 1935 it had done nothing but pass a resolution.

The National Labor Board, the mediating body of the National Recovery Administration, had no real decision-making power, and when the NRA failed Senator Robert Wagner, with AFL support, began designing a board with adequate authority to enforce labor representation. The legislative outcome was the National Labor Relations Act (or Wagner Act) of 1935, which protected the right of workers to organize. The act established a National Labor Relations Board (NLRB) to investigate and enforce labor's rights and to determine appropriate bargaining units.[13] Its passage guaranteed a major role for collective bargaining in the future regulation of employment practices in industry.

In lending support to the Wagner Act, the AFL did not foresee how amenable the legislation would be to industrial unionism. Christopher Tomlins explains:

> By making the National Labor Relations Board responsible for determining the dimensions of the unit from which collective bargaining representatives would be elected, the Wagner Act enabled the Board to ignore the AFL's claim to possess exclusive rights to define the structure and extent of labor representation through the exercise of its jurisdictional rules, and to superimpose its own definition.[14]

If a union received a majority vote in a plant, it was certified by the NLRB. This action gave it legal status that could be withdrawn only if formal evidence could be brought forward showing it lacked majority support. Thus the NLRB was not bound to respect the boundaries of AFL unions in making its unit determinations.[15] Although the Wagner Act threw the power of the state behind the workers' right to organize, it also meant that the state could now determine how that right was to be exercised.

At the 1935 AFL convention the majority report, made by John Frey of the Metal Trades Department, upheld the historical rights of craft unions. The minority report, in which United Mine Workers president John L. Lewis charged the union with a "breach of faith," defended the principle of industrial unionism. Although the strength of the national and international unions defeated the minority position, a majority of the state federations, city centrals and federal labor unions supported it.[16] Three weeks later officers from eight AFL unions set up the Committee for Industrial Organization to promote the organization of workers in mass production industries. In subsequent months the split widened, and after an attempt to unite the two organizations failed, the committee formed a permanent labor organization, the Congress of Industrial Organizations. The AFL's pre–New Deal emphasis on exclusive jurisdiction as well as its other methods of safeguarding its existence became an outmoded form of protection, an obstruction to the realization of the new model of labor relations in which the NLRB would perform all the necessary protection.[17] In industry after industry CIO unions gained majority status, and by 1941 CIO membership stood at 2,850,000.[18]

INDUSTRIAL WORKERS AND MONOPOLY CAPITAL IN THE STATE

Since the 1935 passage of the Social Security Act, Congress had legislated no increases in OASI benefits. At the close of the war, CIO membership stood at 15 million, a fivefold increase since 1933, and with less need to strike over the right to organize, the time was optimal for a big CIO push for Social Security expansion.[19] As the main representative of mass-production workers, the CIO should have served as the focus of radical political action. Yet the union, whose members had much to gain from improved social insurance, was more interested in gaining private pensions than in state benefits. What explains this apparent contradiction in interest?

One factor concerned the collective bargaining structures that evolved in this period, which neutralized labor's political power. The CIO's loss of radical momentum began during World War II when the union, under the authority of the National War Labor Board (NWLB), exchanged a no-strike pledge for maintenance of membership agreements, which bound all workers in war industries to the union. The NWLB also restricted union bargaining power by imposing a virtual wage freeze, which lasted throughout the war.[20]

The NWLB also had a significant impact in nationalizing "a conception of routine and bureaucratic industrial relations" that upheld the authority of the union leadership at the expense of the rank and file.[21] The collective bargaining system removed industrial disputes from the shop floor, where work groups held the greatest leverage, and provided a set of formal, bureaucratic procedures that defused union power and increased managerial authority.[22] When the war ended and collective bargaining returned to the private sector, the model produced during the war years became extended throughout mass-production industry. This model resulted in a set of wage rules, which consisted of formulalike mechanisms to set wages through collective bargaining agreements.[23] The demise of an effective union presence on the local level helped advance the general depoliticization of organized labor in the postwar period.

Another impediment to labor's political participation was the right-wing shift of institutional power that began with the election of a conservative Congress in 1944. Composed of Republicans and southern democrats, the conservative bloc drafted numerous antilabor bills and impeded action on social spending measures.[24] The political scene became even more hostile to benefit expansion after the 1946 midterm election, when the Democrats lost control of Congress.[25] Conservatives blocked proposals for expanding OASI coverage and increasing benefits, and in 1947 Congress passed two measures narrowing Social Security coverage.[26] Thus, political action for expanded benefits appeared to be futile.

The split between the AFL and CIO also impeded labor's political effectiveness. If the two factions of labor had united, they might have been able to achieve some victories by supporting candidates, at least in local politics. But their internal conflicts lessened the ability of either faction to have political input.[27]

A more subtle but equally significant factor was the generalized depoliticization of mass-production unionists. During the war the CIO had engaged in some political action, and the rank and file were eager for some union activity. In 1943, for example, the CIO had formed a political action committee, whose purpose was to support Roosevelt and to deflect internal union agitation for independent political action. And at the war's close, Walter Reuther's brother Victor supported the formation of a labor-based third party to campaign for the social ownership of monopolistic industries.[28] The CIO was internally divided on the merits of direct political action, however, and the 1947 passage of the Taft-Hartley Act, the culmination of a decade-long battle of those who sought to contain the CIO, abruptly terminated labor's waning political activism. Taft-Hartley forced the CIO to rely more heavily on the formalized collective bargaining procedures as the most important mechanism unions could use to improve their members' welfare. The rigidity of the collective bargaining process, which weakened unions at the local level, thwarted the emergence of an independent politically minded cadre.[29]

As labor's political power waned, the monopoly corporations strengthened their position within the state hierarchy. Wartime politics had reinforced the trend toward monopolization in the manufacturing and mining industries begun before the depression. During World War II Roosevelt had appointed businessmen from large corporations to head most major defense mobilization boards. In the first six months of the war, 60 percent of the contracts awarded by the armed services went to twenty firms, and throughout the war production contracts continued to be concentrated in the hands of the large corporations.[30] When the war was nearly over, the War Production Board (WPB) began planning to convert production back to civilian markets. Quick cutbacks in war production would have given the smaller firms, who held subcontracts from the large monopolies, a jump on their competitors in the postwar field. But the WPB delayed reconversion, an act that guaranteed monopolies postwar market dominance.[31]

At the close of the war, then, organized labor had obtained some influence within the corporate political economy, but the breadth of its influence was checked by three factors: the greater power of monopoly corporations, the election of a conservative antilabor Congress, and the structure of union rules, which depoliticized rank-and-file activity.

PENSIONS IN MASS-PRODUCTION INDUSTRY

Because the CIO lacked the political power to achieve welfare state reforms, it began a campaign to obtain them at the sectoral level.[32] Several legislative changes in the 1930s and 1940s made pensions an attractive goal. As noted in chapter 5, until the 1930s private pensions provided few guarantees for employees, but two laws passed during the Roosevelt administration forced businesses to stabilize pension funds. In 1938 a Revenue Act prevented the exemption of company pension funds from federal income taxation unless they were placed in an irrevocable trust for employee benefits. This law closed the tax loopholes that had allowed employers to contribute to pension funds during years of high earnings and then recapture the earnings in poor years by revoking the trust. A sharp increase in corporate income taxes in 1940 stimulated employers' interest in pension plans, leading Congress to further tighten the requirements for qualification. The Revenue Act of 1942 allowed employers to deduct contributions to a pension plan only if the pension was incorporated into a written contract guaranteeing a permanent program for the exclusive benefit of employees and their beneficiaries.[33] The act also exempted income from pension trust funds from taxation.

Wartime events further encouraged the expansion of private pension programs. During the war, the National War Labor Board had placed limits on wage increases but determined that fringe benefits were not inflationary.[34] This decision served as a stimulus to pensions as manufacturers, troubled by the wartime labor shortage, appealed to labor by offering pension benefits in lieu of raises. Thus pensions became a means of eluding the wage freeze.[35] When the war ended so did the labor shortage, and in the postwar prosperity, employers' interest in new plans cooled.

At the war's close the CIO needed some membership inducements, and pensions, defined as deferred wages, were one compensation unions could offer. Pensions could serve another function, not stated as part of union goals but clearly a motivating factor. During the wartime labor shortage, employers had filled in the gap by hiring many older workers and women.[36] Although the union expected that "women and older people would voluntarily withdraw from the labor market" during reconversion, low Social Security benefits and no other pension made workers reluctant to leave their jobs. As a result many men in their sixties and seventies, whose years of service gave them seniority over returning veterans, continued to work in the auto industry after the war.[37] Thus one factor motivating the CIO to secure private pensions was a desire to reduce postwar unemployment.

The CIO was also fully aware of its impotence in the public sector and initially envisioned private pensions as a temporary expedient until Congress was willing to improve public benefits.[38] In 1946 the CIO began a massive campaign to get employers to establish secure pension programs. As Walter Reuther, president of the UAW-CIO, announced to union officers:

> Immediate action must be taken in every Local of the UAW-CIO for a pension program that will assure every worker . . . a decent livelihood when he reaches retirement age. One factor alone has made action now on pensions urgently necessary— Social Security payments, which were niggardly on the basis of the 1937 price level that prevailed at the time they were determined, today provide men and women sixty-five and over with only a purse of pennies for their living expenses. . . . It is also obvious now that the retirement age under the Social Security Law is too long delayed for us in our industry. The pace, the pressure and the physical demands of our work make an earlier retirement age necessary if we are to live to enjoy our pensions.[39]

With the welfare state seemingly beyond reach, union-negotiated pensions would provide an inducement to members and help provide jobs for veterans.

The AFL, by contrast, maintained its earlier mistrust of employer pensions and urged greater reliance on Social Security. In part its objections were based on its long-standing fear that private pensions might "impair other vital trade union aims and functions, while offering relatively little in return."[40] The AFL also found state benefits more attractive because its constituent unions were less able to negotiate pensions through collective bargaining. Because craft workers, especially those in the core building trades, were often in unstable relationships with employers, their unions were not in a strong bargaining position to demand benefits. Further, mobility was critical to many craft workers, and the AFL leadership felt that union-negotiated pensions immobilized the labor force. Thus the politically more conservative AFL took a greater interest in Social Security legislation, whereas the more politically activist CIO geared its energies toward the private sector.[41]

A National Labor Relations Board decision, which altered

collective bargaining rules, reinforced the CIO's drive for private pensions. The case arose out of a grievance filed with the NLRB in 1946, challenging the unilateral action of the Inland Steel Company in enforcing a mandatory retirement policy. The company argued that mandatory retirement was an essential part of the company's pension plan and that pensions fell outside the scope of collective bargaining. The union countered that the company could not take unilateral action on any part of the pension agreement that was also part of a general labor contract. In 1948 the NLRB ruled that under the Labor Management Relations Act of 1947 pensions were subject to collective bargaining, because they were deferred wages and part of the conditions of employment.[42] When the Supreme Court upheld the decision in 1949, the CIO immediately launched a major drive for pensions. The union's goals were to bring all existing benefit schemes under collective bargaining agreements, to establish patterned pension schemes in all union affiliates, and to induce employers to join labor in seeking liberalization of the federal OASI program.[43] The Supreme Court decision had expanded the scope of collective bargaining, and the CIO intended to take full advantage.

Whereas the AFL, in both the public and the private sector, had favored contributory benefits, which the union believed guaranteed greater worker control, the CIO formulated a different strategy. CIO officials designed a model pension for all locals, to be carried out through a unified collective bargaining program. The plan's core features were total employer financing, which would take nothing out of workers' paychecks, and joint administration.[44] Employer-financed, noncontributory pensions were a crucial component of CIO policy not only because of their greater appeal to workers but also because Reuther envisioned them as a mechanism for reducing employers' resistance to Social Security benefit expansion. His intent was to link public and private benefits into one package, allowing employers to reduce private expenditures whenever public benefits increased. As he explained to the Senate Committee on Finance considering benefit increases in 1950,

> And so we said, "We will go to Washington, and we will fight to try to get an increase in Federal Social Security both with respect to benefits and the scope of the coverage." As I say, they [employers] came down here and they blocked that. . . . So we began then to fight on the collective bargaining front for pension plans. We fought for a noncontributory pension plan in industry because we knew that that was the key to getting action at the Federal Government level. We said, "If we can fight to establish pension plans in private industry through collective

bargaining on the principle that then the employer must pay the total cost of such private plans, then the employer will have an incentive to go down to Washington and fight with us to get the Government to meet this problem.[45]

In its model plan, the CIO agreed to deduct Social Security payments from the $100 monthly benefits provided through company pensions.[46]

The CIO also insisted upon joint administration, because company plans, established outside collective bargaining agreements, were paternalistic, "planned and operated with [the employers'] interest primarily in view rather than the interest of the workers." Thus the CIO demanded "equal representation in both the planning of the program and in the administration of benefits." The model plan also called for $100 minimum monthly pensions for employees at age sixty with twenty-five years of service, graduated monthly pensions for those with fewer than twenty-five years service, and the establishment of an actuarially sound trust fund. In the pension guide all unions were clearly warned that "any move toward compromising these basic standards on the part of any Local Union will jeopardize the interests of the rest of the UAW-CIO membership."[47]

THE AUTO WORKERS' VICTORY

Among CIO affiliates, the UAW took the lead. As the largest and strongest of the mass-production unions, the UAW had established a Social Security committee at the close of World War II to pursue wartime gains in collective bargaining for benefits. Although its initial thrust was for employer-financed group insurance, in 1947 it added a pension plan to present to Ford, General Motors, and Chrysler.[48] The union made no headway for two years, but it followed the steel case intently. Within days after the NLRB decision on Inland Steel, it began gearing up for a pension battle. On 9 April 1948, three days before the final NLRB decision was made, Harry Becker, director of the UAW-CIO Social Security department, sent a memo to all regional staff outlining a "standard" pension program. Three weeks after the favorable ruling, he notified all locals that it was "the official UAW-CIO position that employers must bargain collectively on the subject of pensions, life insurance, disability, medical care and other social security matters."[49]

Although the national CIO leadership recognized the value of bargaining for benefits, particularly during the 1949 recession when wage increases were difficult to justify, rank-and-file members, most of whom were well under retirement age, needed convincing. To gain support for the pension issue, the union "called together members who were aged 60 and older in meetings all across the country." Thousands of older workers attended the meetings and adopted the battle cry "Pensions for all."[50] In addition, all locals received an announcement on the UAW Social Security program, the journal *Auto Worker* ran articles on pensions, and the union held educational conferences to convince delegates to bring the message home.[51] Thus the leadership succeeded in convincing workers that industrial pensions, established through collective bargaining, were a necessary supplement to inadequate government protection.[52] Throughout the auto industry at Ford, General Motors, and Chrysler, locals, following the central leadership's agenda, inserted pension benefits into their next contract negotiations.

The first test came in July 1949, immediately after the Supreme Court upheld the NLRB decision. The UAW decided to make the Ford Motor Company a test case, since Ford had offered its workers a contributory pension plan two years earlier.[53] Threatened with a strike, it took only thirty-five hours of bargaining for Ford to adopt an employer-financed pension program for hourly wageworkers.[54] Under the terms of the agreement, retirees were to receive $100 in monthly pensions, including Social Security benefits, at age sixty-five with thirty years of service.[55] Ford also agreed to establish an actuarially sound pension trust fund to cover both past and future service credits of all workers and to allow workers to participate in administering the plan.[56] The contract terms also guaranteed Ford at least fifteen months of labor peace, a worthwhile trade-off in the competitive auto industry. According to the *Detroit Free Press*, "The system was hailed as a pattern-setter for all heavy industry in the United States."[57]

That assessment appeared to be correct as other UAW employers—Nash, Budd Manufacturing, and Kaiser Frazer—quickly fell into line with similar programs. Many employers capitulated quickly on the pension issue because they recognized possible gains for industry. General Motors, for example, had long had a pension for executives but not one for the rank and file. As early as 1944 Charles Wilson, the company's president, had considered the value of establishing a company-financed pension plan. Wilson believed that a company plan integrated with Social Security would minimize government intervention in industry while mollifying organized labor.[58]

The one holdout was the Chrysler Corporation, whose previous contract had barred talks on any subject other than wages.[59] At Ford

FIG. 9 Retired Ford workers picketing in favor of a pension plan during the 1949 negotiations. The Archives of Labor and Urban Affairs, Walter P. Reuther Library, Wayne State University.

workers had won what came to slightly more than ten cents an hour in benefits. The UAW demanded the equivalent at Chrysler, which had just had a year of record-breaking profits, to secure the concept of pattern bargaining.[60] Although Chrysler agreed to a pension plan, the company refused to establish an actuarially sound trust fund or to allow joint administration, the core features of the union proposal, and its total package was worth only three cents an hour. According to Chrysler management, the pension offer was secure enough, "backed up by the good faith of the company."[61] From their experience with earlier company pension plans, workers had learned that without a voice in administration, their benefit rights were entirely at the mercy of the market or the whims of management. After more than two months of fruitless negotiations, Chrysler workers voted eight to one to strike, but actual strike action was delayed for another two months as negotiations continued.[62]

On the eve of the strike, the UAW offered the Chrysler Corporation a compromise proposal for ten cents an hour, either through a flat wage increase or by agreeing to pay the equivalent of six cents an hour for a pension program and four cents an hour for hospital-medical insurance. The company's counteroffer of pensions of $100 a month appeared to satisfy union demands, but the total package was worth only three cents an hour, denied the workers any voice in administering the pension plan, and contained no provision for a trust fund. The union also objected to a clause granting the corporation the right to cancel the plan after five years and to "jokers" in the eligibility rules, which could deny workers with long years of continuous service any pension benefits. As an example, it cited the following hypothetical instance:

> A man hired in a Chrysler Corporation plant in January 1938 and who worked continuously through January 1953 and who is laid off for a period of two years loses all of his 15 years of service credits. Upon his recall to work he would start as a new employee as far as his rights under the pension plan are concerned. This would require his working 25 additional years unless he has a two year break during that period in which case he would again lose all of his service credits.[63]

In a year when Chrylser profits had reached an all-time high, workers were in no mood to compromise, particularly on a plan that still smacked of welfare capitalism. Further, corporation executives were already receiving generous pension benefits. President K. T. Keller, for example, whose annual salary was $250,000, had a $25,000 yearly pension awaiting him on his retirement. Other corporate executives fared equally well, and the union felt it was only justice that "the company extend to them in some small proportion the same concern for the well-being and security of their families as it does for its already wealthy and already secure executives."[64]

The corporation's refusal to provide an actuarially sound pension program that union members had a voice in administering triggered a strike, which began on 25 January 1950.[65] Not until the eighty-second day of the strike, when dealers' inventories had dwindled to a three-week supply and striking employees had been forced to apply for relief, did the company agree to guarantee pension payments by establishing a trust fund and to protect pension credits for laid-off workers. After another two weeks of negotiations, the strike ended on the ninety-ninth day.[66] The final contract gave retiring workers $100 per month, including OASI, at age sixty-five after twenty-five years' service, with early retirees drawing lower benefits. The union agreed that Chrysler payments would be decreased by a like amount if federal OASI benefits were increased.[67] The plan was noncontributory and gave the union a joint voice in administering the fund.[68]

The CIO's success in winning noncontributory pensions had an immediate impact on employers' attitudes toward expanding Social Security. The night before the CIO settled with Ford, Ernest Breech, Ford's executive vice president, made a speech in Youngstown, Ohio, advocating benefit increases. General Motors president Wilson also made a number of speeches suggesting expanded coverage and increased benefits.[69] As Senator Millikin noted during the 1950 hearings, "The system has gained some new and strange adherents in the last year or so."[70]

Within less than a year after the first noncontributory pensions had been won through collective bargaining, the fifteen-year hiatus in Social Security expansion was ended. Because of the resolution of a conflict between workers and capital in the private sector, a factionalized state government was forced to act. "In forty-eight hours in Washington we did what could not be done by Congress in twelve years," declared Walter Reuther. "We took our collective-bargaining process leverage to increase Social Security from thirty-two dollars to a hundred dollars a month for everyone. . . . Congress hadn't been able to raise payments in all those years, but the industrialists suddenly gave the nod to regular increases. They prefer to do it in Washington rather than individually because in Washington they only have to pay half."[71]

The Chrysler pension board, consisting of three union and three company representatives, held its first meeting on 20 July 1950. The first order of business was drafting an agreement to be submitted to the Treasury Department to secure tax exemption for the fund.[72] At the second meeting, held on 16 August 1950, the board examined the first pension applications. To adhere to the agreement of $100 per month for retirees, Chrysler agreed to pay between $54.40 and $67.56, depending on months of credited service, with OASI making up the difference. The board decided to wait before making its first payouts pending the outcome of the congressional hearings.[73] Just one week later Congress legislated a 77 percent increase in Social Security, and Chrysler recomputed its pension benefits. Under the new legislation OASI rose to $68.50 per month, while the company contribution dropped to $31.50.[74] Between the tax savings and the legislated benefit increase, the company's actual pension costs were minimal.

After the other auto manufacturers signed pension contracts, General Motors president Wilson proposed an improved plan that extended worker benefits but also protected the company's investment pool by calling for professional independent management of corporate funds, no investment beyond 5 percent of the company's total capital, and no investment in any company of more than 10 percent of the total fund assets. Wilson did not fear offering a more

FIG. 10 Ben Martin, a seventy-year-old worker from the Ternstedt Division
of General Motors, reading a newspaper account of the 1950 United Auto
Workers-General Motors contract that established a pension plan for
retired workers. The Archives of Labor and Urban Affairs, Walter P.
Reuther Library, Wayne State University.

generous plan, because he knew that the patterned collective
bargaining within the UAW would force his competitors to match it.
Unlike earlier private pensions, which invested in standard life
insurance investments such as mortgages, government bonds, and
other fixed-interest-bearing sources, the General Motors plan was
innovative in defining the pension fund as a trust for investment in

the capital market.[75] When the plan was put into effect, Ford and Chrysler followed suit immediately. Thus pension programs encouraged capital formation by providing large corporations with tax-free funds for market investment.

THE SPREAD OF INDUSTRIAL PENSIONS

The precedents for pensions established by 1950 spread from the basic industries to many small-scale companies by the late 1950s. In the multiemployer plans, labor and management jointly administered employer-financed benefits (in accordance with the terms of the Taft-Hartley Act), which were sometimes integrated with Social Security.[76] The CIO disproved the AFL belief that contributory pensions would give workers more protection and a greater voice in administration. Noncontributory pensions could achieve the same goals with fewer costs to workers.[77] By the late 1950s over half of all unionized employees were covered by pension plans.[78]

As employers began implementing the programs, they took the opportunity to forcibly retire older workers. UAW Local 9, consisting of workers in the Bendix Aviation Corporation, signed a pension agreement on 14 September 1950. Like all UAW contracts, it specified that pension negotiations be handled through the National UAW Pension Board.[79] Fearing that locals would be unable to maintain their bargaining power, the national union insisted on supervising all pension negotiations.

Although the contract required joint worker-management administration, a resistant management made unilateral decisions without consulting representatives. The company retired employees without bringing their names before the pension board and refused to release full figures on the pension fund to the union.[80] At each step workers had to struggle to maintain the gains they had wrested from a reluctant corporation.

Among the contract conditions was a clause stating that "no employee shall be required, by reason of age alone, to retire before his 68th birthday. He may continue working after 68 only with the consent of the employer."[81] The company's first action, to abruptly terminate all employees age sixty-eight or older, took the union by surprise. Although union pension board members did not object to the mandatory retirement of older workers, they did protest the company's methods, arguing that management had told them that "the termination of these employees would be handled on an individual basis." Company representatives pointed out, however, that the Bendix locals were aware of this provision when they ratified the contract and that other large companies had exercised this option.[82] The board denied a union request to extend the time limit to allow these employees to "get their house in order" and forcibly retired sixty-five older workers, who ranged in age from sixty-eight to seventy-eight. Since only twenty-two had acquired the full twenty-five years credit, most retirees received reduced benefits. Several were close to full retirement, but the harsh implementation of the mandatory retirement clauses prevented them from working the extra time necessary to qualify. For example, H. F. Porter, age seventy-four, who had accumulated twenty-four years, ten months of service to Bendix, needed only two more months for full benefits. His forced retirement reduced his pension from the maximum $45.00 to only $37.50 a month. Several men over age seventy-five with less than ten years of service, most likely wartime hirees, received only $15 a month. Only one women was in this first batch of retirees—Emily Brook, who after twenty-two years, eleven months of service chose to retire at age sixty-six with a $34.38 monthly pension.[83]

By the mid-1950s there was also increasing evidence that employers were discriminating against older workers. According to one report, the Detroit auto plants refused to hire any women over age thirty-five. Older men also faced more limited job opportunities.[84] The AFL-CIO, which had merged in 1955, adopted a two-pronged approach to combat the job insecurity of older workers. Recognizing that older workers were potentially more costly for employers, the union suggested setting up a fund to which insurance companies, the government, and employers would contribute: "The fund could be used to equalize the costs of pensions or any other charge related to older worker employment so that the pure age effect upon costs of industrial pensions would be eliminated." For older workers who were laid off because of a plant closing, the United Steelworkers of America suggested that seniority rights be transferable to other plants and that these workers be given preferential re-hiring rights. The fund was never implemented, and both workers and employers resisted hiring workers from other plants when their own employees needed protection.[85] Thus discrimination against older workers appeared to be an unresolvable issue for the private sector. Pension protection for aged workers increased economic insecurity for middle-aged workers, and unions could not devise a viable solution that did not interfere with the work rules negotiated through the complex collective bargaining agreements.

The CIO's willingness to integrate company plans with Social Security with the avowed intent that industry would then stop opposing OASI expansion quickly backfired. When Congress did legislate Social Security benefit increases, retired workers expected to reap the rewards by improving their standard of living or to at least keep up with inflation. Instead, companies simply reduced their own pensions, so that each state benefit increase signified a cost reduction for business. Retired workers immediately recognized the disadvantages of pension integration to their economic security. As a former steel company employee explained in a 1952 letter to his congressman,

> The past two increases given to pensioners, who have an agreement with steel companies, have not received any of these increases. In all actuality the increases have been responsible for steel companies to save a great deal of money. A pensioner under an agreement formed by the union and the steel company received an amount from the steel company the difference of what the government allows a pensioner and $100.00. An Act of Congress (effective Sept. 1, 1952), recently raised the amount by approximately $7.00 per month and by the same token the steel company deducted $7.00 per month. The result was that the pensioner did not receive a penny more, but actually the steel company indirectly received the benefit.[86]

As in other instances where it might have intervened in the private sector, the Social Security Board maintained a neutral stance on the grounds that "the private pension arrangements are contracts between the employer and the union and the employees." As Wilbur Cohen, then technical advisor to the commissioner for Social Security, explained to Congressman Herman Eberharter, "The unions were willing to go along with such a provision. . . . to give the employer an incentive to be in favor of increased social security benefits. As you know employers did not oppose the increased social security benefits in 1950 or 1952 and the unions claim credit for this." The unions had apparently negotiated away economic protection for older workers, and the state was simply unwilling to intervene in what it defined as a private sector issue, even though public and private sector benefits were integrated.[87]

With no help forthcoming from the state on the fairness of pension integration, the CIO began a campaign to separate the private pension benefit from Social Security. In 1950 General Motors traded five years of industrial peace for $125 month pensions along with other income guarantees.[88] In subsequent contract negotiations, unions began including demands for increases in pension benefits, independent of Social Security increases.[89] As the UAW reported to its members in 1955, "even with the improvements achieved since the programs were initially negotiated, the typical retirement benefit plus Social Security does not provide an adequate standard of living for the retired worker. It will be necessary to bargain for some increase in the normal retirement benefit."[90] Markedly successful in improving benefit levels, the union gained increases in workers' pension credits for each year of service, from $1.50 in 1950 to $6.00 by 1970. As a result the maximum monthly benefit increased from $31.50 to $240.[91] By contrast, a 13 percent increase in OASI benefits in 1954 signaled the end of any meaningful public-benefit improvements for more than a decade. Until 1968 benefits were increased only twice, except for a small improvement in widows' benefits.[92]

By the late 1950s union demands went beyond benefit increases to include such items as early-retirement inducements, reduction in service eligibility requirements, survivor benefits, improved disability benefits, and the protection of pension purchasing power. In the next decade many of these demands were granted. By 1970 the UAW pension program included seven options—normal retirement, three versions of early retirement, special early retirement, disability benefits, deferred retirement for unemployed workers between forty and sixty, an optional surviving spouse benefit (55 percent of the reduced basic pension), and a widow's benefit.[93]

Corporations had numerous positive incentives to increase their pension fund, including creating large tax-free investment pools, maintaining a more flexible labor force by retiring older workers, and keeping the unions satisfied with contract negotiations. But independent negotiations for private pensions reduced whatever incentive they might have had to support Social Security benefit increases. With labor's energies deflected and business uninterested, the next decade saw only minor changes in public OASI.[94] Thus developments in the private sector impeded the expansion of the public welfare state.

The concept of pension integration also changed over the next decades from the goal of eliminating all duplication with Social Security through a fixed integration level (originally $100 per month) to a mechanism for counteracting the benefit tilt in OASDI toward replacement rates favoring low-income earners. In a typical integrated plan, a company may now pay its retired employees 50 percent of their final five-year average salary minus a portion of the worker's OASDI benefit. Because of Social Security's benefit tilt, subtracting these benefits has a proportionately greater impact on low earners. In fact, workers below certain earnings levels may receive no company pension at all.[95]

Gaining the Retirement Wage

After a fifteen-year lag a series of amendments to the Social Security Act, passed between 1968 and 1972, brought the American Social Security system up to par with European plans. During these years Congress initially increased benefit levels by 58 percent, raised the wage base substantially, and increased the tax rate.[96] It then ensured that these gains would never be eroded by tying benefit increases to prices and the wage base to earnings. The pattern of incremental policymaking based on cautious consensus building, which characterized the Social Security system throughout its thirty-year history, had broken down, resulting in a major policy shift. While organized labor was not directly responsible for the entire policy change, a faction of the labor movement did provide the momentum to push cautious policymakers in a more radical direction.

Why did it take labor fifteen years to achieve these gains? One factor was a drive in the early 1950s by the Chamber of Commerce to undermine the old age insurance program by reducing the reserve and paying every retiree a flat benefit of $25. The Chamber of Commerce logic was that depleting the reserve would eliminate an inducement to benefit increases. Instead of pushing for program improvements, labor's role became that of defending the existing system.[97] Limited in its access to the state by a Republican administration, organized labor played only a defensive role in national politics, working on the fringes rather than at the core of state policy.

Labor's internal factional split also interfered with a united agenda. As long as the AFL and CIO remained two separate unions, there was little organized labor could achieve through direct political action. By 1958, however, the unions had merged, and the national political scene appeared more promising.

Since the Social Security Act was legislated, the AFL had worked with program bureaucrats in the Social Security Administration, using such tactics as informational campaigns, letters to senators to obtain support for program goals, and technical assistance. The CIO, by contrast, had initially been suspicious of the Social Security Administration's request for union members' names, fearing that employers would use these lists to blacklist unionists. In subsequent years the CIO continued to work for Social Security reform independent of the state bureaucracy. The merger altered the CIO's tactics, however, as the AFL strategy of uniting with program bureaucrats to work for incremental reform predominated. As Katherine Ellickson, a member of the Social Security program staff of the CIO, recalled, "In the merged organization, the AFL techniques prevailed and the AFL attitudes. And the AFL had been a quite different type of organization in which authority flowed downward and you were expected to carry out enunciated policy and not to do too much in the way of moving ahead on your own."[98]

The labor agenda for reforming Social Security emerged out of a conflict within the labor movement over organized labor's political role. After the AFL-CIO merger, the labor movement strengthened its ties to the Democratic party. Encouraged by Walter Reuther's conviction that labor should become more involved in national politics, in each election from 1956 to 1968 Democratic presidential candidates received significant support from the AFL-CIO.[99] During the Eisenhower years labor's political impact was weak, but a shift in the national political agenda began in the 1960s. In the 1960 presidential election, organized labor backed the Kennedy-Johnson ticket, with the UAW, which had forty delegates at that year's Democratic convention, the most politically active of all segments of labor.[100] Labor's influence increased in 1962 when the Democrats showed a net gain of three seats in the Senate. This initial victory was firmly secured in 1964 when a Democratic landslide, which placed thirty-seven members in the House, allowed the Democrats to gain two more seats on the Ways and Means Committee, through which Social Security legislation would pass.[101]

During the battle for medicare, the AFL-CIO had taken its direction from the Social Security Administration, working with program administrators to shape a political plan for reform. While the Republicans were still in office, however, labor's exclusion from the national political scene made it an equal partner with program bureaucrats. As long as the Social Security Administration had no administrative support for program expansion, labor could take the initiative, "exploring problems, recommending action and having the action followed up" by the program bureaucrats. Ironically, when John Kennedy was elected to the presidency, labor's role diminished. As Ellickson explains, "When the Kennedy administration actually took office, then the initiative in this whole field passed over to the administration and the work in the Social Security department became substantially less exhilarating."[102] With the support of national political leaders, the momentum had shifted, and organized labor's political support was needed less than the technical knowledge of program bureaucrats.

Shortly after medicare was passed, program administrators began a campaign for bigger social insurance benefits, based on an incremental strategy of benefit increases to reverse the erosion of benefit levels. In contrast to its previous position of support for administrative proposals, the AFL-CIO responded with a more radical agenda that laid out a major program of change in a single proposal.[103] The stimulus for organized labor's agenda came from the UAW, which pushed the labor movement beyond its liaison with Social Security Administration officials.

The UAW's concern for broader reform for Social Security stemmed from Walter Reuther's commitment to expanding the role of trade unionism beyond its conventional program. His interest in organizing the unorganized and in civil rights as well as his personal fears about the escalating Vietnam War brought him into constant conflict with the more conservative George Meany, who still firmly ruled the AFL-CIO.[104] At the 1965 AFL-CIO convention, Reuther introduced a resolution calling for substantial increases in benefit levels, a higher wage base, and contributions from general revenues to ease the burden on workers.[105] Although the AFL-CIO central body had not planned a new initiative beyond that advocated by the Social Security Administration, Reuther's resolution pushed the convention to adopt a more radical agenda.

Dissatisfied with merely influencing the AFL-CIO's position, the UAW went a step further, setting forth an independent position in a bill introduced by Senator Robert Kennedy in 1966. Although President Lyndon Johnson had announced proposals for improvements in Social Security, Kennedy's proposal, which contained more generous improvements, was announced first.[106] In 1967 Congress began debate on Johnson's proposals, which had the support of the AFL-CIO. H.R. 5710 called for an immediate 20 percent increase in OASI benefits, indexing benefits to the consumer price index, increasing the wage base to $10,800, and raising the tax rate. In addition, it advocated future contributions to the Social Security trust fund from general revenues and gradual progress toward a 50 percent benefit increase.[107] The Kennedy-UAW bill, which was reintroduced in 1967 and set out by Walter Reuther in his testimony on H.R. 5710, went beyond the adminstration's proposal, calling for raising the wage base to $15,000, immediate implementation of general revenue financing and subsequent gradual increases of contributions from general revenues, replacement rates of two-thirds of covered earnings, widow's benefits up to 100 percent of the deceased husband's entitlement, and an immediate 50 percent increase in benefits.[108] As Reuther explained to the committee, "I share the President's real concern about problems of the aged in America. . . . but I am disappointed that his recommendations were not more adequate in dealing with these unmet human needs. . . . we need to raise our sights and stop this endless patchwork approach to Social Security where we tinker over here, we tinker over here, we use a little baling wire over here and then we say, 'Well, we fixed it up until it catches up with us the next time.'"[109]

With the UAW in open dissent and threatening to leave the federation, Meany retreated from the expansive resolution of 1965. The legislation that eventually passed was a compromise hammered out between Democrats and dissenting Republicans in the House Ways and Means Committee. It raised benefits by 13 percent and raised the wage base to $7,800, but it neither indexed benefits to the cost of living nor increased the tax rate.[110] General revenue financing never became a part of the bill.

The following year the UAW withdrew from the AFL-CIO. It went alone, since Reuther failed to enlist any of the CIO unions in his crusade for labor's revitalization. Although Reuther joined with the Teamsters to form the Alliance for Labor Action, his political effectiveness was diminished by Richard Nixon's 1968 election victory.[111]

It was not only labor's internal divisiveness that weakened its political effectiveness; the 1968 elections—in which the "new liberals" of the antiwar movement captured the Democratic party— alienated organized labor, and in 1969 George Meany went so far as to explore the possibility of links with the Republican party. The 1972 elections confirmed the breach between the new liberals and the AFL-CIO, when the executive committee voted not to support the party's nominee, George McGovern.[112]

In spite of labor's alienation from the Democratic party and a Republican victory, the years between 1968 and 1972 represented a turning point in the politics of policymaking for Social Security. With the exception of general revenue financing, nearly all of Walter Reuther's original goals had been enacted. What factors intervened to cause this abrupt shift?

One contributing factor was party rivalry. With a Republican administration and a Democratic Congress, any benefit increases the Republicans proposed were quickly outbid by the Democrats. The result was substantial benefit increases in 1969 and 1972. Internal division within the Nixon administration also prevented it from consistently opposing the increases. With a Social Security Administration committed to program improvements in a period of rapid wage increases, there was no concerted opposition to rationalizing the system by automatically tying Social Security benefits to the cost of living. In fact, Republicans now seized upon the idea of indexing as a means of containing the biennial pressure for expansion and perhaps depoliticizing Social Security as well.[113]

In contrast to many other Social Security measures that were passed after lengthy debate, with input from a wide variety of interest groups, the most significant legislative change since 1935 occurred within the House Ways and Means Committee. Most of the witnesses were technical experts; the bill, so far-reaching yet so complex, simply did not generate the type of heated debate that had characterized previous legislative measures. As Martha Derthick explains, "If there was an issue of principle here, it had been drained of much of its political potency by being rendered in narrow, technical terms and reduced to an issue of degree."[114]

One faction of organized labor, located in the reform-minded UAW, played a role in reshaping Social Security, but its influence was primarily in initiating rather than in enacting vast improvements in benefits. It is impossible to know what would have happened had the

UAW not rejected incrementalism and established an agenda for a true retirement income. Perhaps the political and economic forces already in operation would have stimulated the exact changes that did occur. Because organized labor acted through the Democratic party rather than through an independent labor party, its political fate was tied to environmental forces beyond its control.

CONCLUSION

Organized labor's role in influencing Social Security policy in the postwar era was limited by factionalism within the labor movement. Craft unionists worked within the state bureaucracy for incremental change, whereas mass-production workers feared the state's intrusion into labor's internal affairs. Instead this faction of labor worked to shape public policy indirectly, through private collective bargaining agreements.

The focus of mass production workers on private sector benefits helped maintain a bifurcated welfare state. Wageworkers in mass-production industries received good company benefits in addition to Social Security, whereas competitive sector workers, for the most part, were ineligible for private pensions and, because of their irregular work histories, received the lowest Social Security benefits as well. Organized labor's depoliticization meant decades of undeveloped programs for those workers least able to take advantage of the benefits that unions did win. Although the CIO favored expansion of the welfare state, its ability to mobilize rank-and-file workers for this goal was diminished by the collective bargaining procedures that removed union activity from the shop floor.

The state was not a neutral actor in the battle between labor and capital that heated up during the depression and then stabilized in the postwar era. Rather, a series of legislative decisions influenced the direction that both labor and capital were willing to take. Through tax laws that increased business profits while stabilizing workers' pension security, the state encouraged the growth of private pension schemes. By ruling that pensions were a negotiable item in collective bargaining argeements, the state also provided an incentive for workers to incorporate retirement benefits into contract demands. Finally, legislative action shaped the structure of collective bargaining agreements and contributed to the depoliticization of mass-production workers.

Although the state played a mediating role between labor and capital, it is important to recognize that no single entity of "the state" as a historical actor existed. Rather, different components of the state, often powerfully influenced by private sector actors, took varied and often contradictory policy stances. Nowhere is the state's responsiveness to private sector initiatives more obvious than in the events that culminated in the 1950 amendments to the Social Security Act. In the postwar years "the state," as represented by the Social Security Board, set an agenda of program expansion. But "the state," as represented by a conservative congressional coalition composed of Republicans and southern Democrats, blocked all such legislation. When "the state," as represented by the Supreme Court, legitimated pensions as a subject for collective bargaining, organized labor adopted a strategy of pension integration that reduced employers' opposition to public sector benefit expansion. Thus, as unions struggled with capital for pensions, this private sector activity finally pushed the government to act.

Although the 1950 amendments represented a gain for the working class, this victory was limited. The labor movement failed to adopt a strategy for political action but accepted piecemeal reform—in this instance, a large benefit increase. By thus limiting its agenda, organized labor reinforced the incrementalist strategy of the state bureaucracy. In the long run this meant nearly two more decades of only minimal program improvements.

By the 1960s it was no longer possible to draw a clear distinction between craft and mass-production workers. The merger of the AFL and the CIO, as well as changes in the organization of production, had blurred these lines. In these years labor's coalition with the Democratic party gave it its greatest political potential, yet no unified plan for discarding incrementalism emerged. Rather a single union, the UAW, pushed the entire labor movement toward more liberal reform than had emerged from the state bureaucracy. But a schism within the labor movement crushed support for an effective campaign, and the more conservative faction of the labor movement retreated from the radical agenda. Yet workers did gain substantially through improvements in Social Security benefits, as program bureaucrats within the Social Security Administration used their technical knowledge to take advantage of the political popularity of Social Security. Although the final legislation did not meet all the UAW objectives, it did guarantee workers security in old age.

This analysis confirms the critique of Poulantzas discussed in chapter 1. It indicates that a conception of an autonomous state, mediating between class factions, vastly oversimplifies the policy-making process. Either capital or labor may initiate and attain independent agendas, to which the state must respond, and these private sector events set limits on or even determine the possibilities for state action.

FIG. 11 *American Labor Legislation Review* 20 (June 1930): 207.

8

Explaining American Exceptionalism

Although at the turn of the century the United States had the economic capacity to fund a national old age pension, none was forthcoming until 1935, when Congress legislated a dual program of social insurance and old age assistance. The initial legislation covered only a small fraction of the population, but in succeeding decades program improvements progressed incrementally, a strategy that maintained a bifurcated structure with separate benefits for the poor. Incrementalism is indicative of what Mary Ruggie terms the liberal welfare state model—that is, a welfare state in which the proper sphere of state behavior is circumscribed by market forces. In a corporatist welfare state, by contrast, an integrated labor policy and a commitment to social equality blur the boundaries between state and society.[1] The two tasks of this book have been to explain the comparative lateness of the United States in developing national welfare programs and to determine why America's welfare programs remained firmly market based.

Analyzing the particular pattern of American welfare state development required a more general statement of the origins of welfare states. In formulating an explanation, I drew upon insights from existing theories, discarding those properties that had proved nonviable in previous research. My central argument began with a known but often ignored fact: that welfare programs are not unique features of advanced capitalist societies but have served a dual function in most Western nations since at least the sixteenth century—sustaining the vulnerable and allocating labor. In labor-intensive agrarian societies, welfare performed the latter function through restrictions that locked labor to the land. As industrial capitalism necessitated the free sale and purchase of labor as a commodity, relief requirements loosened to let workers respond to fluctuations in demand. From observing the historical transformation of welfare, I concluded that relief programs were shaped by the social organization of production. If traditional poor laws were a product of feudalistic agrarian societies requiring an immobilized labor force, then national welfare systems emerged from the conflicts generated by the commodification of labor under industrial capitalism.

Although a thesis linking work to welfare might partially explain the growth of the welfare state, it could not account for variability across nations. Even if social production evolved simultaneously in two nations, the timing and structure of their welfare programs could vary considerably. This variation occurs because welfare programs are legislated through a political process. Welfare state variations can be explained only through a dynamic model of the state, which incorporates its emergent, historically shifting properties.

In chapter 1 I proposed a three-tiered model of the state, which provided a format for analyzing the political process without reducing labor-capital relations to a preconceived set of functions. The model's first component, the most readily visible tier, is the arena of decision making, where politicians and political parties compete for electoral victories and decide on social programs and legislation. This level of analysis focuses on the legislative record, which identifies the historical actors who influenced the direction of social benefits and the issues that molded public opinion. At the second tier, the agenda of politics is determined. It is more difficult to identify specific actors on this level, where a matrix of social power shapes the environment of decision making. Here the analysis must proceed beyond the legislative debates to examine the power struggle between labor, capital, and other class factions that might be affected by the initiation of welfare benefits. Finally, there is a third level of politics in which changes occur in the power matrix. Such changes determine the ability of relevant actors to shape the social agenda.[2] They are most difficult to assess, and at this level of politics it is possible that the absence of certain class factions may be as relevant as the presence of others. The task then becomes explaining the lack of political action by some groups. Rather than predetermining the complexion of the matrix of social power, the historical analysis must identify it.

Posing this framework against alternative arguments, I endeavored to explain why the United States failed to enact national welfare legislation until 1935 and why it constructed and maintained bifurcated, market-based benefits that penalized low-wage workers or those outside the industrial marketplace. Rather than pointing to a single variable with sufficient explanatory power, the historical evidence led me to a number of factors that as a composite provided compelling support for the exceptionalism of the American case.

THE DYNAMICS OF AMERICAN WELFARE
STATE DEVELOPMENT
The Late Unionization of Mass-Production Workers

The core social democratic thesis of welfare state development is that workers first gain the right to organize and then carry the struggle over the commodification of labor to the state. Unionized workers form a political party, win electoral victories, and then use the state as a vehicle to modify distributional inequalities. This argument's implication for the development of the American welfare state is that a weak labor movement hindered program development.

The problem with the social democratic model, based as it is on limited data from certain European nations, is that it oversimplifies some key issues. First, most social democrats depict labor as a monolithic entity.[3] In the United States, the history of mass-production workers differed considerably from that of craft workers, and the economic conflicts faced by each faction of labor shaped its stance on public benefits. Dividing labor into its component factions is not incompatible with a social democratic explanation, but it requires a more complex analysis of labor's role. Second, the social democratic argument implies that if labor does not form a political party, its impact on social policy will be minimal. Yet the American data indicate that organized labor did shape the directions of social policy, though often through mechanisms unanticipated by a model attuned solely to the outcome of direct political participation.

Craft workers, who organized first, focused their union activities on preserving workplace autonomy. Autonomy meant self-protection and the rejection of state benefits. Although some unions succeeded in establishing pension programs that remained viable for more than a decade, the demise of trade unionism in the 1920s and the aging of the craft unions placed an unsupportable burden on union funds. By the late 1920s nearly all the union pension funds faced bankruptcy. Craft unions came to view state pensions as a viable option when self-protection failed.

The craft-based organization of the American labor movement in this period also splintered labor's political agenda. One faction of labor, found among the railroad workers, did advocate and win a national pension scheme, but its victory was limited to one industry. The tradition of craft autonomy had dissociated the railroad workers from broad concerns about social equality, and instead of using their political power to press for benefits for all wageworkers, they directed their energies toward federalizing railroad pensions.

In the decades before the passage of the Social Security Act, few mass-production workers were organized. Although they favored a unified program of social insurance, their failure to unionize until after the Social Security Act had laid the basis of the American welfare state gave them little input into the program's structure. The only powerful movement for public pensions arose from the one strong organization of industrial workers, the United Mine Workers, which recognized the futility of self-protection for the unskilled. By joining forces with a fraternal organization, they won some victories at the state level. Although it is impossible to draw definite conclusions from a negative thesis, the evidence suggests that if industrial workers had had a strong voice within the state during the formulation of the Social Security Act, they would have rejected a bifurcated structure that separated benefits to the poor from those available to all citizens. The late unionization of mass-production workers probably delayed the onset of the welfare state, and their exclusion from the arena of decision making reduced the possibilities for a welfare state based on an integrated labor policy.

To all appearances, the 1939 amendments were a victory for labor, particularly the newly organized mass-production workers, who advocated universal social insurance. The amendments extended coverage to dependents and began immediate payouts. Labor achieved these gains, however, only because its agenda matched that of businessmen, who strongly desired a reduction in the size of the reserve. Congress paid scant attention to labor's other, more basic goals—improvements in old age assistance and changes in the structure of the insurance program—legislating only those program improvements that were congruent with what business wanted. Industrial workers were still struggling for collective bargaining and the right to unionize, and though workers set forth a plan for positive political action on public benefits, their bargaining power within the state was weak.

Why, then, did industrial workers not take a more aggressive posture regarding the expansion of public benefits after they had organized and won collective bargaining rights? The answer lies in the depoliticization of mass-production unions in the postwar period. Because a conservative, antilabor congressional coalition blocked welfare state expansion and forced industrial unions to rely on the complex collective bargaining procedures that had developed during the 1940s, the goals of what might have become the radical flank of the American labor movement were directed toward expanding private sector benefits. By integrating private and public pensions within collective bargaining agreements, mass-production unions deflected rank-and-file energy from the expansion of Social Security.

The depoliticization of mass-production unions further reinforced the bifurcation of the welfare state by widening the gap in benefit rights between core and competitive sector workers. The more privileged workers in monopoly industry, whose unions won them consistent wage increases, earned the maximum in public pensions in addition to private pension rights in old age. By combining public pensions with continual improved private sector benefits, these workers won a full retirement income well before the rest of the nation. Those employed in less secure, nonunionized jobs in the competitive sector, by contrast, not only were ineligible for private pensions but also earned lower Social Security benefits, with many of these workers eligible only for means-tested poverty programs.

With the AFL and CIO split until the late 1950s, labor had no unified agenda. The AFL, which accepted a strategy of incremental reform, worked through the state bureaucracy to advocate program improvements. Because it was craft workers who had a voice in the state hierarchy, the United States maintained a market-based welfare state.

In 1972 American citizens finally gained a generous old age insurance program that provided benefits equal to a full retirement income. The momentum for change emerged from one union, the UAW, whose radical agenda pushed the now-unified AFL-CIO toward a stance that challenged incrementalism. Conflicts within the labor movement over labor's political role deflected union energies in other directions, however, and when the UAW withdrew from the national organization, the AFL-CIO retreated to its original position. The election of a Democrat to the presidency expanded the power of the state bureaucrats in the Social Security Administration relative to that of organized labor. Program administrators, who for decades had pursued a strategy of incremental change, won the final battle, using their technical knowledge to push through program change. The price workers paid was the elimination of some key programmatic goals, for in the long run the technical knowledge of state bureaucrats was more powerful than the support of an ambivalent labor movement.

These findings suggest that the argument that the American welfare state was late to develop because of a weak labor movement oversimplifies the complex causal processes. Labor must be examined in terms of its core components—organized workers in skilled-craft and mass-production industries—and in terms of those workers excluded from unionization, whose welfare often depends on the bargain unionized workers are able to strike with other class factions.

American labor participated actively in the process of welfare state formation, but on different terms than its European counterparts. Since unionized workers were excluded from decision making within the state, many of the struggles took place in the market. Private sector initiatives also had a powerful impact on the timing and structure of the American welfare state.

The Impact of Private Sector Initiatives

All the theories of welfare state development fail to take account of private sector programs. Adherents to the "logic of industrialism" view see benefits as arising automatically from the failure of traditional support systems. Social democrats envision private welfare benefits as merely an extension of public benefits, one more component of the wage package to be negotiated. Neo-Marxist theorists presume that the functions of welfare programs can be provided only by the state. In the United States, however, a major dynamic shaping the character of the welfare state has been the extent to which private sector initiatives have affected public sector benefits.

Before any public pensions existed, employers found pensions a useful weapon in the battle between capital and labor. During the initial expansion of wage labor, noncontributory pensions functioned like poor relief, a discretionary gratuity workers might receive from a benevolent employer. In attempting to control an increasingly volatile semiskilled labor force, employers used pensions to inhibit the growth of trade unions, prevent strikes, improve efficiency, and lessen labor mobility. With the growth of monopoly capitalism, the need for a mobile labor force made noncontributory industrial pensions an anachronistic form of employee benefits, more befitting a set of economic relations in which employers depended upon welfare to limit labor mobility. Employers abandoned these punitive tactics in favor of contributory pensions, which eliminated restrictions on labor mobility by basing benefits on contributions rather than years served.

Before the initiation of public benefits, private benefits were part of the wage-setting process negotiated between capital and labor. When private sector benefits failed to perform either the protective or the labor control functions of welfare, however, employers increasingly became more accepting of state intervention. During the 1920s several major employers' organizations proposed that industry and the state could jointly achieve the economic stabilization so vital to maintaining profits for industry. The old age insurance title of the Social Security Act was a proto-Keynesian measure, designed to stabilize aggregate demand for mass-production products concentrated in consumer durables, facilitate the removal of older workers from the labor force, and provide a wage-based benefit for industrial workers that eliminated impediments to labor mobility. Its structure was similar to a proposal developed by private industry a decade earlier.

The Social Security Act of 1935 initiated a market-based welfare state that set an agenda for incremental reform in all future efforts. Its origins lay in the wage-setting process in private industry. Private benefits were not merely a temporary substitute for public benefits but helped shape the emerging welfare state. In the political process, the first tier of the state, the arena of decision making, was less important than the second tier, where the political agenda was determined. When it came time to enact legislation, the business community had no need to influence social policy directly, because those granted the planning capacity were already attuned to its goals. Through the commitment of influential organizations to contributory pensions, business succeeded in affecting the environment of decision making. Both social democrats and neo-Marxists underestimate the potential impact of private sector initiatives on the structure of the welfare state.

The environment of decision making, determined by the matrix of social power before 1935, shaped the structure of the Social Security Act. But the Social Security Act also reshaped the matrix of social power, as the development of old age insurance brought the struggle between labor and capital more directly under the jurisdiction of the state apparatus. Both public and private benefits were now firmly situated within the state, and all future changes in benefit programs took place through interaction between labor, capital, and state officials.

From its inception old age insurance was designed to complement private pensions. Employer members of the legislative-planning Advisory Council recognized the potential gains to industry of integrating public and private benefits and structured the Social Security Act so that it was compatible with pension integration. In subsequent years the initiatives of businessmen in monopoly industries restructured private pensions, making them a tax-free source of funds for capital investment. Because tax laws made them a deductible business expense and because increases in Social Security allowed for reductions in pension expenditures, in the long run private pensions cost employers little.

It was not just the actions of employers, however, that brought the private sector agenda into the public sphere. The unionization of mass-production workers also changed the complexion of private sector benefits. Although mass-production unionists initially were interested in universal social insurance, a conservative congressional coalition composed of Republicans and southern Democrats blocked program improvements for a decade. As a result, industrial workers focused on improving the scope of private benefits, a goal that appeared more accessible during the expansionary phase of collective bargaining. Their success in achieving industrywide pensions, which were integrated with public pensions, reduced employers' opposition to Social Security expansion. In 1950 Congress legislated substantial improvements in Social Security after a fifteen-year lag. Labor's victory was only temporary, however, for the labor movement's inability to construct an agenda for direct action on public benefits reinforced the incrementalist strategy of the state bureaucracy. Both labor and capital had a vested interest in pension integration, and the extent to which public and private benefits are intertwined—a distinguishing characteristic of the American welfare state—impeded the expansion of public welfare programs.

Although both public and private pensions did come to perform those functions that neo-Marxists attribute to welfare benefits, they were not merely repressive social control mechanisms. Pressures from unionized workers, both in the political sphere and through private collective bargaining agreements, did lead to real gains for workers. Welfare benefits represent neither concessions to capitalism nor victories for labor in any pure sense. They contain components of both, to a greater or lesser degree, depending on the structure of the power matrix in both the state and the marketplace.

The Coexistence of Two Economic Formations

Many of the generalizations about welfare state formation, whether supporting the "logic of industrialism" argument, the social democratic perspective, or a neo-Marxist thesis, are based on quantitative, comparative data. In each case the researcher uses a few measures to capture the level of economic development of the entire nation. The problem with such gross measures is that they distort regional variations in levels of development within nations. If welfare programs do arise in response to economic development, however it is theorized, then less developed regions should have different welfare needs. Although undeveloped, labor-intensive agrarian areas may still rely on traditional poor law measures to lock a labor supply to the land, industrializing regions are likely to demand welfare measures that enhance labor mobility. To the extent that regional variations in economic development are reflected in political processes, they can be crucial factors in the timing of national welfare programs.

In the United States the coexistence of two distinct economic formations within the boundaries of a single nation-state was the third dynamic shaping the character of the American welfare state. While labor and capital were waging a battle throughout the industrializing Northeast, the South maintained a plantation mode of production until well into the twentieth century. At critical turning points in history, southern congressmen used their political power to hinder the growth of a national welfare state. Since the region was subject to none of the conditions transforming social production elsewhere in the nation, southern resistance to national benefits became a strategy for protecting the labor control prerogatives of the southern planter class.

Whereas European nations began debating the merits of national old age pensions in the late nineteenth century, a generous military pension system muted public support for federal pensions in the United States. Since southerners, for the most part, were ineligible for Civil War pensions, a pension movement might have arisen from the South, where tremendous poverty existed. But the disfranchise-ment of southern citizens prevented the people from making political demands at either the state or the national level. Southern congress-men, who represented the planter class, resented federal inter-vention into local affairs and resisted national spending measures, which had thus far benefited the North at the expense of the South.

Southern planters gained political power through the establish-ment of a one-party South, which effectively stifled opposition to planter dominance, and through the structure of the committee system in Congress, which allowed southern representatives to exercise a controlling negative influence on national legislation. Because they controlled key congressional committees, they were able to block proposals for old age pension legislation.

During the 1930s, when Congress legislated the first national welfare programs, the political economy of the cotton South continued to impede American welfare state development. In the initial formulation of the Social Security Act, southern congressmen insisted that agricultural laborers be excluded from OAI coverage and that the old age assistance title remain under local control. They had no intention of letting federal funds undermine planters' paternalistic control of a primarily black tenant labor force.

The mechanization of cotton gradually replaced tenants with day laborers and then lessened the demand for those workers too, who migrated in massive numbers to the industrial centers of the North and Midwest. Left behind were increasing numbers of older blacks and poor whites whose presence turned OAA into an anachronistic burden. As the South industrialized, industrialists demanding a free and mobile labor force and relief from the burden of welfare expenditures challenged the planters' political power. These demographic and economic changes occurred in conjunction with a decline in the veto power of southern congressmen. By the time the southern agenda had changed from a demand for local autonomy to a plea for federal relief, a bifurcated welfare state structure had already been firmly established as a core feature of American welfare policy.

A more indirect effect of the existence of two economic formations was the South's impact on the labor movement. Although this topic has been touched upon only briefly in the book, the antilabor policies of southern states and the subsequent almost total absence of organized labor in the South splintered the labor movement and made it more difficult for workers to advocate a unified national labor policy. And as Mary Ruggie has suggested, a national labor policy, the outcome of a unified labor movement with access to the state hierarchy, is the best predictor of the generosity of public welfare programs.[4]

WELFARE AND THE SOCIAL ORGANIZATION OF PRODUCTION

Throughout American history welfare has responded to changes in the social organization of production. The poor laws, the precursor to a national system of economic support for the aged, provided the earliest form of relief to the needy. In a labor-scarce economy where communities retained a *gemeinschaft* character, poor laws primarily served the most vulnerable—the sick, the widowed, the aged. With the expansion of a wage-labor force, however, the functions of poor relief changed. The traditional labor control mechanisms embedded in the earliest English poor laws—residency requirements, family responsibility clauses, and local administration—were applied with increasing harshness. Townships tightened regulations regarding the distribution of outrelief, and the beginnings of a bifurcated structure of public welfare emerged as almshouses became peopled with immigrants, blacks, and older women.

It was not industrialization per se that caused poor law authorities to implement relief with increasing harshness, as those who adhere to the "logic of industrialism" thesis might argue. Rather, as capitalist expansion in the nineteenth century proletarianized the labor force and made wage labor the prevalent way of organizing production, the poor law responded by shifting from a minimal system of relief for the most helpless members of society to a harshly administered program of labor control for unemployed wageworkers.

The first old age pensions were passed by states, the locus of political action in the early twentieth century, and all retained the labor control mechanisms of the poor law. When Congress began debating the merits of a national old age pension, these proposals were modeled after the state legislation. They incorporated all the poor law regulations and envisioned national welfare as a minimal program of relief for the aged poor. Before 1935, then, all proposals conceived of public pensions as a form of relief. This was true of most state pension laws and of the proposed national legislation. Yet when Congress passed the Social Security Act, it established a dual structure: a wage-based program of social insurance for industrial wageworkers and traditional relief for the aged poor. By tying benefits to wages, the insurance program maintained class-based inequalities in the distribution of benefits for the aged and ensured that benefits would not undermine wages in low-wage industries. At the same time the relief program (OAA) contained the labor control mechanisms of agrarian poor laws.

Although it is possible to view old age insurance as a radical departure from the relief tradition of the poor laws, it did not signify an end to the link betwen work and welfare. Rather, old age insurance emerged out of the conflicts between labor and capital over the commodification of wage labor. It was the private sector agenda that labor and capital brought to the bargaining table when the option of state action appeared viable. The struggle for old age pensions was part of a broader process of class struggle, shaped first within the marketplace and later within the electoral-representative political system.

THE STRUCTURE OF THE STATE

The unique development of American industrial capitalism and the particular history of the American labor movement were primary factors affecting the timing and subsequent development of Social Security. But program structure was also the product of the changing positions of labor and capital within the state hierarchy. In the first three decades of the twentieth century business dominated, and labor had little influence within the state. When labor did gain some ability to affect legislation during the New Deal, the state did not respond by directly capitulating to its demands. Legislation appeased labor while still taking economic stabilization as its main goal. The lack of a single labor agenda also made it easier for the state to co-opt the more radical demands that emerged from rank-and-file mass-production workers. Although the state's authority benefited labor by legitimating unions and by setting the ground rules for collective bargaining, it also contained labor's agenda within a narrow framework. The issue of old age pensions got encapsulated at the most fundamental level of politics, the struggle for the redistribution of social power. Because monopoly capital dominated that struggle, labor's goals, defined differently by skilled and mass-production workers, were compromised.

Although this analysis has focused upon the state as a composite of class factions, it has also examined the validity of the concept of the state as an autonomous body. Even ignoring the salient fact that different elements within the state structure are influenced by class factions in civil society, it is apparent that such no entity as "the state" exists. Such different components of government as the executive, Congress, the courts, political parties, and the state bureaucracy all, either directly or indirectly, influenced the formation of social benefit programs, not infrequently in conflicting directions. While at times the state took direct action to mediate conflicts between capital and labor, the evidence indicates that just as often events in the private sector galvanized the state into action. To the extent that the state set an agenda, it reflected pressures from civil society—often, but not always, those of monopoly businessmen. More typically events in the private sector set limits upon or even determined the course of state action.

What is also apparent is the fruitlessness of attempting to explain welfare state development by analyzing only the most basic level of politics, the arena of decision making. Although this level of analysis, where the actions of particular historical actors are visible, is most accessible to the historian, this strategy ignores the broader agenda-setting process, available only through interpretation. Both the lack of input from mass-production workers and the ability of southern politicians to impede legislation shaped the structure of the American welfare state, and yet very little confirming evidence appears in the historical record. Although negative hypotheses are difficult to prove conclusively, I am convinced that these factors constitute a powerful explanation of American exceptionalism.

CAUSALITY IN HISTORICAL EXPLANATION

In attempting to isolate the most significant factors in welfare state development, political theorists have devised causal models advocating one set of variables or sequence of events as having the greatest explanatory power. These models attribute public benefit expansion to such forces as the strength of organized labor, the dominance of monopoly capital, the logic of industrialization, or the agenda of the state bureaucracy. Most of the analyses measuring a given argument. be it the logic of industrialism or the power of social democracy, have attempted to quantify what the researcher identifies as the salient variables. Although these analyses appear to take history into account in that they follow a sequence of political events over a long period, history is not embedded in the analysis as a variable in itself. By denying history, such models often lose sight of how relationships between the variables change or, more important, how the variables themselves alter in character. Thus it becomes possible to argue that organized labor is responsible for creating welfare programs in Western capitalist democracies and to subsequently attempt to identify the relative significance of this variable. Undoubtedly, labor movements have taken an active role in shaping social policy in certain nations at certain points in history—but not always, and not always the same faction of the labor movement. We should not expect that any single factor is invariably responsible, because the very definition of history implies movement and change. This is not to deny the sociological quest for underlying conditions, but rather to situate that quest in history. Historical change must become the core focus of the analysis, and the causal generalizations that arise must be derived from regularities in the historical evidence.

Notes

Preface

1. Charles Tilly, *Big Structures, Large Processes, Huge Comparisons* (New York: Russell Sage Foundation, 1984), pp. 87–96.

2. Ibid., p. 145.

3. Ibid., p. 116.

Chapter One

1. Guy Perrin, "Reflections on Fifty Years of Social Security," *International Labour Review* 99 (February 1969): 253; Gaston V. Rimlinger, *Welfare Policy and Industrialization in Europe, America and Russia* (New York: John Wiley, 1971), p. 121; Jill Quadagno, *Aging in Early Industrial Society: Work, Family and Social Policy in Nineteenth Century England* (New York: Academic Press, 1982), p. 115; Hugh Heclo, *Modern Social Politics in Britain and Sweden* (New Haven: Yale University Press, 1974), p. 194.

2. Ann Shola Orloff and Theda Skocpol, "Why Not Equal Protection? Explaining the Politics of Public Social Spending in Britain, 1900–1911, and the United States, 1880s–1920s," *American Sociological Review* 49 (December 1984): 742; Jill Quadagno, "From Poor Laws to Pensions: The Evolution of Economic Support for the Aged in England and America," *Milbank Memorial Fund Quarterly* 62 (Summer 1984): 437.

3. Perrin, "Reflections on Fifty Years of Social Security," p. 263; John Myles, "The Retirement Wage in the Postwar Capitalist Democracies," paper presented to the American Sociological Association, San Antonio, 1984, p. 3.

4. Richard F. Tomasson, "Government Old Age Pensions under Affluence and Austerity: West Germany, Sweden, the Netherlands and the United States," *Research in Social Problems and Public Policy* 3 (1984): 232.

5. John Myles, *Old Age in the Welfare State* (Boston: Little, Brown, 1984), p. 40; Robert T. Kudrle and Theodore R. Marmor, "The Development of the Welfare State in North America," in *The Development of Welfare States in Europe and America*, ed. Peter Flora and Arnold Heidenheimer (New Brunswick, N.J.: Transaction Books, 1981), p. 85.

6. Tomasson, "Government Old Age Pensions," p. 224.

7. Jill Quadagno, "Welfare Capitalism and the Social Security Act of 1935," *American Sociological Review* 49 (October 1984): 634.

8. Martha Derthick, *Policymaking for Social Security* (Washington, D.C.: Brookings Institution, 1979), pp. 267, 357.

9. U.S. Social Security Administration, *Social Security Bulletin, Annual Statistical Supplement* (Washington, D.C.: Government Printing Office, 1982), tables 34, 37.

10. Theda Skocpol, "America's Incomplete Welfare State: The Limits of New Deal Reforms and the Origins of the Present Crisis," paper presented to the American Sociological Association, San Antonio, 1984, p. 8.

11. Clark Kerr, John T. Dunlop, Frederick Harbison, and Charles A. Myers, *Industrialism and Industrial Man: The Problems of Labor and Management in Economic Growth* (New York: Oxford University Press, 1964); Daniel Lerner, *The Passing of Traditional Society: Modernizing the Middle East* (Glencoe, Ill.: Free Press, 1958).

12. Donald Cowgill, "The Aging of Populations and Societies," in *Aging, the Individual and Society: Readings in Social Gerontology,* ed. Jill Quadagno (New York: St. Martin's Press, 1982), pp. 15–33; William Form, "Comparative Industrial Sociology and the Convergence Hypothesis," *Annual Review of Sociology* 5 (1979): 1–25; Fred Pampel and Jane Weiss, "Economic Development, Pension Policies, and the Labor Force Participation of Aged Males: A Cross-National Longitudinal Analysis," *American Journal of Sociology* 89 (1983): 350–72.

13. Phillips Cutright, "Political Structure, Economic Development and National Social Security Programs," *American Journal of Sociology* 70 (1965): 537–48; Robert Jackman, *Politics and Social Equality: A Comparative Analysis* (New York: John Wiley, 1975); Harold Wilensky, *The Welfare State and Equality: Structural and Ideological Roots of Public Expenditures* (Berkeley: University of California Press, 1975), p. xiii.

14. Edwin Amenta and Theda Skocpol, "States and Social Policies," *Annual Review of Sociology* 12 (1986): 131–57; Peter Flora and Jens Alber, "Modernization, Democratization and the Development of Welfare States in Western Europe," in *The Development of Welfare States in Europe and America,* ed. Peter Flora and Arnold Heidenheimer (New Brunswick, N.J.: Transaction Books, 1981), pp. 37–80; David Collier and Richard Messick, "Prerequisites versus Diffusion: Testing Alternative Explanations of Social Security Adoption," *American Political Science Review* 69 (1975): 1299–1315.

15. Goran Therborn, "The Rule of Capital and the Rise of Democracy," in *States and Societies,* ed. Thomas Held, James Anderson, Bram Gieben, Stuart Hall, Laurence Harris, Paul Lewis, Noel Parker, and Ben Turok (New York: New York University Press, 1983), pp. 261–71.

16. Michael Shalev, "The Social Democratic Model and Beyond: Two Generations of Comparative Research on the Welfare State," in *Comparative Social Research Annual,* vol. 6, ed. Richard F. Tomasson (Greenwich, Conn.: JAI Press, 1983), pp. 319–20; David R. Cameron, "The Expansion of the

Public Economy," *American Political Science Review* 72 (December 1978); 1243–60.

17. Walter Korpi, "Social Policy and Distributional Conflict in the Capitalist Democracies," *West European Politics* 3 (October 1980): 296–315; John Stephens, *The Transition from Capitalism to Socialism* (London: Macmillan, 1979), p. 89; Cameron, "Expansion of the Public Economy," pp. 1243–60; Francis Castles, *The Impact of Parties* (Beverly Hills, Calif.: Sage, 1983); Francis Castles and Richard McKinlay, "Public Welfare Provision and the Sheer Futility of the Sociological Approach to Politics," *British Journal of Political Science* 9 (1979): 157–72.

18. Shalev, "Social Democratic Model," p. 324; Frank Parkin, *Class Inequality and Political Order* (New York: Praeger, 1971), pp. 121, 124; Martin Carnoy, *The State and Political Theory* (Princeton: Princeton University Press, 1984), p. 255.

19. Claus Offe, *Contradictions of the Welfare State* (Cambridge: MIT Press, 1984), p. 186.

20. Ian Gough, *The Political Economy of the Welfare State* (London: Macmillan, 1979), p. 11.

21. James O'Connor, *The Fiscal Crisis of the State* (New York: St. Martin's Press, 1973), p. 124; Fred Block, "Beyond Corporate Liberalism," *Social Problems* 24 (1977): 352–61; Chris Phillipson, "The State, the Economy and Retirement," in *Old Age and the Welfare State*, ed. Anne Marie Guillemard (Beverly Hills, Calif.: Sage, 1983), p. 134; Laura Katz Olson, *The Political Economy of Aging* (New York: Columbia University Press, 1982), pp. 21–22; Rolande Trempe, "The Struggles of French Miners for the Creation of Retirement Funds in the Nineteenth Century," in *Old Age and the Welfare State*, ed. Anne Marie Guillemard (Beverly Hills, Calif.: Sage, 1983), p. 107.

22. Gough, *Political Economy of the Welfare State*, p. 12.

23. Rimlinger, *Welfare Policy and Industrialization*, p. 116; Quadagno, "Welfare Capitalism and the Social Security Act of 1935," pp. 632–47; Shalev, "Social Democratic Model and Beyond," p. 341.

24. Theda Skocpol, "Political Response to Capitalist Crisis: Neo-Marxist Theories of the State and the Case of the New Deal," *Politics and Society* 10 (1980): 181.

25. Nelson Lichtenstein, *Labor's War at Home* (Cambridge: Cambridge University Press, 1982), p. 5.

26. Frances Fox Piven and Richard A. Cloward, *Regulating the Poor: The Functions of Public Welfare* (New York: Vintage Books, 1971), p. 8; Ernest W. Martin, "From Parish to Union: Poor Law Administration, 1601–1865," in *Comparative Development in Social Welfare*, ed. Ernest W. Martin (London: George Allen and Unwin, 1972), p. 28; Derek Fraser, *The Evolution of the British Welfare State* (London: Macmillan, 1973), p. 30.

27. Rimlinger, *Welfare Policy and Industrialization*, p. 19; Quadagno, *Aging in Early Industrial Society*, p. 96; Anthony Brundage, *The Making of the New Poor Law* (New Brunswick, N.J.: Rutgers University Press, 1978), p. 5.

28. Rimlinger, *Welfare Policy and Industrialization,* p. 23; Piven and Cloward, *Regulating the Poor,* p. 30.

29. June Axinn and Herman Levin, *Social Welfare: A History of the American Response to Need* (New York: Harper and Row, 1982), p. 21.

30. Rimlinger, *Welfare Policy and Industrialization,* p. 327.

31. Karl Marx, "A Contribution to the Critique of Political Economy," in *The Marx-Engels Reader,* ed. Robert C. Tucker (New York: W. W. Norton, 1972), p. 4.

32. Collier and Messick, "Prerequisites versus Diffusion," p. 1310.

33. Jerald Hage and Robert A. Hanneman, "The Growth of the Welfare State in Britain, France, Germany, and Italy: A Comparison of Three Paradigms," *Comparative Social Research* 3 (1980): 68.

34. John Williamson and Jane Weiss, "Egalitarian Political Movements, Social Welfare Effort and Convergence Theory: A Cross-National Analysis," *Comparative Social Research* 2 (1979): 299.

35. Shalev, "Social Democratic Model and Beyond," p. 319; Myles, *Old Age in the Welfare State,* p. 77.

36. Mary Ruggie, *The State and Working Women* (Princeton: Princeton University Press, 1984), p. 15.

37. Nicos Poulantzas, *State, Power, Socialism,* (London: NLB, 1978), pp. 132–35.

38. Offe, *Contradictions of the Welfare State,* p. 159.

39. Ibid., p. 160.

40. Stephens, *Transition from Capitalism to Socialism,* p. 89; Rimlinger, *Welfare Policy and Industrialization,* p. 80.

41. Werner Sombart, *Why Is There No Socialism in America?* (White Plains, N.Y.: M. E. Sharpe, 1976); Louis Hartz, "The Liberal Tradition," in *Failure of a Dream?* ed. John Laslett and Seymour M. Lipset (Garden City, N.Y.: Anchor Press, 1974), pp. 401, 406; Seymour M. Lipset, "The Labor Movement and American Values," in *Failure of a Dream,* ed. Laslett and Lipset, p. 553; John M. Laslett, "The American Tradition of Labor Theory and Its Relevance to the Contemporary Working Class," in *The American Working Class,* ed. Irving Louis Horowitz, John C. Leggett, and Martin Oppenheimer (New Brunswick, N.J.: Transaction Books, 1979), pp. 5–26; Jerome Karabel, "The Reasons Why," *New York Review of Books* 29 (February 1979): 22–25; Mike Davis, "Why the US Working Class Is Different," *New Left Review* 123 (September–October 1980): 3–44; Ira Katznelson, *City Trenches: Urban Politics and the Patterning of Class in the United States* (New York: Pantheon Books, 1981), p. 10.

42. Gosta Esping-Anderson, *Politics against Markets: The Social Democratic Road to Power* (Princeton: Princeton University Press, 1985), p. 245; see also Stephens, *Transition from Capitalism to Socialism,* p. 150.

43. Christopher Tomlins, *The State and the Unions: Labor Relations, Law and the Organized Labor Movement in America, 1880–1960* (Cambridge: Cambridge University Press, 1985), p. 16; David M. Gordon, Richard Edwards, and Michael Reich, *Segmented Work, Divided Workers: The Historical Transformation*

of Labor in the United States (Cambridge: Cambridge University Press, 1982). p. 91.

44. Selig Perlman and Philip Taft, *History of Labor in the United States, 1896–1932* (New York: Macmillan, 1935), pp. 8, 25.

45. David Brody, *Workers in Industrial America* (New York: Basic Books, 1984), p. 115.

46. Orloff and Skocpol, "Why Not Equal Protection?" pp. 730–31.

47. Ibid., p. 742.

48. Tomlins, *State and the Unions*, p. 22; Gianfranco Poggi, *The Development of the Modern State: A Sociological Introduction* (Stanford, Calif.: Stanford University Press, 1978), pp. 60–117.

49. Tomlins, *State and the Unions*, pp. 26, 28.

50. Ibid., p. 30.

51. Robert Wiebe, *Businessmen and Reform: A Study of the Progressive Movement* (Chicago: Quadrangle Books, 1968), p. 43.

52. Neil Fligstein, "State and Markets: The Transformation of the Large Corporation, 1880–1985," University of Arizona, unpublished manuscript, p. 24.

53. Ibid., pp. 25–26.

54. Gabriel Kolko, *The Triumph of Conservativism: A Reinterpretation of American History, 1900–1916* (New York: Free Press, 1977), p. 56.

55. Ibid., p. 3.

56. Wiebe, *Businessmen and Reform*, pp. 22–23.

57. Tomlins, *State and the Unions*, p. 11.

58. Jay R. Mandle, *The Roots of Black Poverty: The Southern Plantation Economy after the Civil War* (Durham, N.C.: Duke University Press, 1978). pp. 11, 46.

59. F. Ray Marshall, *Labor in the South* (Cambridge,: Harvard University Press, 1967), pp. 27, 299.

60. Avery O. Craven, *The Growth of Southern Nationalism, 1848–1861* (Baton Rouge: Louisiana State University Press, 1953), pp. 159–61.

61. C. Vann Woodward, *Origins of the New South, 1877–1913* (Baton Rouge: Louisiana State University Press, 1951), p. 345; V. O. Key, *Southern Politics in State and Nation* (New York: Alfred A. Knopf, 1949), p. 20.

62. J. Morgan Kousser, *The Shaping of Southern Politics: Suffrage Restriction and the Establishment of the One-Party South, 1880–1910* (New Haven: Yale University Press, 1974), p. 246.

63. Key, *Southern Politics*, p. 10.

64. Charles S. Sydnor, *The Development of Southern Sectionalism, 1819–1848* (Baton Rouge: Louisiana State University Press, 1948), p. 213; David M. Potter, *The South and the Concurrent Majority* (Baton Rouge: Louisiana State University Press, 1972), p. 32.

65. Potter, *South and the Concurrent Majority*, pp. 10, 16, 48, 49.

66. Ibid., pp. 51, 31.

67. Ibid., p. 32.

68. Ibid., p. 68.

69. Gavin Wright, *The Political Economy of the Cotton South: Households, Markets, and Wealth in the Nineteenth Century* (New York: W. W. Norton, 1978), p. 4.

70. For a detailed discussion of this point see William Graebner, *A History of Retirement: The Meaning and Function of an American Institution, 1885–1978* (New Haven: Yale University Press, 1980).

CHAPTER TWO

1. David Hackett Fischer, *Growing Old in America* (New York: Oxford University Press, 1978), pp. 162, 168.

2. W. Andrew Achenbaum, *Old Age in the New Land: The American Experience since 1790* (Baltimore: Johns Hopkins University Press, 1978), pp. 85, 127.

3. Lee Welling Squier, *Old Age Dependency in the United States* (New York: Macmillan, 1912), p. 320; Charles Richmond Henderson, *Industrial Insurance in the United States* (Chicago: University of Chicago Press, 1909), p. 308; Robert Howe, "Industry and the Aged," *Harvard Business Review* 8 (1929): 438.

4. Ann Shola Orloff and Theda Skocpol, "Why Not Equal Protection? Explaining the Politics of Public Social Spending in Britain, 1900–1911, and the United States, 1880s–1920s," *American Sociological Review* 49 (December 1984): 742; Ann Shola Orloff, "The Politics of Pensions: A Comparative Analysis of the Origins of Pensions and Old Age Insurance in Canada, Great Britain and the United States, 1880s–1930s," Ph.D. diss., Princeton University, 1985, pp. 35–214.

5. Jill Quadagno, "State Structures and the Administration of Old Age Assistance," paper presented to the Social Science History Association, Toronto, October 1984.

6. Orloff, "Politics of Pensions," p. 112.

7. Maurice Dobb, "Transition from Feudalism to Capitalism," in *Papers on Capitalism, Development and Planning,* ed. Maurice Dobb (New York: International Publishers, 1967), p. 7.

8. Jay R. Mandle, *The Roots of Black Poverty: The Southern Plantation Economy after the Civil War* (Durham, N.C.: Duke University Press, 1978). p. 10.

9. Ibid., p. 11. The use of the term "plantation mode of production" is historically narrow in that these characteristics also existed in preindustrial European nations, like England in the eighteenth century, independent of plantations per se. Rather, this type of farmer-laborer relationship was often associated with large-scale, market-oriented, agricultural production. Nonetheless, the distinctive features of the plantation mode of production, as opposed to either capitalism or feudalism, need to be specified, and Mandle's terminology will be used here.

10. Gavin Wright, *The Political Economy of the Cotton South: Households, Markets, and Wealth in the Nineteenth Century* (New York: W. W. Norton, 1978). p. 6.

11. The exception was the town of Taunton in Plymouth Colony, which was cited for not providing relief during the 1650s. See Charles R. Lee, "Public Poor Relief and the Massachusetts Community, 1620–1715," *New England Quarterly* 55, 4 (1982): 564–85.

12. Jill S. Quadagno, "From Poor Laws to Pensions: The Evolution of Economic Support for the Aged in England and America," *Milbank Memorial Fund Quarterly* 62 (Summer 1984): 423.

13. Margaret D. Creech, *Three Centuries of Poor Law Administration* (Chicago: University of Chicago Press, 1936), p. 28.

14. Robert Kelso, *The History of Public Poor Relief in Massachusetts, 1620–1920* (Boston: Houghton Mifflin, 1922), p. 102.

15. June Axinn and Herman Levin, *Social Welfare: A History of the American Response to Need* (New York: Harper and Row, 1982), p. 21.

16. Douglas Lamar Jones, "The Strolling Poor: Transiency in Eighteenth Century Massachusetts," *Journal of Social History* 8 (Spring 1975): 28; idem, "Poverty and Vagabondage: The Process of Survival in Eighteenth-Century Massachusetts," *New England Historical and Genealogical Register* 83 (October 1979): 243.

17. David M. Gordon, Richard Edwards, and Michael Reich, *Segmented Work, Divided Workers: The Historical Transformation of Labor in the United States* (Cambridge: Cambridge University Press, 1982), pp. 55, 61, 67, 73. See chap. 2 for a more detailed discussion of the growth of capitalist forms of production.

18. Louis J. Piccarello, "Social Structure and Public Welfare Policy in Danvers, Massachusetts: 1750–1850," *Essex Institute Historical Collections* 118 (October 1982): 255, 257.

19. David Rothman, *The Discovery of the Asylum* (Boston: Little, Brown, 1971), p. 183.

20. Brian Gratton, "The Invention of Social Work: Welfare Reform in the Antebellum City," *Urban and Social Change Review* 18 (Winter, 1985): 6.

21. Byers argues that the extent of almshouse use in this period is exaggerated. Similarly, Piccarello demonstrates that the use of an almshouse by a village varied according to the nature of the town's poor and that in the eighteenth century some towns with large numbers of unemployed built almshouses to care for them. Thus the nature of the local economy was more important than any single reform movement. See Edward Byers, "America's Almshouse Experience: Dependent Poverty in Salem, Massachusetts, 1750–1920," unpublished manuscript, Department of History, Brandeis University, p. 3; and Louis Piccarello, "The Administration of Public Welfare: A Comparative Analysis of Salem, Danvers, Deerfield and Greenfield," *Historical Journal of Massachusetts* 10 (June 1982): 30–42, table 6.

22. Priscilla Ferguson Clement, "The Response to Need, Welfare and Poverty in Philadelphia, 1800 to 1850," Ph.D. diss., University of Pennsylvania, 1977, p. 184.

23. Rothman, *Discovery*, p. 196.

24. Clement, "Response to Need," p. 184; Brian Gratton, *Urban Elders: Family, Work and Welfare among Boston's Aged, 1890–1950* (Philadelphia:

Temple University Press, 1986), p. 129. Economic factors also propelled more and more of the aged into institutions in California, where the passage of an act by the state legislature in 1883 appropriated the sum of $100 yearly for the support of every indigent person over sixty years of age. See Mary Roberts Smith, "Almshouse Women," *American Statistical Association* 31 (September 1895): 223. Since the average cost per inmate in California almshouses was less than $100 per person per year, it became financially advantageous for institutions to admit old as opposed to young residents. The result was a substantial increase in the average age of inmates from fifty in 1882 to fifty-nine by 1894. As was true elsewhere, most of these residents were Irish immigrants. Statistics indicate that older people also received an increasingly disproportionate share of outdoor relief. In 1826, 61 percent of those on outdoor relief in Philadelphia were over fifty; by 1859 this figure had risen to 80 percent. And 48 percent of the almshouse residents were also old. See Clement, "Response to Need," p. 240. This act was repealed in 1894. In 1830 Philadelphia supported 549 outdoor paupers at an average rate of 46½ cents per week, and 390 of those were over sixty years of age. See Matthew Carey, *Appeal to the Wealthy of the Land* (Philadelphia: L. Johnson, 1833), pp. 3–34.

25. Michael B. Katz, *Poverty and Policy in American History* (New York: Academic Press, 1983), p. 10; Edward Berkowitz and Kim McQuaid, *Creating the Welfare State* (New York: Praeger, 1980), p. 26; Alice Shaffer and Mary Wysor Keefer, *The Indiana Poor Law* (Chicago: University of Chicago Press, 1936), p. 14.

26. Elizabeth Wisner, *Social Welfare in the South: From Colonial Times to World War I* (Baton Rouge: Louisiana State University Press, 1970), p. 12.

27. Ibid., p. 14.

28. Ibid., p. 36.

29. Axinn and Levin, *Social Welfare*, p. 42.

30. Charles Sydnor, *The Development of Southern Sectionalism, 1819–1848* (Baton Rouge: Louisiana State University Press, 1948), p. 93.

31. Henry Rogers Seager, *Social Insurance: A Program of Reform* (New York: Macmillan, 1910), p. 5. See chapter 5 for a more detailed discussion of early twentieth-century pension proposals.

32. See chapter 6 for a more detailed discussion of tenancy in the South.

33. Richard F. Bensel, *Sectionalism and American Political Development, 1880–1980* (Madison: University of Wisconsin Press, 1984), p. 4.

34. Wright, *Political Economy of the Cotton South*, p. 37.

35. Bensel, *Sectionalism and American Political Development*, p. 6.

36. Ibid., pp. 14, 91.

37. Ibid., p. 23.

38. Ibid., p. 35.

39. Ibid., p. 46.

40. Allan G. Bogue, *From Prairie to Corn Belt* (Chicago: University of Chicago Press, 1963), p. 154.

41. Wright, *Political Economy of the Cotton South*, p. 55.

42. Ibid., p. 219.

43. William Glasson, *Federal Military Pensions in the United States* (New York: Oxford University Press, 1918), p. 16.

44. Ibid., pp. 20, 23.

45. Ibid., p. 65; Sydnor, *Development of Southern Sectionalism*, p. 140.

46. Ira Katznelson, *City Trenches: Urban Politics and the Patterning of Class in the United States* (New York: Pantheon Books, 1981), p. 46.

47. Glasson, *Federal Military Pensions*, p. 64.

48. *Annals of Congress*, 15th Cong., 1st sess., 1825, 1:140–50.

49. Glasson, *Federal Military Pensions*, p. 70; Edward Stanwood, *American Tariff Controversies in the Nineteenth Century* (Boston: Houghton Mifflin, 1903), 1:179–91.

50. Sydnor, *Development of Southern Sectionalism*, pp. 144, 187, 189.

51. Glasson, *Federal Military Pensions*, p. 77; William Glasson, "The South and Service Pension Laws," *South Atlantic Quarterly* 1 (October 1902): 354.

52. *Register of Debates in Congress*, 22d Cong., 1st sess., 1832, 7, (part 2): 2498, 2393, 2372–73.

53. Glasson, *Federal Military Pensions*, p. 80.

54. Glasson "South and Service Pension Laws," p. 356.

55. Martin Shefter, "Party, Bureaucracy and Political Change in the United States," in *Political Parties: Development and Decay*, ed. Louis Maisel and Joseph Cooper (Beverly Hills, Calif.: Sage, 1978), p. 218.

56. Stephen Skowronek, *Building a New American State: The Expansion of National Administrative Capacities, 1877–1920* (Cambridge: Cambridge University Press, 1982), p. 25.

57. Carl R. Fish, *The Civil Service and Patronage* (New York: Longmans, Green, 1905), p. 166.

58. Sydnor, *Development of Southern Sectionalism*, p. 284.

59. Avery O. Craven, *The Growth of Southern Nationalism, 1848–1861* (Baton Rouge: Louisiana State University Press, 1953), p. 161.

60. Sydnor, *Development of Southern Sectionalism*, pp. 285, 288.

61. Craven, *Growth of Southern Nationalism*, p. 161.

62. J. Mills Thornton, *Politics and Power in a Slave Society: Alabama, 1800–1860* (Baton Rouge: Louisiana State University Press, 1978), pp. 67, 138.

63. Bennett D. Baack and Edward J. Ray, "Tariff Policy and Income Distribution: The Case of the United States, 1830–1860," *Explorations in Economic History* 11 (Winter 1973–4): 103–22. Robert Royal Russel, *Economic Aspects of Southern Sectionalism, 1840–1861*, Studies in the Social Sciences, vol. 11, no. 1 (Urbana: University of Illinois, 1922; reprinted New York: Arno Press, 1973), p. 165.

64. C. Vann Woodward, *Origins of the New South, 1877–1913* (Baton Rouge: Louisiana State University Press, 1951), p. 186; Bensel, *Sectionalism and American Political Development*, p. 60.

65. Tom E. Terrill, *The Tariff, Politics, and American Foreign Policy, 1874–1901* (Westport, Conn.: Greenwood Press, 1973), p. 4.

66. John W. Oliver, *History of the Civil War Military Pensions, 1861–1885*, History Series 1 (Madison: University of Wisconsin, 1917), pp. 6, 7.

67. Ibid., p. 10.

68. Mary Beth Norton, David M. Katzman, Paul D. Escott, Howard P. Chudacoff, Thomas G. Patterson, and William M. Tuttle, *A People and a Nation* (Boston: Houghton Mifflin, 1982), pp. 380–81.

69. Bensel, *Sectionalism and American Political Development*, pp. 62, 22.

70. Oliver, "History of Civil War Military Pensions," p. 24.

71. Ibid., pp. 51, 53, 56.

72. Heywood T. Sanders, "Paying for the Bloody Shirt: The Politics of Civil War Pensions," in *Political Benefits*, ed. Barry Rundquist (Lexington, Mass.: Lexington Books, 1980), p. 139.

73. David Potter, *The South and the Concurrent Majority* (Baton Rouge: Louisiana State University Press, 1972), p. 37.

74. *Congressional Record*, 47th Cong., 1st sess., Senate, 22 February, 1881, pp. 913–17, 918.

75. Oliver, "Civil War Pensions," pp. 93, 95.

76. *National Tribune*, 24 January 1884, p. 1.

77. Bensel, *Sectionalism and American Political Development*, p. 49.

78. Oliver, "Civil War Pensions," p. 104.

79. Ibid., pp. 106–13.

80. Ibid., p. 117.

81. Allan Nevins, *Grover Cleveland: A Study in Courage* (New York: Dodd, Mead, 1944), p. 328; Bensel, *Sectionalism and American Political Development*, p. 71.

82. *Congressional Record*, 49th Cong. 2d sess., House, 11 February 1887, p. 1639.

83. Nevins, *Grover Cleveland*, p. 332; Glasson, *Federal Military Pensions*, p. 205.

84. *National Tribune*, 31 March 1887, p. 3.

85. *Congressional Record*, 50th Cong., 1st sess., Senate, 1 March 1888, p. 1626.

86. Terrill, *Tariffs, Politics and American Foreign Policy*, p. 134.

87. *Congressional Record*, 47th Cong., 1st sess., Senate, part 1, 6 February 1882, p. 915; Robert Hunter, *Labor in Politics* (Chicago: Socialist Party, 1915), pp. 97–98; *Congressional Record*, 50th Cong., 1st sess., Senate, 1 March 1888, p. 1628.

88. Terrill, *Tariffs, Politics and American Foreign Policy*, pp. 103, 121, 133.

89. Glasson, *Federal Military Pensions*, p. 225.

90. Stanwood, *American Tariff Controversies*, pp. 262, 264, 286.

91. U.S. Congress, House of Representatives, 51st Cong., 1st sess., House Report 3732, *The Raum Investigation*, 26 July 1890.

92. Glasson, *Federal Military Pensions*, p. 229.

93. *Congressional Record*, 51st Cong., 1st sess., Senate, 31 March 1890, pp. 2835, 2836.

94. Bensel, *Sectionalism and American Political Development*, p. 67; Glasson, *Federal Military Pensions*, p. 273.

95. Terrill, *Tariff, Politics and American Foreign Competition*, pp. 111, 209, 120.

96. Robert H. Wiebe, *Businessmen and Reform: A Study of the Progressive Movement* (Chicago: Quadrangle Books, 1968), pp. 20, 26, 34.

97. *Congressional Record,* 51st Cong., 1st sess., Senate, 31 March 1890, pp. 2837, 2838, 2840.

98. Ibid., pp. 2844, 2846.

99. *Congressional Record,* 51st Cong., 1st sess., House, 1890, pp. 5944, 5949, 5950.

100. For a more detailed discussion, see William Glasson, "The National Pension System as Applied to the Civil War and the War with Spain," *Annals of the American Academy of Political and Social Sciences* 19 (March 1902): 220.

101. Bensel, *Sectionalism and American Political Development,* p. 67; John DeWitt Warner, "Half a Million Dollars a Day for Pensions," *Forum* 15 (June 1893): 439.

102. For examples of protests against the law, see Alan R. Foote, "Degradation by Pensions: The Protest of Loyal Volunteers," *Forum* 12 (December 1891): 423–32; H. W. Slocum, "Pensions: Time to Call a Halt," *Forum* 12 (January 1892): 646–51.

103. S. N. Clark, "Some Weak Places in Our Pension System," *Forum* 26 (1898): 315, 307.

104. William Graebner, *A History of Retirement: The Meaning and Function of an American Institution, 1885–1978* (New Haven: Yale University Press, 1980), p. 58.

105. John H. Girdner, "To Purge the Pension List," *North American Review* 166 (March 1898): 374.

106. Glasson, "South and Service Pension Laws," p. 359.

107. M. B. Morton, "Federal and Confederate Pensions Contrasted," *Forum* 16 (September 1893): 73; Glasson, *Federal Military Pensions,* p. 269.

108. *Congressional Record,* 59th Cong., 1st sess., 1906, p. 687; Orloff, *Politics of Pensions,* p. 77; Glasson, *Federal Military Pensions,* p. 271.

CHAPTER THREE

1. Ann Shola Orloff, "The Politics of Pensions: A Comparative Analysis of the Origins of Pensions and Old Age Insurance in Canada, Great Britain and the United States, 1880s–1930s," Ph.D diss., Princeton University, 1985, pp. 76, 78; Priscilla Ferguson Clement, "Women and the Welfare System in 19th Century America," paper presented to the Social Science History Association, Saint Louis, October 1986, p. 5.

2. Orloff, "Politics of Pensions," p. 136.

3. Christopher Anglim and Brian Gratton, "Organized Labor and Old Age Pensions," *International Journal of Aging and Human Development,* in press.

4. Gosta Esping-Anderson, *Politics against Markets: The Social Democratic Road to Power* (Princeton: Princeton University Press, 1985), p. 60.

5. Richard Edwards, *Contested Terrain: The Transformation of the Workplace in the Twentieth Century* (New York: Basic Books, 1979), p. 19.

6. David M. Gordon, Richard Edwards, and Michael Reich, *Segmented*

Work, Divided Workers: The Historical Transformation of Labor in the United States (Cambridge: Cambridge University Press, 1982), p. 100.

7. Robert M. Jackson, *The Formation of Craft Labor Markets* (Orlando, Fla.: Academic Press, 1984), p. 18.

8. Ibid., pp. 3–7.

9. Christopher Tomlins, *The State and the Unions: Labor Relations, Law and the Organized Labor Movement in America, 1880–1960* (Cambridge: Cambridge University Press, 1985), p. 16.

10. Letter from Samuel Gompers to the Committee on Miners' Home and Pensions. Quoted in Abraham Epstein, *Facing Old Age* (New York: Alfred Knopf, 1922; reprinted by Arno Press, 1972), p. 193.

11. David Montgomery, *Workers' Control in America: Studies in the History of Work, Technology, and Labor Struggles* (Cambridge: Cambridge University Press, 1979), p. 15.

12. Ibid., p. 18.

13. Ibid., p. 22.

14. U.S. Department of Labor, "Care of the Aged by Labor Organizations," *Bulletin of the Bureau of Labor Statistics* 489 (October 1929): 86.

15. Ibid., p. 87.

16. Tomlins, *State and the Unions*, pp. 69–70.

17. Selig Perlman and Philip Taft, *History of Labor in the United States, 1986–1952* (New York: Macmillan, 1935), pp. 410, 84.

18. Murray Webb Latimer, *Trade Union Pension Systems* (New York: Industrial Relations Counselors, 1932), p. 8.

19. Irving Bernstein, *The Lean Years* (Boston: Houghton Mifflin, 1960), p. 84.

20. Edwards, *Contested Terrain*, p. 71.

21. Stuart Brandes, *American Welfare Capitalism* (Chicago: University of Chicago Press, 1976), pp. 103–48.

22. Mark Perlman, "Labor in Eclipse," in *Change and Continuity in Twentieth Century America: The 1920s*, ed. John Braeman, Robert Bremner, and David Brody (Columbus: Ohio State University Press, 1968), p. 122; Bernstein, *Lean Years*, pp. 87–89.

23. U.S. Department of Labor, "Care of the Aged," p. 95.

24. *Proceedings of the Fifth Triennial Convention of the Brotherhood of Railroad Trainmen*, 1919, p. 777; *Proceedings of the Thirty-first Annual Convention of the Brotherhood of Locomotive Firemen and Enginemen*, 1928, pp. 1075, 1079.

25. Bryant Putney, "Federal Assistance to the Aged," Editorial Research Report, vol. 2, no. 18, 1934, Franklin Delano Roosevelt Papers, Official Files, 494a, Hyde Park, New York, FDR Library, p. 329.

26. *Proceedings of the American Federation of Labor*, 1929, p. 99.

27. Perlman and Taft, *History of Labor*, p. 51.

28. Latimer, *Trade Union Pension Systems*, p. 22. According to William Graebner, the ITU instituted a pension because it recognized that technological change had undermined the earning power of the older worker. See his discussion in *A History of Retirement: The Meaning and Function*

of an American Institution, 1885–1978 (New Haven: Yale University Press, 1980), p. 135.

29. Epstein, *Facing Old Age*, p. 196; Latimer, *Trade Union Pension Systems*, p. 59.

30. *Reports of Officers to the Sixty-sixth Session of the International Typographical Union*, 1921, p. 23.

31. James M. Lynch, "Pensions Are Superior to Poorhouses," *American Labor Legislation Review* 15 (September 1925): 262.

32. *Report of Officers to the Seventieth Session of the International Typographical Union*, 1925, pp. 82–83.

33. *Report of Officers to the Seventy-first Session of the International Typographical Union*, 1926, p. 93.

34. *Report, Seventieth Session*, p. 77; *Report, Seventy-first Session*, p. 50.

35. U.S. Department of Labor, "Beneficial Activities of American Trade Unions," *Bulletin of the Bureau of Labor Statistics* 465 (September 1928): 41.

36. *Proceedings of the Seventy-second Convention of the International Typographical Union*, 1928, p. 12.

37. Ibid., pp. 54, 67.

38. *Report of Officers to the Seventy-third Session of the International Typographical Union*, 1929, p. 8.

39. Ibid., p. 80.

40. Bernstein, *Lean Years*, p. 254.

41. *Report of Officers to the Seventy-sixth Session of the International Typographical Union*, 1931, pp. 5, 40.

42. *Report of Officers to the Seventy-seventh Session of the International Typographical Union*, 1932, pp. 2, 37.

43. Ibid., p. 74.

44. Ibid., p. 34.

45. *Report of Officers to the Seventy-eighth Session of the International Typographical Union*, 1934, p. 4.

46. Robert Hunter, *Labor in Politics* (Chicago: Socialist Party, 1915), p. 12.

47. Vivian Vale, *Labour in American Politics* (London: Routledge and Kegan Paul, 1971), p. 33.

48. Hunter, *Labor in Politics*, p. 15.

49. Robert H. Wiebe, *Businessmen and Reform: A Study of the Progressive Movement* (Chicago: Quadrangle Books, 1968), p. 26; Gabriel Kolko, *The Triumph of Conservatism: A Reinterpretation of American History, 1900–1916* (New York: Free Press, 1977), p. 62.

50. Wiebe, *Businessmen and Reform*, p. 19.

51. Montgomery, *Workers' Control in America*, p. 59.

52. Mike Davis, "Why the US Working Class Is Different," *New Left Review* 123 (September–October 1980): 32; Jerome Karabel, "The Reason Why," *New York Review of Books* 26 (February 1979): 22; Martin Oppenheimer, *White Collar Politics* (New York: Monthly Review Press, 1985), p. 40.

53. Samual P. Hays, *The Response to Industrialism, 1885–1914* (Chicago: University of Chicago Press, 1957), p. 151.

54. I. M. Rubinow, *Social Insurance* (New York: Henry Holt, 1913), p. 500.

55. David Hackett Fischer, *Growing Old in America* (New York: Oxford University Press, 1978), p. 171.

56. Orloff, *Politics of Pensions*, p. 103; Charles Richmond Henderson, *Industrial Insurance in the United States* (Chicago: University of Chicago Press, 1909), p. 61.

57. Samuel Gompers, "Voluntary Social Insurance vs. Compulsory," *American Federationist* 23 (May and August 1916): 340, 677.

58. Samuel Gompers, "Not Even Compulsory Benevolence Will Do," *American Federationist* 24 (January 1917): 48.

59. Gompers, "Voluntary Social Insurance vs. Compulsory," pp. 341, 680.

60. Gary L. Fink, ed., *State Labor Proceedings: A Bibliography of the AFL, CIO and AFL-CIO Proceedings, 1885–1974, Held in the AFL-CIO Library* (Westport, Conn.: Greenwood Press, 1975), pp. ix–x.

61. *Proceedings of the Ninth Annual Convention of the Arkansas State Federation of Labor*, 1911, p. 78.

62. *Proceedings of the Seventeenth Annual Convention of the California State Federation of Labor*, 1916, p. 98.

63. Gompers, "Voluntary Social Insurance vs. Compulsory," p. 675.

64. William Green, "Trade Union Sick Funds and Compulsory Health Insurance," *American Labor Legislation Review* 7 (1917): 92.

65. Vale, *Labour in American Politics*, p. 36.

66. Ibid., pp. 38–39.

67. Perlman and Taft, *History of Labor*, p. 403.

68. Charles Tilly, *From Mobilization to Revolution* (Reading, Mass.: Addison-Wesley, 1978), p. 70; Mayer Zald and John McCarthy, "Resource Mobilization and Social Movements: A Partial Theory," *American Journal of Sociology* 82 (May 1977): 1225.

69. Anglim and Gratton, "Organized Labor and Old Age Pensions," p. 2.

70. *United Mine Workers Journal*, 8 August 1918, pp. 11, 13; 1 September 1918, p. 2; 1 December 1918, p. 3.

71. *United Mine Workers Journal*, 15 September 1918, p. 17. For a discussion of the issues involved in cooperation between social movement organizations, see Mayer Zald and John McCarthy, "Social Movement Industries: Competition and Cooperation among Movement Organizations," *Research in Social Movements, Conflicts and Change* 3 (1980): 1–20.

72. *United Mine Workers Journal*, 1 February 1919; 1 October 1919, p. 2.

73. *United Mine Workers Journal*, 1 January 1920, p. 12; 15 June 1920, p. 7; 1 August 1920, p. 9.

74. *United Mine Workers Journal*, 1 August 1920, p. 9; 15 August 1920, p. 17.

75. Bernstein, *Lean Years*, pp. 127–36.

76. Charles K. Knight, "Fraternal Life Insurance," *Annals of the American Academy of Political and Social Science* 130 (March 1927): 97.

77. Walter S. Nichols, "Fraternal Insurance in the United States: Its Origin, Development, Character and Existing Status," *Annals of the American Academy of Political and Social Science* 70 (March 1917): 111.

78. *Eagle Magazine* 11 (August 1923): 5. For a summary of research indicating that commitment to a moral purpose is more binding on individuals and more successful in generating loyalty than material incentives, see Craig Jenkins, "Resource Mobilization Theory and the Study of Social Movements," *Annual Review of Sociology* 9 (1983): 537.

79. *Eagle Magazine* 11 (March 1923): 15; 12 (June 1924): 16; 13 (June 1925: 7; Earl R. Beckner, *A History of Labor Legislation in Illinois* (Chicago: University of Chicago Press, 1929), p. 486.

80. *Eagle Magazine* 10 (February 1922): 8; 10 (June 1922): 12; 12 (June 1924): 16.

81. *Eagle Magazine* 10 (January 1922): 20; "Ohio Joins Pension States," *American Labor Legislation Review* 23 (March 1923): 191.

82. *Eagle Magazine* 10 (January 1922): 20; Epstein, *Facing Old Age*, p. 207.

83. *Eagle Magazine* 10 (May 1922): 30; 10 (February 1922): 22, 9.

84. *Eagle Magazine* 11 (March 1923): 4.

85. Tilly, *From Mobilization to Revolution*, pp. 125–33.

86. *Eagle Magazine* 10 (July 1922): 15.

87. *Eagle Magazine* 10 (April 1922): 22; 12 (August 1924): 8.

88. *Eagle Magazine* 12 (April 1924): 26; 10 (April 1922): 22.

89. Quoted in Anglim and Gratton, "Organized Labor and Old Age Pensions," p. 11.

90. Pennsylvania Manufacturers' Association, *Monthly Bulletin,* 1 May 1927, p. 1.

91. U.S. Congress, House Committee on Labor, *Old Age Pensions,* 71st Cong., 2d sess., February 1930, Washington, D.C., p. 245.

92. "Public Pensions for Aged Dependents," *Monthly Labor Review* 22 (June 1926): 1180; Abraham Epstein. "Experience under State Old-Age Pension Laws in 1932," *Monthly Labor Review* 37 (August 1933): 255; Florence E. Parker, "Experience under State Old-Age Pension Acts in 1933," *Monthly Labor Review* 39 (August 1934): 263.

93. John R. Commons, *History of Labor in the United States, 1896–1932* (New York: Macmillan 1935), p. 613; Edward F. McGrady, "Old Age Pensions," *American Federationist* 37 (1930): 546.

94. I. M. Rubinow, The Quest for Security (New York: Henry Holt, 1934), pp. 279, 278.

95. Illinois State Federation of Labor, *Weekly News Letter,* 17 March 1923.

96. John H. Walker, "Labor's Point of View," in *The Care of the Aged,* ed. I. M. Rubinow (New York: Arno, 1980 [1930]), pp. 24–25.

97. *Proceedings of the American Federation of Labor,* 1929, p. 261.

98. Nelson Cruickshank Memoirs, Columbia University Oral History Collection, New York, Butler Library, p. 54.

99. *Proceedings of the American Federation of Labor,* 1928, p. 258.

100. *Proceedings of the American Federation of Labor,* 1929, pp. 258–59.

101. Louis Stark, "Labor on Relief and Insurance," *Survey Magazine,* 1931, p. 187.

102. Epstein, "Experience under State Old-Age Pension Laws," pp. 259, 131; Parker, "Experience under State Old-Age Pension Acts," p. 256.

103. Florence Peterson, *American Labor Unions* (New York: Harper and Row, 1945), pp. 53–55.

104. See chapter 4 for a detailed discussion of the railroad pension.

105. Quoted in Graebner, *History of Retirement,* p. 167.

106. Ibid., p. 172.

107. "U.S. May Take over Railroad Pension Plans," *Railway Age* 97 (1934): 143; Graebner, *History of Retirement,* pp. 179–80; "Railway Pension Bill Approved by President," *Railway Age* 97 (1934): 6.

108. "Hearing on Pension Legislation," *Railway Age* 94 (1933): 112; "U.S. May Take over Railroad Pension Plans," p. 147.

109. Hayes Robbins, "Clearances Needed in Railroad Pension Financing," *Railway Age* 89 (1930): 485; Graebner, *History of Retirement,* p. 165.

110. *Congressional Record,* Senate, 19 August 1935, pp. 136–46; House, August 1935, pp. 16673.

111. U.S. Congress, Senate, Subcommittee of the Committee on Interstate Commerce, *Hearings on S. 3151: Retirement System for Employees of Carriers,* 74th Cong., 1st sess. (Washington, D.C.: Government Printing Office, 1935), p. 13, 2–4.

CHAPTER FOUR

1. For a critique of the logic of industrialism argument and systematic analysis of the support systems for the aged in the past, see Peter Laslett, "Societal Development and Aging," in *Handbook of Aging and the Social Sciences,* ed. Robert H. Binstock and Ethel Shanas (New York: Van Nostrand Reinhold, 1985), pp. 199–230.

2. John Myles, *Old Age in the Welfare State: The Political Economy of Public Pensions* (Boston: Little, Brown, 1984). p. 77.

3. Ian Gough, *The Political Economy of the Welfare State* (London: Macmillan, 1979), p. 33.

4. Richard Edwards, *Contested Terrain: The Transformation of the Workplace in the Twentieth Century* (New York: Basic Books, 1979), pp. 24, 19.

5. William Graebner, *A History of Retirement: The Meaning and Function of an American Institution, 1885–1978* (New Haven: Yale University Press, 1980), p. 38.

6. Dan Clawson, *Bureaucracy and the Labor Process: The Transformation of U.S. Industry, 1860–1920* (New York: Monthly Review Press, 1980), pp. 71, 75, 108.

7. Burton J. Hendrick, "The Superannuated Man," *McClure's Magazine* 32 (December 1908): 121.

8. Quoted in Arthur D. Cloud, *Pensions in Modern Industry* (Chicago: Hawkins and Loomis, 1930), pp. 122–23.

9. Paul Monroe, "An American System of Labor Pensions and Insurance," *American Journal of Sociology* 2 (January 1897): 507.

10. Alfred Dolge, *The Plan of Earnings-Division: An Excerpt from "Economic Theories Practically Applied"* (Dolgeville, N.Y.: Dolgeville Herald, 1896), p. 2.

11. Monroe, "An American System," p. 510.

12. Charles Richmond Henderson, *Industrial Insurance in the United States* (Chicago: University of Chicago Press, 1909), p. 204.

13. Murray Webb Latimer, *Industrial Pension Systems in the United States and Canada* (New York: Industrial Relations Counselors, 1932), p. 1010.

14. Quoted in Luther Conant, *A Critical Analysis of Industrial Pension Systems* (New York: Macmillan, 1922), p. 18.

15. David Brody, *Workers in Industrial America* (New York: Basic Books, 1984), p. 24; Robert H. Wiebe, *Businessmen and Reform: A Study of the Progressive Movement* (Chicago: Quadrangle Books, 1968), p. 19.

16. Wiebe, *Businessmen and Reform*, p. 25; see also David Montgomery, *Workers' Control in America: Studies in the History of Work, Technology, and Labor Struggles* (Cambridge: Cambridge University Press, 1979), p. 26.

17. Brody, *Workers in Industrial America*, p. 25; Larry J. Griffin, Michael E. Wallace, and Beth A. Rubin, "Capitalist Resistance to the Organization of Labor before the New Deal: Why? How? Success?" *American Sociological Review* 51 (April 1986): 160; Selig Perlman and Philip Taft, *History of Labor in the United States, 1896–1932* (New York: Macmillan, 1935), p. 134.

18. Perlman and Taft, *History of Labor,* pp. 109, 123.

19. Brody, *Workers in Industrial America,* p. 30; Robert M. Jackson, *The Formation of Craft Labor Markets* (Orlando, Fla.: Academic Press, 1984), p. 321.

20. Cloud, *Pensions in Modern Industry,* pp. 52–53.

21. Carol Haber, *Beyond Sixty-five: The Dilemma of Old Age in America's Past* (Cambridge: Cambridge University Press, 1983), p. 114; Latimer, *Industrial Pension Systems,* p. 20; Henderson, *Industrial Insurance in the United States,* p. 233.

22. "Invalidity and Old Age Insurance," *Bulletin of the U.S. Bureau of Labor Statistics* 212 (June 1917): 740.

23. Emory P. Johnson, "Railway Relief Departments," *Annals of the American Academy of Political and Social Science* 6 (1895): 424–26; "Notes: Charities and Social Problems," *Annals of the American Academy of Political and Social Science* 18 (1901): 183; M. Riebenack, "Pennsylvania Railroad Pension Departments: Systems East and West of Pittsburgh and Erie, Pa. Status to and Including the Year, 1907," *Annals of the American Academy of Political and Social Science* 33 (1909): 258–64.

24. E. B. Erskine, "United States Steel and Carnegie Pension Fund," *Bulletin of the U.S. Bureau of Labor Statistics* 212 (June 1917): 742; Perlman and Taft, *History of Labor,* p. 100.

25. Cloud, *Pensions in Modern Industry,* p. 139; "Welfare Work for Employees in Industrial Establishments," *Bulletin of the U.S. Bureau of Labor Statistics* 250 (1919): 109.

26. Mary Conyngton, "Industrial Pensions for Old Age and Disability," *Monthly Labor Review* 22 (1926): 53.

27. "Invalidity and Old Age Insurance," p. 736; Latimer, *Industrial Pension Plans,* p. 1090.

28. A. Johnston, "Heroic Pensioners," *Locomotive Engineers Journal* 60 (January 1926): 14; see also "A Congressman's Tribute to Engineers," *Locomotive Engineers Journal* 60 (January 1926): 8.

29. Conyngton, "Industrial Pensions for Old Age and Disability," p. 50; Graebner, *History of Retirement,* p. 167.

30. E. A. Vanderlip, "Insurance from the Employer's Standpoint," *Proceedings of the Thirty-third National Conference of Charities and Corrections,* 1906, p. 463.

31. See Latimer, *Industrial Pension Systems,* pp. 998–1051.

32. Montgomery, *Workers' Control in America,* p. 119.

33. Quoted in Cloud, *Pensions in Modern Industry,* p. 131.

34. "Invalidity and Old-Age Insurance, Pensions, and Retirement Allowances," *Bulletin of the U. S. Bureau of Labor Statistics* 212 (June 1917): 742.

35. Riebenack, "Pennsylvania Railroad Pension Departments," p. 38.

36. Quoted in Cloud, *Industrial Pension Systems,* p. 45.

37. Ibid., pp. 162–65.

38. "Another Union to Adopt Pension Scheme," *Locomotive Engineers Journal* 61 (September 1927): 688.

39. For an extended discussion of the use of pensions as a means of rationalizing the labor force, see Graebner, *History of Retirement.*

40. Hendrick, "Superannuated Man," p. 120.

41. Henderson, *Industrial Insurance in the United States,* p. 238.

42. From 1914 to 1919, the percentage of employees in manufacturing who regularly worked no more than forty-eight hours a week increased from 11.8 to 48.7. United States Bureau of the Census, *Biennial Census of Manufacturers, 1923* (Washington, D.C.: Government Printing Office, 1926).

43. P. F. Brissenden and E. Frankel, *Labor Turnover in Industry* (New York: Macmillan, 1922), pp. 88–89; U.S. Bureau of Labor Statistics, "Labor and Laboring Classes," *Handbook of Labor Statistics, 1924–1926* (Washington, D.C.: Government Printing Office, 1927), p. 570; Leo Wolman, *The Growth of Trades Unions, 1880–1923* (New York: National Bureau of Economic Research, 1924), p. 33. See chapter 3 for a more extensive discussion of changes in the position of labor.

44. Edwards, *Contested Terrain,* p. 70.

45. David M. Gordon, Richard Edwards, and Michael Reich, *Segmented Work, Divided Workers: The Historical Transformation of Labor in the United States* (Cambridge: Cambridge University Press, 1982), p. 163.

46. Brody, *Workers in Industrial America,* p. 5.

47. Magnus W. Alexander, "Hiring and Firing: Its Economic Waste and How to Avoid It," *Annals of the American Academy of Political and Social Sciences* 65 (May 1916): 130; Gordon, Edwards, and Reich, *Segmented Work, Divided Workers,* p. 163.

48. Alexander, "Hiring and Firing," p. 143.

49. David Brody, "The Rise and Decline of Welfare Capitalism," in *Change and Continuity in Twentieth Century America: The 1920s,* ed. John Braeman, Robert Bremner, and David Brody (Columbus: Ohio State University Press, 1968), pp. 147–48; Brody, *Workers in Industrial America,* p. 53; Clarence J. Hicks, "What Can the Employer Do to Encourage Saving and Wise Investment by Industrial Employees," *Harvard Business Review* 2 (January 1924): 200.

50. Sumner H. Slichter, "The Current Labor Policies of American Industry," *Quarterly Journal of Economics* 43 (May 1929): 396.

51. The Standard Oil (SO) companies that initiated pensions included SO of California, SO of New Jersey, SO of Indiana, SO of Kansas, SO of Nebraska, SO of Ohio, SO of New York, Vacuum Oil, a subsidiary of SO of New York, SO of Kentucky, and Humble Oil, another Standard Oil subsidiary. See Latimer, *Industrial Pension Systems,* pp. 1010–12, 1055; William J. Kemnitzer, *Rebirth of Monopoly: A Critical Analysis of Economic Conduct in the Petroleum Industry in the United States* (New York: Harper, 1938), p. 43; Bennett H. Wall and George S. Gibb, *Teagle of Jersey Standard* (New Orleans: Tulane University Press, 1974), p. 209.

52. Henrietta M. Larson, "The Rise of Big Business in the Oil Industry," in *Oil's First Century: Papers Given at the Centennial Seminar on the History of the Petroleum Industry* (Cambridge: Harvard Graduate School of Business Administration, 1960), p. 27; Kemnitzer, *Rebirth of Monopoly,* p. 11.

53. Kemnitzer, *Rebirth of Monopoly,* p. 18.

54. Wall and Gibb, *Teagle of Jersey Standard,* p. 131.

55. Irving Bernstein, *The Turbulent Years: A History of the American Worker, 1933–1941* (Boston: Houghton Mifflin, 1970), p. 109. Standard Oil of California had previously initiated a pension in 1916; see *1879–1979: One Hundred Years Helping to Create the Future* (N.p.: Standard Oil Company of California, 1979), p. 23.

56. Wall and Gibb, *Teagle of Jersey Standard,* p. 132.

57. Albert deRoode, "Pensions as Wages," *American Economic Review* 3 (June 1913): 290.

58. "Phelps Dodge Modified Employees' Pension System at Bisbee," *Mining News* 116 (15 December 1923): 1042; see also "Old Age Pension Plan for Ashland Employees," *Electric Railway Journal* 63 (12 January 1924): 80; and "Half Pay Pensions for New Jersey Employees," *Electric Railway Journal* 68 (16 October 1926): 744.

59. Conyngton, "Industrial Pensions for Old Age and Disability," p. 52; "Defrauding Yourselves," *Locomotive Engineers Journal* 60 (June 1926): 409.

60. "Pensions Stir Labor Unions," *Locomotive Engineers Journal* 60 (February 1926): 408.

61. Robert Howe, "Industry and the Aged," *Harvard Business Review* 8 (October 1929): 437.

62. H. P. Daugherty, "Company Pension Plans," *Locomotive Engineers Journal* 61 (April 1927): 250.

63. Calculated From Latimer, *Industrial Pension Systems,* pp. 1052–65.

64. Latimer, *Industrial Pension Systems,* p. 614; Daugherty, "Company Pension Plans," p. 250.

65. "Employee Pension Plans," *American Machinist* 66 (June 1927): 989; E. R. Renaud, "Old Age Pensions on a Sound Basis—Discussion," *American Machinist* 78 (October 1934): 735.

66. "New Pension Plan Announced by General Electric," *Electric Railway Journal* 70 (31 December 1927): 1213; "Annuity Plan of a Large Manufacturing Company," *Monthly Labor Review* 30 (February 1930): 255; G.

Chauncey Parsons, "Old Age Pensions on a Sound Basis," *American Machinist* 780 (15 August 1934): 567.

67. Latimer, *Industrial Pension Systems*, p. 881; "Employee Pension Plans," p. 989.

68. "Labor Laws and Court Decisions," *Monthly Labor Review* 38 (1934): 1102.

69. "Insurance and Pension Plans," *Monthly Labor Review* [U.S. Bureau of Labor Statistics] 36, no. 1 (1933): 1064.

70. "Beware of 'Company' Group Insurance," *Brotherhood of Locomotive Firemen and Enginemen's Magazine* 76 (June 1924): 23. For a discussion of pensions as wages, see deRoode, "Pensions as Wages"; Conyngton, "Industrial Pensions for Old Age and Disability," p. 22.

71. Conant, *Industrial Pension Systems*, p. 107.

72. *Proceedings of the American Federation of Labor*, 1928, p. 102.

73. Gordon, Edwards, and Reich, *Segmented Work, Divided Workers*, pp. 174–75.

74. Ibid., pp. 174–75.

75. Conant, *Industrial Pension Systems*, pp. 249–50.

76. Parsons, "Old Age Pensions on a Sound Basis," p. 568; Ingalls Kimball, "Industrial Pensions vs. State Poor Relief," *Annalist* 27 (January 1926): 150.

77. Albert M. Linton, "Life Insurance Companies and Pension Plans," *Annals of the American Academy of Political and Social Sciences* 130 (March 1927): 39.

78. Latimer, *Industrial Pension Systems*, pp. 615, 724–25.

79. Gurden Edwards, "Industrial Pension Plans Collapsing," *Annalist* 26 (20 November 1925): 637, 638.

80. Linton, "Life Insurance Companies and Pension Plans," p. 34.

81. Gurden Edwards, "The Way out of the Industrial Pension Crisis," *Annalist* 26 (27 November 1925): 667.

82. Emerson P. Schmidt, "Industrial Pensions and Trade Unions," *American Federationist* 36 (1929): 417.

83. Murray Webb Latimer, "Old Age Pensions in America," *American Labor Legislation Review* 19 (March 1929): 62. For a similar analysis, see Conyngton, "Industrial Pensions for Old Age and Disability," p. 50.

84. Latimer, "Old Age Pensions in America," p. 62.

85. Latimer, *Industrial Pension Systems*, p. 847.

CHAPTER FIVE

1. Jerry Cates, *Insuring Inequality: Administrative Leadership in Social Security, 1935–1954* (Ann Arbor: University of Michigan Press, 1982), p. 23.

2. Theda Skocpol and John Ikenberry, "The Political Formation of the American Welfare State in Historical and Comparative Perspective," *Comparative Social Research* 6 (1983): 117, 119.

3. Theda Skocpol and Edwin Amenta, "Did Capitalists Shape Social Security?" *American Sociological Review* 50 (1985): 573.

4. Henry Rogers Seager, *Social Insurance: A Program of Reform* (New York: Macmillan, 1910), pp. 5, 18.

5. F. Spencer Baldwin, "The Work of the Massachusetts Commission on Old Age Pensions," *American Statistical Association* 85 (March 1909): 417.

6. Massachusetts Commission on Old Age Pensions, Annuities, and Insurance, *House Report No. 1400* (Boston, January 1910), p. 301.

7. Ibid., p. 322.

8. See chapter 4 for a more detailed discussion of business opposition.

9. Robert H. Wiebe, *Businessmen and Reform: A Study of the Progressive Movement* (Chicago: Quadrangle Books, 1968), pp. 32–33.

10. Publications by the NICB included *Rest Periods for Industrial Workers* (Research Report no. 13, 1919); *The Eight Hour Day Defined* (Research Report no. 11, 1918); *Hours of Work as Related to Output and Health of Workers* (Research Report no. 18, 1919), and numerous other specialized reports on labor issues.

11. See chapter 4 for a more detailed discussion of the problems of industrial pensions in the 1920s.

12. "Pensions for Industrial Workers a Problem for Executives Today," *American Machinist* 64 (18 February 1926): 298; D. B. Wedge, "Why the Government in Pensions," *American Machinist* 70 (3 January 1929): 2.

13. Charles L. Edgar, William R. Willcox, and P. Tecumseh Sherman, *Old Age Pensions Conference* (New York: National Civic Federation, 1927), pp. 6–7.

14. Robert Howe, "Industry and the Aged," *Harvard Business Review* 8 (October 1929): 436, 439, 441; see also Wedge, "Why the Government in Pensions," p. 2.

15. American Association for Social Security Archives, 1928, "Letter from Owen D. Young to Bishop Francis F. McConnell," Abraham Epstein Papers, Old Age Pension-Industrial Plans Folder, Ithaca, N.Y., Cornell University, 1928; See also Gurden Edwards, "The Benefits to Employees of Sound Pension Plans," *Annalist* 26 (4 December 1925): 876.

16. David Brody, *Workers in Industrial America* (New York: Basic Books, 1984), p. 53.

17. Murray Webb Latimer, *Industrial Pension Systems in the United States and Canada* (New York: Industrial Relations Counselors, 1932), p. 42.

18. H. P. Mulford, *Incidence and Effects of the Payroll Tax* (Washington, D.C.: Social Security Board, 1936), p. 5.

19. Latimer, *Industrial Pension Systems*, p. 789.

20. "Industrial Pension Plans in the Depression, United States and Canada," *Monthly Labor Review* 36 (January 1933): 1062.

21. Latimer, *Industrial Pension Systems*, pp. 846–48.

22. Michael Piore and Charles F. Sabel, *The Second Industrial Divide* (New York: Basic Books, 1984), p. 55.

23. Ibid., pp. 56–57, 63.

24. Ibid., p. 74.

25. Henry I. Harriman, "The Stabilization of Business and Employment," *American Economic Review* 22 (1932): 63–74; Gerard Swope, "The Stabilization of Industry," in *America Faces the Future,* ed. Charles Beard

(Boston: Houghton Mifflin, 1932), pp. 160–85; Barbara Brents, "Policy Formation in Capitalist Society: The Social Security Act of 1935," master's thesis, Department of Sociology, University of Missouri, Columbia, 1983, app. 2.

26. Swope, "The Stabilization of Industry," p. 163; Harriman, "Stabilization of Business and Employment," p. 74.

27. Swope, "Stabilization of Industry," pp. 167–68.

28. Ibid., p. 184.

29. Herman E. Kroos, *Executive Opinion* (Garden City, N.J.: Doubleday, 1970), pp. 152, 153.

30. Raymond Moley, *After Seven Years* (New York: Harper, 1939), p. 187; Christopher Tomlins, *The State and the Unions: Labor Relations, Law, and the Organized Labor Movement in America, 1880–1960* (Cambridge: Cambridge University Press, 1985), pp. 105–7.

31. Edward Berkowitz and Kim McQuaid, *Creating the Welfare State* (New York: Praeger, 1980), p. 85.

32. David Loth, *Swope of G.E.* (New York: Simon and Schuster, 1958), p. 232.

33. Gabriel Kolko, *The Triumph of Conservatism: A Reinterpretation of American History, 1900–1916* (New York: Free Press, 1977), p. 129; Barton J. Bernstein, "The New Deal: The Conservative Achievements of Liberal Reform," in *Toward the New Past*, ed. Barton J. Bernstein (New York: Random House, 1968), p. 269.

34. Kolko, *Triumph of Conservatism*, p. 138.

35. U.S. Congress, House, Committee on Labor, *Old Age Pensions*, 71st Cong., 2d sess. (Washington, D.C.: Government Printing Office, 1930).

36. Philip Burch, "The NAM as an Interest Group," *Politics and Society* 4 (1973): 99, 102; testimony of Noel Sargent of the National Association of Manufacturers, U.S. Congress, House, Committee on Labor, *Old Age Pensions*, p. 192.

37. U.S. Congress, Senate, Subcommittee of the Committee on Pensions, *Hearings on S. 3257: A Bill to Encourage and Assist the States in Providing Pensions to the Aged*, 71st Cong., 2d sess. (Washington, D.C.: Government Printing Office, 1931).

38. Ibid., p. 64.

39. Francis E. Townsend, *New Horizons* (Chicago: J. L. Stewart, 1943).

40. Committee on Economic Security, *The Townsend Crusade* (New York: Twentieth Century Fund, 1936), p. 16.

41. Franklin Delano Roosevelt papers, Official Files, 494a, Hyde Park, New York, FDR Library.

42. Committee on Economic Security, *Townsend Crusade*, p. 18.

43. William Graebner, *A History of Retirement: The Meaning and Function of an American Institution, 1885–1978* (New Haven: Yale University Press, 1980), p. 192.

44. U.S. Congress, House Subcommittee of the Committee on Labor, *Hearings on H.R. 2827: Unemployment, Old Age and Social Insurance*, 74th

Cong., 1st sess. (Washington, D.C.: Government Printing Office, 1935), pp. 1–2.

45. Testimony of Elmer Johnson, representing the Chicago Branch of the American Federation of Labor, ibid., p. 522.

46. Testimony of Herbert Benjamin, executive secretary, National Joint Action Committee for Genuine Social Insurance, ibid., p. 183.

47. See chapter 3 for a discussion of labor's stance on state benefits.

48. Clarke A. Chambers, *Seedtime of Reform* (Minneapolis: University of Minnesota Press, 1963), p. 166.

49. Loth, *Swope of G.E.*, p. 235.

50. Ibid., p. 236; see also William Domhoff, *The Higher Circles* (New York: Random House, 1970), pp. 211–12.

51. Frank Bane Memoirs, Columbia University Oral History Collection, New York, Butler Library, p. 22; Thomas Eliot Memoirs, Columbia University Oral History Collection, New York, Butler Library, p. 13.

52. Roosevelt papers, Official Files, 494a, box 1.

53. Skocpol and Ikenberry, "Political Formation of the American Welfare State," p. 124.

54. J. Douglas Brown, "Philosophical Basis of the National Old Age Insurance Program," in *Social Security and Private Pension Plans*, ed. Dan McGill (Homewood, Ill: Richard D. Irwin, 1977), p. 5.

55. Arthur Altmeyer, *The Formative Years of Social Security* (Madison: University of Wisconsin Press, 1966), p. xi.

56. Marion Folsom Memoirs, Columbia University Oral History Collection, New York, Butler Library, p. 95.

57. Edwin Witte, *The Development of the Social Security Act* (Madison: University of Wisconsin Press, 1963), pp. 12, 29; letter from Arthur Altmeyer to Frances Perkins, July 1935, National Archives, RG 47, Chairman's Files, box 9, file 020.

58. Witte, *Development of the Social Security Act,* p. 19.

59. Ibid., p. 89.

60. Brents, "Policy Formation in Capitalist Society," appendix.

61. Ibid.

62. "Suggestions for an Advisory Council," Arthur Altmeyer Papers, CES File 2, box 1, Madison, State Historical Society of Wisconsin Library.

63. U.S. Congress, Senate Committee on Finance, *Economic Security Act: Hearings on S. 1130: A Bill to Alleviate the Hazards of Old Age Unemployment, Illness and Dependency, to Establish a Social Insurance Board in the Department of Labor, to Raise Revenue, and for Other Purposes,* 74th Cong., 1st sess. (Washington, D.C.: Government Printing Office, 1935), p. 284.

64. Folsom, Memoirs, p. 54.

65. Ibid., pp. 68–69.

66. J. Douglas Brown, *Am American Philosophy of Social Security* (Princeton: Princeton University Press, 1972), p. 21.

67. U.S. Senate, Committee on Finance, *Hearings on S. 1130.* p. 926.

68. Ibid., p. 686.

69. Arthur Schlesinger, *The Coming of the New Deal* (Boston: Houghton Mifflin, 1958), p. 312.

70. Lee J. Alston and Joseph P. Ferrie, "Labor Costs, Paternalism, and Loyalty in Southern Agriculture: A Constraint on the Growth of the Welfare State," *Journal of Economic History* 45 (March 1985): 110, 112.

71. Austria, Belgium, Bulgaria, Czechoslovakia, France, Great Britain, Italy, the Netherlands, and Spain all had coverage for agricultural workers and domestics in their pension plans. U.S. Senate, Committee on Finance, *Hearings on S. 1130,* p. 51.

72. Ibid., p. 71.

73. Raymond Wolters, "The New Deal and the Negro," in *The New Deal,* ed. John Braeman, Robert H. Bremmer, and David Brody (Columbus: Ohio State University Press, 1975), p. 194.

74. Mulford, *Incidence and Effects of the Payroll Tax,* p. 17.

75. Ibid., p. 489.

76. "What Business Thinks," *Fortune,* October 1939, pp. 52–53, 90.

77. Charles McKinley and Robert W. Frase, *Launching Social Security: A Capture-and-Record Account* (Madison: University of Wisconsin, 1970), p. 347; Brown, *American Philosophy,* p. 23.

78. Marion Folsom, "Coordination of Pension Plans with Social Security Provisions," *Personnel* 16 (1939): 42, 41.

79. Social Security Act in Relation to Private Plans for Employees Benefits, 29 April 1936. National Archives, RG 47, Chairman's File, box 12, file 025.

80. Murray Webb Latimer and Karl Tufel, *Trends in Industrial Pensions* (New York: Industrial Relations Counselors, 1940), pp. 7, 29, 73–74.

81. Ibid., p. 40.

82. Letter from Charles Schottland to Congressman Victor Wickersham, 1 April 1955. Federal Archives and Records Center, Suitland, Md., RG 47, Chairman's Files, box 37, file 050.317.

83. Nelson Cruickshank Memoirs, Columbia University Oral History Collection, New York, Butler Library, p. 27.

84. *Reports of Officers to the Twenty-seventh Session of the International Typographical Union,* 1935, p. 6.

85. Letter from William Green to All Central Labor Unions, 29 August 1939, National Archives, RG 47, Chairman's Files, box 119, file 095.

86. Informational Service memo from Louis Resnick to Frank Bane, 12 May 1936, National Archives, RG 47, Central Files, box 65, file 062; see also "Labor Information Program for Application by Regional Staff, 18 March 1938," National Archives, RG 47, Central Files, box 65, file 062.81.

87. Memorandum from Joseph Kovner, executive secretary, CIO Committee on Social Security, National Archives, RG 47, Central Files, box 65, file 062.81.

88. Abraham Epstein, "The Turning Point in Social Security," in *Social Security in the United States,* Eleventh National Conference on Social Security (New York: American Association for Social Security, 1938), pp. 2–3.

89. Testimony of Abraham Epstein, U.S. Congress, House Com-

mittee on Ways and Means, *Hearings on H.R. 6635,* 76th Cong., 1st sess. (Washington, D.C.: Government Printing Office, 1939), pp. 1022–23.

90. Statement of CIO before House Ways and Means Committee on Proposed Changes in the Social Security Act, National Archives, RG 47, Chariman's Files, box 119, file 011.1.

91. Resolution 219, International Ladies Garment Workers Union, Convention Proceedings, May 1937; Letter from Freemand Cochran, executive secretary Tacoma Industrial Union Council to the president; Resolution from United Automobile Workers of America, May 1938; National Archives, RG 47, Central Files, box 6, file 011.4.

92. J. Douglas Brown, "Next Steps in Old Age Insurance," in *Social Security in the United States* (New York: American Association for Social Security, 1938), p. 46.

93. U.S. Congress, Senate Committee on Finance, *Hearings on S. Con. Res. 4: A Concurrent Resolution Calling for the Amendment of Certain Provisions of the Social Security Act,* 75th Cong., 1st sess. (Washington, D.C.: Government Printing Office, 1937).

94. Ibid., p. 28.

95. Folsom Memoirs, p. 33.

96. Board Meeting Minutes, Discussion of Amendments to Title II, 6 February 1937, p. 3. National Archives, RG 47, Chairman's Files, box 7, file 001.1.

97. Altmeyer, *Formative Years,* p. 91.

Chapter Six

1. Claus Offe, *Contradictions of the Welfare State* (Cambridge: MIT Press, 1984), pp. 106–7.

2. Jerry Cates, *Insuring Inequality: Administrative Leadership in Social Security, 1935–1954* (Ann Arbor: University of Michigan Press, 1982), p. 18.

3. David M. Potter, *The South and the Concurrent Majority* (Baton Rouge: Louisiana State University Press, 1972), pp. 10, 16, 48.

4. Richard F. Bensel, *Sectionalism and American Political Development, 1880–1980* (Madison: University of Wisconsin Press, 1984), pp. 153, 150, 160.

5. Ibid., p. 153; Jack Temple Kirby, "The Transformation of Southern Plantations ca. 1920–1960," *Agricultural History* 57 (July 1983): 267.

6. Gunnar Myrdal, *An American Dilemma* (New York: McGraw-Hill, 1964), p. 224); Oscar Zeichner, "The Legal Status of the Agricultural Laborer in the South," *Political Science Quarterly* 55 (1940): 412.

7. Orville V. Burton, *In My Father's House Are Many Mansions: Family and Community in Edgefield, South Carolina* (Chapel Hill: University of North Carolina Press, 1985), pp. 260–311; Jacqueline Jones, *Labor of Love, Labor of Sorrow: Black Women, Work, and the Family from Slavery to the Present* (New York: Basic Books, 1985), pp. 81–95; Brian Gratton, "The Labor Force Participation of Older Men: 1890–1950," *Journal of Social History* 21 (June 1987): 7.

8. Lee J. Alston and Joseph P. Ferrie, "Labor Costs, Paternalism, and

Loyalty in Southern Agriculture: A Constraint on the Growth of the Welfare State," *Journal of Economic History* 45 (March 1985): 100; Zeichner, "Legal Status of the Agricultural Laborer," pp. 414, 422.

9. U.S. Bureau of the Census, *Fifteenth Census of the United States, 1930, Agriculture,* vol. 2, part 2, county table 1. Data on wage laborers are from the *Fifteenth Census of the United States, 1930, Population,* vol. 4, state table 11.

10. Jay R. Mandle, "The Plantation States as a Sub-region of the Post-bellum South," *Journal of Economic History* 34 (1974): 733.

11. J. Morgan Kousser, *The Shaping of Southern Politics: Suffrage Restriction and the Establishment of the One-Party South, 1880–1910* (New Haven: Yale University Press, 1974), p. 239.

12. C. Vann Woodward, *Origins of the New South, 1877–1913* (Baton Rouge: Louisiana State University Press, 1951), p. 345; V. O. Key, *Southern Politics in State and Nation* (New York: Alfred A. Knopf, 1949), p. 20.

13. Key, *Southern Politics,* p. 10.

14. Ibid., p. 20.

15. Potter, *South and the Concurrent Majority,* p. 49.

16. Woodward, *Origins of the New South,* p. 346.

17. See chapter 2 for a comparison between relief in the South and that in the rest of the nation before the depression.

18. Elizabeth Wisner, *Social Welfare in the South: From Colonial Times to World War I* (Baton Rouge: Louisiana State University Press, 1970), p. 45.

19. Thomas J. Woofter, *Landlord and Tenant on the Cotton Plantation* (Washington, D.C.: Works Progress Administration, 1936), p. 151; Howard B. Myers, "Relief in the South," *Southern Economic Journal* 3 (1937): 282.

20. Woofter, *Landlord and Tenant,* p. 150.

21. John Samuel Ezell, *The South since 1865* (New York: Macmillan, 1975), pp. 430, 432. Southerners also strongly resented the work relief programs in such agencies as the WPA and CCC because they offered shorter hours, lighter work, and year-round employment that interfered with the labor supply.

22. Ibid., p. 169.

23. Ibid., p. 433.

24. Kirby, "Transformation of Southern Plantations," p. 263.

25. Ezell, *South since 1865,* p. 152.

26. Arthur J. Altmeyer, *The Formative Years of Social Security* (Madison: University of Wisconsin Press, 1966), p. 59.

27. Letter from A. J. Hatfield to Frances Perkins, 22 January 1936. Office Memo, n.d., National Archives, RG 47, State Files, box 58, file 092.

28. Social Security Board Interoffice Communication, 17 March 1937, National Archives, RG 47, Records of the Executive Director, box 278, file 631.301.

29. Social Security Board, Bureau of Research and Statistics, National Archives, RG 47, Records of the Executive Director, box 278, file 631.301.

30. Mississippi Old Age Assistance Act, National Archives, RG 47, State Files, box 34, file 600.

31. Louisiana—Revised Plans for Old Age Assistance, 8 October 1936, National Archives, RG 47, State Files, box 26, file 622.203.

32. Ibid.

33. Jill Quadagno, *Aging in Early Industrial Society: Work, Family and Social Policy in Nineteenth Century England* (New York: Academic Press, 1982).

34. Jane Hooey Memoirs, Columbia University Oral History Collection, Butler Library, New York, p. 28.

35. U.S. Congress, House Committee on Ways and Means, *Hearings on H.R. 6635,* 76th Cong., 1st sess. (Washington, D.C.: Government Printing Office, 1939), p. 1038.

36. Letter from Mrs. Frank Pou, 20 October 1941, Franklin Delano Roosevelt papers, Official Files 494a, Pensions, Hyde Park, New York.

37. Memo on Louisiana old age assistance payments for the months of June and July, 9 December 1937, National Archives, RG 47, State Files, box 26, file 600.0413.

38. U.S. Bureau of Research and Statistics, *Trends in Public Assistance, 1933–1939,* Bureau Report no. 8 (Washington, D.C.: Social Security Board, 1940), pp. 57, 75–76.

39. Agenda of the meeting of the commissioners of public welfare from Arkansas, Georgia, Tennessee, Alabama, North Carolina, Virginia, and West Virginia, 25 November 1939, National Archives, RG 47, Records of the Executive Director, box 272, file 600.

40. Charles Richmond Henderson, *Industrial Insurance in the United States* (Chicago: University of Chicago Press, 1909), pp. 283–86.

41. In some states Confederate pensions were set at even higher levels, but regardless of benefit size, the federal government contributed only $15.

42. Payment of Federal Funds in Relation to Grants to Needy Confederate Veterans, 6 December 1937, National Archives, RG 47, Records of the Executive Director, box 273, file 600.045.

43. Bensel, *Sectionalism and American Political Development,* p. 149.

44. John Corson, "Insurance against Old Age Dependency," *Annals of the American Academy of Political and Social Science* 202 (March 1939): 63. Numerous instances of similar remarks appear in the records. For example, I. S. Falk, director of the Bureau of Research and Statistics, acknowledged that "in States in which the average payment to Negroes is higher than to whites it may be assumed that the Negro recipients are more needy. In States in which the average payment to Negroes is lower than to whites in all probability there is a differential in the standards of determining the amount of grant for Negro and white families" (interoffice communication from I. S. Falk to Oscar Powell, 18 May 1940, National Archives, RG 47, Records of the Executive Director, box 279, file 640). Similarly, a report from Industrial Relations Counselors justified lower grants to blacks on the grounds that "for certain racial groups in rural areas of the South and Southwest, long accustomed to an extremely low standard of living, even these small sums undoubtedly represent a standard considerably above that to which they

have been accustomed and which are locally considered more than adequate"
(U.S. Congress, House Committee on Ways and Means, *Hearings on H.R.
6635*, p. 807).

45. Key, *Southern Politics*, pp. 299–301.

46. U.S. Congress, House Committee on Ways and Means, *Hearings on
H.R. 6635*, p. 764.

47. Non-black-belt representatives in Georgia had also passed a
resolution supporting a national old age pension financed solely by federal
taxation (Resolution, 18 March 1939, National Archives, RG 47, Central
Files, box 6, file 011.4).

48. U.S. Congress, House Committee on Ways and Means, *Hearings on
H.R. 6635*, p. 2123. Colmer's affiliation, as well as that of other Southern
congressmen, was determined by examining U.S. Congress, *Biographical
Directory of the American Congress, 1774–1971* (Washington, D.C.: Government Printing Office, 1971), p. 769.

49. Variable Grants, National Archives, RG 47, Records of the Executive
Director, box 274, file 622.

50. Possible revision of the formula for assistance grants to the states, 15
January 1938, National Archives, RG 47, Records of the Executive Director,
box 274, file 622.

51. Ibid.

52. Altmeyer, *Formative Years*, pp. 105, 111.

53. Letter from Homer Atkins, governor of Arkansas, to Arthur
Altmeyer, 4 December 1941, National Archives, RG 47, State Files, box 5, file
092.

54. "Public Assistance," *Social Security Bulletin* 10 (December 1947): 29–
30.

55. Key, *Southern Politics*, p. 307.

56. "Social Security," *Congressional Quarterly Almanac* 14 (1958): 157.
Katherine Ellickson Collection, Archives of Labor History and Urban
Affairs, box 66, folder 9, Social Security–Political Developments, 1957–58.

57. Neil Fligstein, *Going North: Migration of Blacks and Whites from the South,
1900–1950* (New York: Academic Press, 1981), pp. 139–40; Kirby,
"Transformation of Southern Plantations," p. 266.

58. Arthur M. Ford, *Political Economics of Rural Poverty in the South*
(Cambridge: Ballinger, 1973), p. 39; Woofter, *Landlord and Tenant on the
Cotton Plantation*, p. 157.

59. Fligstein, *Going North*, p. 140; Ford, *Political Economics of Rural Poverty*,
p. 40; Myrdal. *American Dilemma*, p. 260.

60. John L. Fulmer, *Agricultural Progress in the Cotton Belt since 1920*
(Chapel Hill: University of North Carolina Press, 1950), p. 58.

61. Richard Day, "The Economics of Technological Change and the
Demise of the Sharecropper," *American Economic Review* 57 (1967): 435.

62. Ford, *Political Economics of Rural Poverty*, p. 22.

63. Kirby, "Transformation of Southern Plantations," p. 270.

64. Daniel M. Johnson and Rex R. Campbell, *Black Migration in America*
(Durham, N.C.: Duke University Press, 1981), p. 118.

65. Jack Bass and Walter DeVries, *The Transformation of Southern Politics: Social Change and Political Consequences since 1945* (New York: New American Library, 1976), p. 504.

66. Ibid., p. 508.

67. Ray Marshall, "The Old South and the New," in *Employment of Blacks in the South*, ed. Ray Marshall and Virgil Christian (Austin: University of Texas Press, 1978), p. 15.

68. Ibid., pp. 118, 119, 134.

69. Potter, *South and the Concurrent Majority*, pp. 60, 67.

70. Ibid., pp. 74, 75.

71. Bass and DeVries, *Transformation*, pp. 402–3.

72. Bensel, *Sectionalism and American Political Development*, p. 242.

73. Key, *Southern Politics*, pp. 644, 657; David Campbell and Joe R. Feagin, "Black Politics in the South: A Descriptive Analysis," *Journal of Politics* 37 (February 1975): 133.

74. Ezell, *South since 1865*, p. 447.

75. David James, "The Transformation of Local State and Class Structures," Ph.D. diss., University of Wisconsin, 1980, pp. 206, 300.

76. David F. Ross, "State and Local Governments," in *Employment of Blacks in the South*, ed. Ray Marshall and Virgil L. Christian (Austin: University of Texas Press 1978), pp. 89, 91.

77. Potter, *South and the Concurrent Majority*, pp. 78, 81, 87.

78. U.S. Bureau of the Census, *Population: Characteristics of the Population*, part 1, *United States Summary, Reports to the States* (Washington, D.C.: Government Printing Office, 1940).

79. Ford, *Political Economics of Rural Poverty in the South*, pp. 63–64.

80. J. Douglas Brown, "Next Steps in Old Age Insurance," in *Social Security in the United States* (New York: American Association for Social Security, 1938), p. 46. See chapter 5 for a more detailed discussion of factors leading to the 1939 amendments.

81. Board Meeting Minutes, 6 February 1937, National Archives, RG 47, Chairman's Files, box 12, file 011.1.

82. Statement of CIO before House Ways and Means Committee on proposed changes in the Social Security Act, National Archives, RG 47, Chairman's Files, box 119, file 011.1; letter from C. H. Jordan, secretary, Los Angeles Industrial Union Council, to Arthur Altmeyer, 16 June 1938, National Archives, RG 47, Central Files, box 6, file 011.4.

83. Altmeyer, *Formative Years*, p. 103.

84. "Social Security Act, H.R. 6000–P.L. 734, Summary," *Congressional Quarterly Almanac* 6 (1950): 166.

85. Altmeyer, *Formative Years* p. 169.

86. *Congressional Record*, 81st Cong., 1st sess., House, H.R. 6000 (Washington, D.C.: Government Printing Office, 1949), p. 13808.

87. "Social Security Extension, H.R. 6000, Summary," *Congressional Quarterly Almanac* 5 (1949): 289.

88. *Congressional Record*, H.R. 6000, pp. 13817, 13838, 13840, 13845, 13915, 13918.

89. U.S. Congress, House Committee on Ways and Means, *Hearings on H.R. 6000: Social Security Revision*, 81st Cong., 2d sess. (Washington, D.C.: Government Printing Office, 1950), pp. 1929–31, 2365, 195; Daniel Sanders, *The Impact of Reform Movements on Social Policy Change: The Case of Social Insurance* (Fairlawn, N.J.: R. E. Burdick, 1973), p. 149.

90. Testimony of Broughton Lamberth, U.S. Congress, House Committee on Ways and Means *Hearings on H.R. 6000*, pp. 196–197, 202; see also the Testimony of Commissioners of Public Welfare from Louisiana, p. 231, Tennessee, p. 223, and Texas, p. 241.

91. Testimony of Herschel C. Atkinson, executive vice president, Ohio Chamber of Commerce, ibid., pp. 1489–90.

92. Wilbur J. Cohen and Robert J. Myers, "Social Security Act Amendments of 1950: A Summary and Legislative History," *Social Security Bulletin* 13 (October 1950): 3.

93. "Social Security Act, H.R. 6000–P.L. 734, Summary," p. 171; Wilbur J. Cohen, Robert M. Ball, and Robert Myers, "Social Security Act Amendments of 1954: A Summary and Legislative History," *Social Security Bulletin* 17 (September 1954): 4.

94. Day, "Economics of Technological Change," p. 441.

95. Altmeyer, *Formative Years*, p. 241.

96. *Congressional Record*, 83d Cong., 2d sess., H.R. 9366, House (Washington, D.C.: Government Printing Office, 1954), pp. 7446, 7447, 7448, 7454.

97. Altmeyer, *Formative Years*, p. 245.

98. *Congressional Record*, 83d Cong., 2d sess., H.R. 9366, Senate, pp. 14413, 14433–35, 14382.

99. Cohen, Ball, and Myers, "Social Security Act Amendments," p. 4.

100. Altmeyer, *Formative Years*, p. 247.

101. "Money Income Sources of Aged Persons, December 1959," *Social Security Bulletin* 23 (1960): 16.

102. Frances Fox Piven and Richard A. Cloward, *Regulating the Poor: The Functions of Public Welfare* (New York: Vintage Books, 1971), p. 186.

103. "Legislative History, Trends, and Adequacy of the Supplemental Security Income (SSI) Program," in *The Supplemental Security Income Program: A Ten-Year Overview* (Washington, D.C.: Special Committee on Aging, United States Senate, 1984), p. 116.

104. Ibid., pp. 117, 151–52.

105. Ibid., pp. 121, 140.

106. Quoted in William Lammers, *Public Policy and the Aging* (Washington, D.C.: CQ Press, 1983), p. 101.

CHAPTER SEVEN

1. For a detailed historical analysis of the complex reasons why the Social Security Board favored expanding OAI, see Jerry Cates, *Insuring Inequality: Administrative Leadership in Social Security, 1935–1954* (Ann Arbor: University of Michigan Press, 1982).

2. Martha Derthick, *Policymaking for Social Security* (Washington, D.C.: Brookings Institution, 1979), p. 430. See chapter 7 for a more extensive discussion of factors leading to the 1950 amendments.

3. James H. Schulz, "To Old Folks with Love: Aged Income Maintenance in America," *Gerontologist* 5 (October 1985): 467; Derthick, *Policymaking for Social Security*, p. 432.

4. Mary Ruggie, *The State and Working Women: A Comparative Study of Britain and Sweden* (Princeton: Princeton University Press, 1984). pp. 13, 299.

5. Gosta Esping-Anderson, *Politics against Markets: The Social Democratic Road to Power* (Princeton: Princeton University Press, 1985), p. 60.

6. David Brody, *Workers in Industrial America* (New York: Basic Books, 1984), p. 82.

7. Michael J. Piore and Charles F. Sabel, *The Second Industrial Divide* (New York: Basic Books, 1984), p. 73.

8. Christopher L. Tomlins, *The State and the Unions: Labor Relations, Law, and the Organized Labor Movement in America, 1880–1960* (Cambridge: Cambridge University Press, 1985), p. 99; Piore and Sabel, *Second Industrial Divide*, p. 74; Irving Bernstein, *The Turbulent Years: A History of the American Worker, 1933–1941* (Boston: Houghton Mifflin, 1970), p. 26.

9. Tomlins, *State and the Unions*, pp. 105, 107.

10. Bernstein, *Turbulent Years*, pp. 41, 66, 77.

11. Tomlins, *State and the Unions*, p. 108.

12. Bernstein, *Turbulent Years*, p. 40; Tomlins, *State and the Unions*, p. 2.

13. Brody, *Workers in Industrial America*, p. 100; Bernstein, *Turbulent Years*, p. 346.

14. Tomlins, *State and the Unions*, p. 144.

15. Ibid., p. 145.

16. Bernstein, *Turbulent Years*, p. 395; Everett Johnson Burtt, *Labor Markets, Unions, and Government Policies* (New York: St. Martin's Press, 1963), p. 140.

17. Bernstein, *Turbulent Years*, p. 401; Burtt, *Labor Markets*, p. 140; Tomlins, *State and the Unions*, p. 147.

18. Brody, *Workers in Industrial America*, p. 113.

19. Ibid., p. 173.

20. Nelson Lichtenstein, *Labor's War at Home: The CIO in World War II* (Cambridge: Cambridge University Press, 1982), pp. 79, 72, 138, 171.

21. Ibid., p. 51; Tomlins, *State and the Unions*, p. 199.

22. Lichtenstein, *Labor's War at Home*, p. 179.

23. Harry C. Katz, *Shifting Gears: Changing Labor Relations in the U.S. Automobile Industry* (Cambridge: MIT Press, 1985), pp. 14–16.

24. Brody, *Workers in Industrial America*, p. 222; *Proceedings of the Twenty-sixth Convention, International Ladies Garment Workers Union*, 1947, p. 38.

25. Derthick, *Policymaking for Social Security*, p. 147.

26. Truman vetoed the first; ibid., p. 146. U.S. Congress, House Committee on Ways and Means, *Hearings on H.R. 6000: Social Security Revision*, 81st Cong., 2d sess. (Washington, D.C.: Government Printing Office, 1950), testimony of Walter Reuther, president of the UAW, p. 1907.

27. Katherine Ellickson Memoirs, Columbia University Oral History Collection, New York, Butler Library, p. 28.

28. Lichtenstein, *Labor's War at Home*, pp. 172, 225.

29. Ibid., pp. 238, 243.

30. Ibid., pp. 39, 204.

31. Ibid., pp. 204–6; Barton J. Bernstein, "The Debate on Industrial Reconversion: The Protection of Oligopoly and Military Control of the Economy," *American Journal of Economics and Sociology* 26 (1967): 172.

32. For a discussion of factors influencing the CIO to press for private pensions, see Beth Stevens, "Blurring the Boundaries: How Federal Social Policy Has Influenced Welfare Benefits in the Private Sector," in *The Politics of Social Policy in the United States*, ed. Ann Orloff, Margaret Weir, and Theda Skocpol (Princeton: Princeton University Press, 1988).

33. Dan M. McGill, *Fundamentals of Private Pensions* (Homewood, Ill.: Richard D. Irwin, 1955), pp. 20, 22.

34. Lichtenstein, *Labor's War at Home*, p. 78; Memoirs of Nelson Cruickshank, Columbia University Oral History Collection, Butler Library, p. 60.

35. Stephen Raushenbush, *Pensions in Our Economy* (Washington, D.C.: Public Affairs Institute, 1955), p. 55.

36. U.S. Congress, House Committee on Ways and Means, *Hearings on H.R. 6000*, testimony of A. D. Marshall, Chamber of Commerce, p. 1501.

37. Warner Pflug, *The UAW in Pictures* (Detroit, Mich.: Wayne State University Press, 1971), p. 104.

38. U.S. Congress, House Committee on Ways and Means, *Hearings on H.R. 6000*, testimony of Walter Reuther, p. 1840.

39. Arthur Hughes Collection, Archives of Labor History and Urban Affairs (hereafter ALUA), Wayne State University, Detroit, Michigan, box 37, folder 15, Social Security Program, 15 November 1946.

40. American Federation of Labor, *Pension Plans under Collective Bargaining*, p. v. Quoted in McGill, *Fundamentals of Private Pensions*, p. 27.

41. Derthick, *Policymaking for Social Security*, pp. 119–20.

42. McGill, *Fundamentals of Private Pensions*, p. 25.

43. Hughes Collection, ALUA, box 8, folder 9, memo from Harry Becker, Social Security Department, Social Security in Contract Negotiations, May 11, 1948.

44. *A Promise Made, a Promise Kept: The Story of the UAW Pension Program* (Detroit, Mich.: UAW Education Department, Solidarity House, 1978).

45. U.S. Congress, House Committee on Ways and Means, *Hearings on H.R. 6000*, testimony of Walter Reuther, pp. 1907–8.

46. Hughes Collection, ALUA, box 8, folder 4, UAW Chrysler Negotiations; Social Security Issue.

47. Hughes Collection, ALUA, box 8, folder 9, Guide to Collective Bargaining, 1949.

48. Hughes Collection, ALUA, box 37, folder 15, Social Security Programs, 1946; box 37, folder 16, Social Security Programs, 1947.

49. Hughes Collection, ALUA, box 8, folder 4, memo from Harry Becker

to all regional directors and staff members 9 April 1948; Memo from Harry Becker to all UAW-CIO local unions, 11 May 1948.

50. *Promise Made.*

51. Hughes Collection, ALUA, box 37, folder 16, memo from Walter Reuther, "The Need for a Specific Plan," 17 March 1947.

52. Hughes Collection, ALUA, box 8, folder 9, UAW-CIO Guide to Collective Bargaining, 1949.

53. John Barnard, *Walter Reuther and the Rise of the Auto Workers* (Boston: Little, Brown, 1983), p. 140.

54. Hughes Collection, ALUA, box 9, folder 10, *Detroit Times,* 25 September 1949.

55. Hughes Collection, ALUA, box 9, folder 19, *Detroit Free Press,* 30 September 1949.

56. Hughes Collection, ALUA, box 9, folder 9, Calendar of Union Gains.

57. Hughes Collection, ALUA, box 9, folder 10. *Detroit Free Press,* 30 September 1949.

58. Peter F. Drucker, *The Unseen Revolution* (New York: Harper and Row, 1976), p. 7; Memoirs of Marion Folsom, Columbia University Oral History Collection, Butler Library, p. 60.

59. Hughes Collection, ALUA, box 9, folder 10, *Detroit Free Press,* 30 September 1949.

60. Hughes Collection, ALUA, box 9, folder 7, proposal by the UAW-CIO to the Chrysler Corporation, 23 January 1950; letter from Walter Reuther to Robert Condor, director of industrial relations, Chrysler Corporation, 3 March 1950.

61. Hughes Collection, ALUA, box 9, folder 9, Calendar of Union Gains.

62. Hughes Collection, ALUA, box 9, folder 10, *Detroit Times,* 25 September 1949.

63. Hughes Collection, box 9, folder 7, statement by Walter Reuther, 25 January 1950.

64. Hughes Collection, ALUA, box 9, folder 7, UAW proposal to the Chrysler Corporation, 23 January 1950.

65. Ibid.

66. Hughes Collection, ALUA, box 9, folder 12, *Detroit Free Press,* February 1950; box 9, folder 9, Calendar of Union Gains during the Strike.

67. Hughes Collection, ALUA, box 9, folder 9, Chrysler Strike.

68. Hughes Collection, ALUA, box 35, folder 8, Pension Plan Agreement, 1950.

69. U.S. Congress, House Committee on Ways and Means, *Hearings on H.R. 6000,* testimony of Walter Reuther, pp. 1840, 1908.

70. U.S. Congress, House Committee on Ways and Means, *Hearings on H.R. 6000,* testimony of Herschel C. Atkinson, executive vice president, Ohio Chamber of Commerce, p. 1493.

71. Jean Gould and Lorena Hickok, *Walter Reuther: Labour's Rugged Individualist* (New York: Dodd, Mead, 1972), p. 281.

72. Hughes Collection, ALUA, box 35, folder 12, Chrysler UAW-CIO Pension Board of Administration.

73. Ibid., Applications for Pensions.

74. Ibid., 24 August 1950.

75. Drucker, *Unseen Revolution,* pp. 10, 7.

76. Over half of all private plans are integrated with Social Security, but collectively bargained multiemployer plans are less likely to be integrated than those in small firms. Pension integration has become a complex issue, and many variations in plans exist. For a detailed discussion of these issues, see James H. Schulz and Thomas D. Leavitt, *Pension Integration: Concepts, Issues and Proposals* (Washington, D.C.: Employee Benefit Research Institute, 1983), p. 25.

77. This is not to say that private pension plans guarantee economic security for older workers. Inadequate pension funding, misuse of pension funds, and the termination of plans because of plant closures or bankruptcy plagued the private pension business for decades, and even though the passage of the Employee Retirement Income Security Act of 1974 set up comprehensive safeguards, problems in private pension plans still remain. See James H. Schulz, *The Economics of Aging* (New York: Van Nostrand Reinhold, 1985), pp. 159–60.

78. Brody, *Workers in Industrial America,* p. 193. Most of the growth occurred in the 1940s and 1950s. Since then the growth rate has slowed to a little over 3 percent a year. Schulz, *Economics of Aging,* p. 150; also Schulz, "To Old Folks with Love," pp. 468–69.

79. UAW Local 9 Collection, ALUA, box 25, folder: Pension 1950–55, Contract.

80. UAW Local 9 Collection, ALUA, box 82, folder: Pension 1952, 10 March 1952.

81. Ibid., p. 4.

82. UAW Local 9, ALUA, box 60, folder: Pension Board 1952, 24 June 1952.

83. UAW Local 9, ALUA, box 82, folder: Pension 1952, 14 February 1952.

84. Nancy Gabon, "Women Workers and the UAW in the Post–World War II Period: 1945–1954," *Labor History* 21 (Winter 1979–80): 26.

85. Hughes Collection, ALUA, box 1, folder 12, "The Unions, Collective Bargaining and the Older Worker," by Philip Taft.

86. Letter from Joseph Jennison to Congressman Herman Eberharter, 5 September 1952, Federal Archives and Records Center, Suitland, Md., RG 47, Chairman's Files, box 37, file 050.317.

87. Memo from Wilbur Cohen to Herman Eberharter, 19 September 1952. Federal Archives and Records Center, RG 47, Suitland, Md., Chairman's Files, box 37, file 050.317.

88. Walter Cormier and William J. Eaton, *Reuther* (Englewood Cliffs, N.J.: Prentice-Hall, 1970), p. 298. The guarantee of labor peace lasted only two years. When the war fueled price hikes, Reuther reopened negotiations in 1952, demanding, among other things, bigger pensions.

89. *Promise Made.*

90. Hughes Collection, ALUA, box 3, folder 11, UAW: Retirement and Health Security Program.

91. Hughes Collection, ALUA, box 20, folder 8, UAW Chrysler Negotiations, Pensions.

92. Derthick, *Policymaking for Social Security*, pp. 431–32.

93. Hughes Collection, ALUA, box 22, folder 8, UAW Chrysler Pension Plan Agreement.

94. Derthick, *Policymaking for Social Security*, pp. 431–32.

95. Schulz and Leavitt, *Pension Integration*, pp. 39, 41, 7, 12.

96. Derthick, *Policymaking for Social Security*, p. 368.

97. Ellickson Memoirs, p. 85.

98. Ibid., pp. 194–95, 3, 216.

99. Graham K. Wilson, *Unions in American National Politics* (London: Macmillan, 1979), p. 37; Gould and Hickok, *Walter Reuther*, p. 313; Barnard, *Walter Reuther and the Rise of the Auto Workers*, p. 175.

100. Cormier and Eaton, *Reuther*, pp. 372, 375.

101. James Sundquist, *Politics and Policy: The Eisenhower, Kennedy and Johnson Years* (Washington, D.C.: Brookings Institution, 1968), pp. 314, 317.

102. Ellickson Memoirs, Columbia University Oral History Collection, p. 216.

103. Robert M. Ball, "Policy Issues in Social Security," *Social Security Bulletin* 29 (June 1966): 5; Derthick, *Policymaking for Social Security*, p. 129.

104. Gould and Hickok, *Walter Reuther*, pp. 334–35; Cormier and Eaton, *Reuther*, pp. 384–86.

105. *Proceedings of the Sixth Annual Convention of the AFL-CIO*, 1965, p. 493.

106. Derthick, *Policymaking for Social Security*, p. 130.

107. U.S. Congress, House Committee on Ways and Means, *Hearings on H.R. 5710: Amendments to the Social Security Act* (Washington, D.C.: Government Printing Office, 1967), pp. 576–77.

108. Lillian Hatcher Collection, ALUA, box 15, folder 11, Social Security, 1957–67.

109. U.S. Congress, House Committee on Ways and Means, *Hearings on H.R. 5710*, pp. 1421–22.

110. Derthick, *Policymaking for Social Security*, pp. 345, 432.

111. Barnard, *Rise of the Auto Workers*, pp. 197–98.

112. Ibid., pp. 41–43.

113. The preceding discussion summarizes the main points of a very detailed analysis by Derthick, *Policymaking for Social Security*, pp. 339–68.

114. Ibid., p. 363.

Chapter Eight

1. Mary Ruggie, *The State and Working Women: A Comparative Study of Britain and Sweden* (Princeton: Princeton University Press, 1984), pp. 13, 299.

2. Claus Offe, *Contradictions of the Welfare State* (Cambridge: MIT Press, 1984), p. 159.

3. An exception is Gosta Esping-Anderson, *Politics against Markets: The Social Democratic Road to Power* (Princeton: Princeton University Press, 1985), pp. 60–62, and to a lesser extent Stephens, *Transition from Capitalism to Socialism,* p. 150.

4. Ruggie, *State and Working Women,* p. 14.

Bibliography

BOOKS AND ARTICLES

Achenbaum, W. Andrew. *Old Age in the New Land: The American Experience since 1790.* Baltimore: Johns Hopkins University Press, 1978.

Alexander, Magnus W. "Hiring and Firing: Its Economic Waste and How to Avoid It." *Annals of the American Academy of Political and Social Sciences* 65 (May 1916): 128–54.

Alston, Lee J., and Joseph P. Ferrie. "Labor Costs, Paternalism, and Loyalty in Southern Agriculture: A Constraint on the Growth of the Welfare State." *Journal of Economic History* 45 (March 1985): 95–117.

Altmeyer, Arthur. *The Formative Years of Social Security.* Madison: University of Wisconsin Press, 1966.

Amenta, Edwin, and Theda Skocpol. "States and Social Policies." *Annual Review of Sociology* 12 (1986): 131–57.

Anglim, Christopher, and Brian Gratton. "Organized Labor and Old Age Pensions." *International Journal of Aging and Human Development.* In press.

"Annuity Plan of a Large Manufacturing Company." *Monthly Labor Review* 30 (February 1930): 255.

"Another Union to Adopt Pension Scheme." *Locomotive Engineers Journal* 61 (September 1927): 688.

Axinn, June, and Herman Levin. *Social Welfare: A History of the American Response to Need.* New York: Harper and Row, 1982.

Baack, Bennett D., and Edward J. Ray. "Tariff Policy and Income Distribution: The Case of the United States, 1830–1860." *Explorations in Economic History* 11 (Winter 1973–74): 103–22.

Baldwin, F. Spencer. "The Work of the Massachusetts Commission on Old Age Pensions." *American Statistical Association* 85 (March 1909): 417–30.

Ball, Robert M. "Policy Issues in Social Security." *Social Security Bulletin* 29 (June 1966): 5.

Barnard, John. *Walter Reuther and the Rise of the Auto Workers.* Boston: Little, Brown, 1983.

Bass, Jack, and Walter DeVries. *The Transformation of Southern Politics: Social Change and Political Consequences since 1945.* New York: New American Library, 1976.

Beckner, Earl R. *A History of Labor Legislation in Illinois.* Chicago: University of Chicago Press, 1929.

"Beneficial Activities of American Trade Unions." *Bulletin of the U.S. Bureau of Labor Statistics,* no. 465 (September 1928): 27–44.

Bensel, Richard F. *Sectionalism and American Political Development, 1880–1980.* Madison: University of Wisconsin Press, 1984.

Berkowitz, Edward, and Kim McQuaid. *Creating the Welfare State.* New York: Praeger, 1980.

Bernstein, Barton J. "The Debate on Industrial Reconversion: The Protection of Oligopoly and Military Control of the Economy." *American Journal of Economics and Sociology* 26 (1967): 159–72.

———. "The New Deal: The Conservative Achievements of Liberal Reform." In *Toward the New Past,* ed. Barton J. Bernstein. New York: Random House, 1968.

Bernstein, Irving. *The Lean Years.* Boston: Houghton Mifflin, 1960.

———. *The Turbulent Years: A History of the American Worker, 1933–1941.* Boston: Houghton Mifflin, 1970.

"Beware of 'Company' Group Insurance." *Brotherhood of Locomotive Firemen and Enginemen's Magazine* 76 (June 1924): 23.

Block, Fred. "Beyond Corporate Liberalism." *Social Problems* 24 (1977): 352–61.

Bogue, Allan G. *From Prairie to Corn Belt.* Chicago: University of Chicago Press, 1963.

Brandes, Stuart. *American Welfare Capitalism.* Chicago: University of Chicago Press, 1976.

Braverman, Harry. *Labor and Monopoly Capital: The Degradation of Work in the Twentieth Century.* New York: Monthly Review Press, 1974.

Brents, Barbara. "Policy Formation in Capitalist Society: The Social Security Act of 1935." Master's thesis, Department of Sociology, University of Missouri, Columbia, 1983.

Brissenden, P. F., and E. Frankel. *Labor Turnover in Industry.* New York: Macmillan, 1922.

Brody, David. "The Rise and Decline of Welfare Capitalism." In *Change and Continuity in Twentieth Century America: The 1920s,* ed. John Braeman, Robert Bremner, and David Brody. Columbus: Ohio State University Press, 1968.

———. *Workers in Industrial America.* New York: Basic Books, 1984.

Brown, J. Douglas. *An American Philosophy of Social Security.* Princeton: Princeton University Press, 1972.

———. "Next Steps in Old Age Insurance." In *Social Security in the United States.* New York: American Association for Social Security, 1938.

———. "Philosophical Basis of the National Old Age Insurance Program." In *Social Security and Private Pension Plans,* ed. Dan McGill. Homewood, Ill: Richard D. Irwin, 1977.

Brundage, Anthony. *The Making of the New Poor Law.* New Brunswick, N.J.: Rutgers University Press, 1978.

Burawoy, Michael. *Manufacturing Consent: Changes in the Labor Process under Monopoly Capitalism.* Chicago: University of Chicago Press, 1979.

Burch, Philip. "The NAM as an Interest Group." *Politics and Society* 4 (1973): 97–130.

Burton, Orville V. *In My Father's House Are Many Mansions: Family and Community in Edgefield, South Carolina.* Chapel Hill: University of North Carolina Press, 1985.

Burtt, Everett Johnson. *Labor Markets, Unions, and Government Policies.* New York: St. Martin's Press, 1963.

Byers, Edward. "America's Almshouse Experience: Dependent Poverty in Salem, Massachusetts, 1750–1920." Manuscript, Department of History, Brandeis University.

Cameron, David R. "The Expansion of the Public Economy." *American Political Science Review* 72 (December 1978): 1243–60.

Campbell, David, and Joe R. Feagin. "Black Politics in the South: A Descriptive Analysis." *Journal of Politics* 37 (February 1975): 129–39.

"Care of the Aged by Labor Organizations." *Bulletin of the Bureau of Labor Statistics,* no. 489, (October 1929): 86–109.

Carey, Matthew. *Appeal to the Wealthy of the Land.* Philadelphia: L. Johnson, 1833.

Carnoy, Martin. *The State and Political Theory.* Princeton: Princeton University Press, 1984.

Castles, Francis. *The Impact of Parties.* Beverly Hills, Calif.: Sage, 1983.

Castles, Francis, and Richard McKinlay. "Public Welfare Provision and the Sheer Futility of the Sociological Approach to Politics." *British Journal of Political Science* 9 (1979): 157–72.

Cates, Jerry. *Insuring Inequality: Administrative Leadership in Social Security, 1935–1954.* Ann Arbor: University of Michigan Press, 1982.

Chambers, Clarke A. *Seedtime of Reform.* Minneapolis: University of Minnesota Press, 1963.

Clark, S. N. "Some Weak Places in Our Pension System." *Forum* 26 (1898): 306–19.

Clawson, Dan. *Bureaucracy and the Labor Process: The Transformation of U.S. Industry, 1860–1920.* New York: Monthly Review Press, 1980.

Clement, Priscilla Ferguson. "The Response to Need, Welfare and Poverty in Philadelphia, 1800 to 1850. Ph.D. diss., University of Pennsylvania, 1977.

———. "Women and the Welfare System in 19th Century America." Paper presented to the Social Science History Association, Saint Louis, October 1986.

Cloud, Arthur D. *Pensions in Modern Industry.* Chicago: Hawkins and Loomis, 1930.

Cohen, Wilbur J., Robert M. Ball, and Robert Myers. "Social Security Act Amendments of 1954: A Summary and Legislative History." *Social Security Bulletin* 17 (September 1954): 3–4.

Cohen, Wilbur J., and Robert J. Myers. "Social Security Act Amendments of

1950: A Summary and Legislative History." *Social Security Bulletin* 13 (October 1950): 3.

Collier, David, and Richard Messick. "Prerequisites versus Diffusion: Testing Alternative Explanations of Social Security Adoption." *American Political Sciences Review* 69 (1975): 1299–1315.

Committee on Economic Security. *The Townsend Crusade*. New York: Twentieth Century Fund, 1936.

Commons, John R. *History of Labor in the United States, 1896–1932*. New York: Macmillan, 1935.

"Company Pension Plans." *Locomotive Engineers Journal* 61 (April 1927): 250, 252.

Conant, Luther. *A Critical Analysis of Industrial Pension Systems*. New York: Macmillan, 1922.

"A Congressman's Tribute to Engineers." *Locomotive Engineers Journal* 60 (January 1926): 8.

Conyngton, Mary "Industrial Pensions for Old Age and Disability." *Monthly Labor Review* 22 (1926): 21–56.

Cormier, Walter, and William J. Eaton. *Reuther*. Englewood Cliffs, N.J.: Prentice-Hall, 1970.

Corson, John. "Insurance against Old Age Dependency." *Annals of the American Academy of Political and Social Science* 202 (March 1939): 61–65.

Cowgill, Donald. "The Aging of Populations and Societies." In *Aging, the Individual and Society: Readings in Social Gerontology*, ed. Jill Quadagno. New York: St. Martin's Press, 1982.

Craven, Avery O. *The Growth of Southern Nationalism, 1848–1861*. Baton Rouge: Louisiana State University Press, 1953.

Creech, Margaret D. *Three Centuries of Poor Law Administration*. Chicago: University of Chicago Press, 1936.

Cutright, Phillips. "Political Structure, Economic Development and National Social Security Programs." *American Journal of Sociology* 70 (1965): 537–50.

Daugherty, H. P. "Company Pension Plans." *Locomotive Engineers Journal* 61 (April 1927): 250, 252.

Davis, Mike. "Why the US Working Class Is Different." *New Left Review* 123 (September–October 1980): 3–44.

Day, Richard. "The Economics of Technological Change and the Demise of the Sharecropper." *American Economic Review* 57 (1967): 427–37.

"Defrauding Yourselves." *Locomotive Engineers Journal* 60 (June 1926): 409.

deRoode, Albert. "Pensions as Wages." *American Economic Review* 3 (June 1913): 287–95.

Derthick, Martha. *Policymaking for Social Security*. Washington, D.C.: Brookings Institution, 1979.

Dobb, Maurice. *Papers on Capitalism, Development and Planning*. New York: International Publishers, 1967.

Dolge, Alfred. *The Plan of Earnings-Division: An Excerpt from "Economic Theories Practically Applied."* Dolgeville, N.Y.: Dolgeville Herald, 1896.

Domhoff, William. *The Higher Circles*. New York: Random House, 1970.

Drucker, Peter F. *The Unseen Revolution*. New York: Harper and Row, 1976.

Edgar, Charles L., William R. Willcox, and P. Tecumseh Sherman. *Old Age Pensions Conference*. New York: National Civic Federation, 1927.

Edwards, Gurden. "The Benefits to Employees of Sound Pension Plans." *Annalist* 26 (4 December 1925): 876.

———. "Industrial Pension Plans Collapsing." *Annalist* 26 (20 November 1925): 637–41.

———. "The Way out of the Industrial Pension Crisis." *Annalist* 26 (27 November 1925): 667–69.

Edwards, Richard. *Contested Terrain: The Transformation of the Workplace in the Twentieth Century*. New York: Basic Books, 1979.

1879–1979: One Hundred Years Helping to Create the Future. N.p.: Standard Oil Company of California, 1979.

"Employee Pension Plans." *American Machinist* 66 (June 1927): 989.

Epstein, Abraham. "Experience under State Old-Age Pension Laws in 1932." *Monthly Labor Review* 37 (August 1933): 251–61.

———. *Facing Old Age*. New York: Alfred Knopf, 1922; reprinted Arno Press, 1972.

———. "The Turning Point in Social Security." In *Social Security in the United States*. Eleventh National Conference on Social Security. New York: American Association for Social Security, 1938.

Erskine, E. B. "United States Steel and Carnegie Pension Fund." *Bulletin of the U.S. Bureau of Labor Statistics* 212 (June 1917): 742.

Esping-Anderson, Gosta. *Politics against Markets: The Social Democratic Road to Power*. Princeton: Princeton University Press, 1985.

Ezell, John Samuel. *The South since 1865*. New York: Macmillan, 1975.

Fink, Gary L., ed. *State Labor Proceedings: A Bibliography of the AFL, CIO and AFL-CIO Proceedings 1885–1974, Held in the AFL-CIO Library*. Westport, Conn.: Greenwood Press, 1975.

Fischer, David Hackett. *Growing Old in America*. New York: Oxford University Press, 1978.

Fish, Carl R. *The Civil Service and Patronage*. New York: Longmans, Green, 1905.

Fligstein, Neil. *Going North: Migration of Blacks and Whites from the South, 1900–1950*. New York: Academic Press, 1981.

———. "State and Markets: The Transformation of the Large Corporation, 1880–1985." University of Arizona, unpublished manuscript.

Flora, Peter, and Jens Alber. "Modernization, Democratization and the Development of Welfare States in Western Europe." In *The Development of Welfare States in Europe and America*, ed. Peter Flora and Arnold Heidenheimer. New Brunswick, N.J.: Transaction Books, 1981.

Folsom, Marion. "Coordination of Pension Plans with Social Security Provisions." *Personnel* 16 (1939): 41–43.

Foote, Alan R. "Degradation by Pensions: The Protest of Loyal Volunteers." *Forum* 12 (December 1891): 423–32.

Ford, Arthur M. *Political Economics of Rural Poverty in the South*. Cambridge, Mass.: Ballinger, 1973.

Form, William. "Comparative Industrial Sociology and the Convergence Hypothesis." *Annual Review of Sociology* 5 (1979): 1–25.

Fraser, Derek. *The Evolution of the British Welfare State*. London: Macmillan, 1973.

Fulmer, John L. *Agricultural Progress in the Cotton Belt since 1920*. Chapel Hill: University of North Carolina Press, 1950.

Gabon, Nancy. "Women Workers and the UAW in the Post–World War II Period: 1945–1954." *Labor History* 21 (Winter 1979–80): 5–30.

Girdner, John H. "To Purge the Pension List." *North American Review* 166 (March 1898): 374–75.

Glasson, William. *Federal Military Pensions in the United States*. New York: Oxford University Press, 1918.

————. "The National Pension System as Applied to the Civil War and the War with Spain." *Annals of the American Academy of Political and Social Sciences* 19 (March 1902): 204–26.

————. "The South and Service Pension Laws." *South Atlantic Quarterly* 1 (October 1902): 351–60.

Gompers, Samuel. "Not Even Compulsory Benevolence Will Do." *American Federationist* 24 (January 1917): 47–48.

————. "Voluntary Social Insurance vs. Compulsory." *American Federationist* 23 (May and August 1916): 333–57, 669–81.

Gordon, David M., Richard Edwards, and Michael Reich. *Segmented Work, Divided Workers: The Historical Transformation of Labor in the United States*. Cambridge: Cambridge University Press, 1982.

Gough, Ian. *The Political Economy of the Welfare State*. London: Macmillan, 1979.

Gould, Jean, and Lorena Hickok. *Walter Reuther: Labour's Rugged Individualist*. New York: Dodd, Mead, 1972.

Graebner, William. *A History of Retirement: The Meaning and Function of an American Institution, 1885–1978*. New Haven: Yale University Press, 1980.

Gratton, Brian. "The Invention of Social Work: Welfare Reform in the Antebellum City." *Urban and Social Change Review* 18 (Winter 1985): 3–8.

————. "The Labor Force Participation of Older Men: 1890–1950." *Journal of Social History* 21 (Summer 1987): 689–710.

————. *Urban Elders: Family, Work and Welfare among Boston's Aged, 1890–1950*. Philadelphia: Temple University Press, 1986.

Green, William. "Trade Union Sick Funds and Compulsory Health Insurance." *American Labor Legislation Review* 7 (1917): 91–95.

Griffin, Larry J., Michael E. Wallace, and Beth A. Rubin. "Capitalist Resistance to the Organization of Labor before the New Deal: Why? How? Success? *American Sociological Review* 51 (April 1986): 147–67.

Haber, Carol. *Beyond Sixty-five: The Dilemma of Old Age in America's Past*. Cambridge: Cambridge University Press, 1983.

Hage, Jerald, and Robert A. Hanneman. "The Growth of the Welfare State in Britain, France, Germany, and Italy: A Comparison of Three Paradigms." *Comparative Social Research* 3 (1980): 45–70.

"Half Pay Pensions for New Jersey Employees." *Electric Railway Journal* 68 (16 October 1926): 744.

Harriman, Henry I. "The Stabilization of Business and Employment." *American Economic Review* 22 (1932): 63–74.

Hartz, Louis. "The Liberal Tradition." In *Failure of a Dream?* ed. John Laslett and Seymour M. Lipset. Garden City, N.Y.: Anchor Press, 1974.

Hays, Samuel P. *The Response to Industrialism, 1885–1914.* Chicago: University of Chicago Press, 1957.

"Hearings on Pension Legislation." *Railway Age.* 94 (1933): 112.

Heclo, Hugh. *Modern Social Politics in Britain and Sweden.* New Haven: Yale University Press, 1974.

Henderson, Charles Richmond. *Industrial Insurance in the United States.* Chicago: University of Chicago Press, 1909.

Hendrick, Burton J. "The Superannuated Man." *McClure's Magazine* 32 (December 1908): 115–27.

Hicks, Clarence J. "What Can the Employer Do to Encourage Saving and Wise Investment by Industrial Employees." *Harvard Business Review* 2 (January 1924): 194–200.

Hildebrand, George H. *American Unionism: An Historical and Analytical Survey.* Reading, Mass.: Addison-Wesley, 1979.

Howe, Robert. "Industry and the Aged." *Harvard Business Review* 8 (October 1929): 435–42.

Hunter, Robert. *Labor in Politics.* Chicago: Socialist Party, 1915.

"Industrial Pension Plans in the Depression, United States and Canada." *Monthly Labor Review* 36 (January 1933): 1062.

"Insurance and Pension Plans." *Monthly Labor Review* [U.S. Bureau of Labor Statistics] 36, no. 1 (1933): 1062–64.

"Invalidity and Old-Age Insurance, Pensions, and Retirement Allowances." *Bulletin of the U.S. Bureau of Labor Statistics* 212 (June 1917): 742.

Jackman, Robert. *Politics and Social Equality: A Comparative Analysis.* New York: John Wiley, 1975.

Jackson, Robert M. *The Formation of Craft Labor Markets.* Orlando, Fla.: Academic Press, 1984.

James, David. "The Transformation of Local State and Class Structures." Ph.D. diss., University of Wisconsin, 1980.

Jenkins, Craig. "Resource Mobilization Theory and the Study of Social Movements." *Annual Review of Sociology* 9 (1983): 527–53.

Jerome, H. *Migration and Business Cycles.* New York: National Bureau of Economic Research, 1926.

Johnson, Daniel M., and Rex R. Campbell. *Black Migration in America.* Durham, N.C.: Duke University Press, 1981.

Johnson, Emory P. "Railway Relief Departments." *Annals of the American Academy of Political and Social Science* 6 (1895): 424–49.

Johnston, A. "Heroic Pensioners." *Locomotive Engineers Journal* 60 (January 1926): 14.

Jones, Douglas Lamar. "Poverty and Vagabondage: The Process of Survival in Eighteenth-Century Massachusetts." *New England Historical and Genealogical Register* 83 (October 1979): 243–54.

―――. "The Strolling Poor: Transiency in Eighteenth Century Massachusetts." *Journal of Social History* 8 (Spring 1975): 28–54.

Jones, Jacqueline. *Labor of Love, Labor of Sorrow: Black Women, Work, and the Family from Slavery to the Present.* New York: Basic Books, 1985.

Karabel, Jerome. "The Reasons Why." *New York Review of Books* 26 (February 1979): 22–25.

Katz, Harry C. *Shifting Gears: Changing Labor Relations in the U.S. Automobile Industry.* Cambridge: MIT Press, 1985.

Katz, Michael B. *Poverty and Policy in American History.* New York: Academic Press, 1983.

Katzelson, Ira. *City Trenches: Urban Politics and the Patterning of Class in the United States.* New York: Pantheon Books, 1981.

Kelso, Robert. *The History of Public Poor Relief in Massachusetts, 1620–1920.* Boston: Houghton Mifflin, 1922.

Kemnitzer, William J. *Rebirth of Monopoly: A Critical Analysis of Economic Conduct in the Petroleum Industry in the United States.* New York: Harper, 1938.

Kerr, Clark, John T. Dunlop, Frederick Harbison, and Charles A. Myers. *Industrialism and Industrial Man: The Problems of Labor and Management in Economic Growth.* New York: Oxford University Press, 1964.

Key, V. O. *Southern Politics in State and Nation.* New York: Alfred A. Knopf, 1949.

Kimball, Ingalls. "Industrial Pensions vs. State Poor Relief." *Annalist* 27 (January 1926): 149–51.

Kirby, Jack Temple. "The Transformation of Southern Plantations ca. 1920–1960." *Agricultural History* 57 (July 1983): 257–76.

Knight, Charles K. "Fraternal Life Insurance." *Annals of the American Academy of Political and Social Science* 130 (March 1927): 97–102.

Kolko, Gabriel. *The Triumph of Conservatism: A Reinterpretation of American History, 1900–1916.* New York: Free Press, 1977.

Korpi, Walter. "Social Policy and Distributional Conflict in the Capitalist Democracies." *West European Politics* 3 (October 1980): 296–315.

Kousser, J. Morgan. *The Shaping of Southern Politics: Suffrage Restriction and the Establishment of the One-Party South, 1880–1910.* New Haven: Yale University Press, 1974.

Kroos, Herman E. *Executive Opinion.* Garden City, N.J.: Doubleday, 1970.

Kudrle, Robert T., and Theodore R. Marmor. "The Development of the Welfare State in North America." In *The Development of Welfare States in Europe and America,* ed. Peter Flora and Arnold Heidenheimer. New Brunswick, N.J.: Transaction Books, 1981.

"Labor and Laboring Classes." *Handbook of Labor Statistics, 1924–1926. Bulletin of the U.S. Bureau of Labor Statistics,* no. 439 (June 1927): 436–44.

"Labor Laws and Court Decisions." *Monthly Labor Review* 38 (1934): 1102.

Lammers, William. *Public Policy and the Aging.* Washington, D.C.: CQ Press, 1983.

Larson, Henrietta M. "The Rise of Big Business in the Oil Industry." In *Oil's First Century: Papers Given at the Centennial Seminar on the History of the Petroleum Industry*. Cambridge: Harvard Graduate School of Business Administration, 1960.

Laslett, John M. "The American Tradition of Labor Theory and Its Relevance to the Contemporary Working Class." In *The American Working Class*, ed. Irving Louis Horowitz, John C. Leggett, and Martin Oppenheimer. New Brunswick, N.J.: Transaction Books, 1979.

Laslett, Peter. "Societal Development and Aging." In *Handbook of Aging and the Social Sciences*, ed. Robert H. Binstock and Ethel Shanas, pp. 199–230. New York: Van Nostrand Reinhold, 1985.

Latimer, Murray Webb. *Industrial Pension Systems in the United States and Canada*. New York: Industrial Relations Counselors, 1932.

———. "Old Age Pensions in America." *American Labor Legislation Review* 19 (March 1929): 55–66.

———. *Trade Union Pension Systems*. New York: Industrial Relations Counselors, 1932.

Latimer, Murray Webb, and Karl Tufel. *Trends in Industrial Pensions*. New York: Industrial Relations Counselors, 1940.

Lee, Charles R. "Public Poor Relief and the Massachusetts Community, 1620–1715." *New England Quarterly* 55, 4 (1982):564–85.

"Legislative History, Trends, and Adequacy of the Supplemental Security Income (SSI) Program." In *The Supplemental Security Income Program: A Ten-Year Overview*. Washington, D.C.: Special Committee on Aging, United States Senate, 1984.

Lerner, Daniel. *The Passing of Traditional Society: Modernizing the Middle East*. Glencoe, Ill.: Free Press, 1958.

Lichtenstein, Nelson. *Labor's War at Home: The CIO in World War II*. Cambridge: Cambridge University Press, 1982.

Linton, M. Albert "Life Insurance Companies and Pension Plans." *Annals of the American Academy of Political and Social Sciences* 130 (March 1927): 34–41.

Lipset, Seymour M. "The Labor Movement and American Values." In *Failure of a Dream?* ed. John Laslett and Seymour M. Lipset. Garden City, N.Y.: Anchor Press, 1974.

Loth, David. *Swope of G.E.* New York: Simon and Schuster, 1958.

Lynch, James M. "Pensions Are Superior to Poorhouses." *American Labor Legislation Review* 15 (September 1925): 262–66.

McCarthy, John, and Mayer Zald. "Resource Mobilization and Social Movements: A Partial Theory." *American Journal of Sociology* 82 (May 1977): 1212–40.

McGill, Dan M. *Fundamentals of Private Pensions*. Homewood, Ill.: Richard D. Irwin, 1955.

McGrady, Edward F. "Old Age Pensions," *American Federationist* 37 (1930): 544–47.

McKinley, Charles, and Robert W. Frase. 1970. *Launching Social Security: A Capture-and-Record Account*. Madison: University of Wisconsin, 1970.

Mandle, Jay R. "The Plantation States as a Sub-region of the Post-bellum South." *Journal of Economic History* 34 (1974): 732–38.

———. *The Roots of Black Poverty: The Southern Plantation Economy after the Civil War*. Durham, N.C.: Duke University Press, 1978.

Marshall, F. Ray. *Labor in the South*. Cambridge: Harvard University Press, 1967.

Marshall, Ray. "The Old South and the New." In *Employment of Blacks in the South*, ed. Ray Marshall and Virgil Christian. Austin: University of Texas Press, 1978.

Martin, Ernest W. "From Parish to Union: Poor Law Administration, 1601–1865." In *Comparative Development in Social Welfare*, ed. Ernest W. Martin. London: George Allen and Unwin, 1972.

Marx, Karl. "A Contribution to the Critique of Political Economy." In *The Marx-Engels Reader*, ed. Robert C. Tucker. New York: W.W. Norton, 1972.

Moley, Raymond. *After Seven Years*. New York: Harper, 1939.

"Money Income Sources of Aged Persons, December 1959." *Social Security Bulletin* 23 (1960): 16.

Monroe, Paul. "An American System of Labor Pensions and Insurance." *American Journal of Sociology* 2 (January 1897): 501–14.

Montgomery, David. *Workers' Control in America: Studies in the History of Work, Technology, and Labor Struggles*. Cambridge: Cambridge University Press, 1979.

Morton, M. B. "Federal and Confederate Pensions Contrasted." *Forum* 16 (September 1893): 68–74.

Mulford, H. P. *Incidence and Effects of the Payroll Tax*. Washington, D.C.: Social Security Board, 1936.

Myers, Howard B. "Relief in the South." *Southern Economic Journal* 3 (1937): 281–91.

Myles, John. *Old Age in the Welfare State: The Political Economy of Public Pensions*. Boston: Little, Brown, 1984.

———. "The Retirement Wage in the Postwar Capitalist Democracies." Paper presented to the American Sociological Association, San Antonio, 1984.

Myrdal, Gunnar. *An American Dilemma*. New York: McGraw-Hill, 1964.

Nevins, Allan. *Grover Cleveland: A Study in Courage*. New York: Dodd, Mead, 1944.

"New Pension Plan Announced by General Electric." *Electric Railway Journal* 70 (31 December 1927): 1213.

Nichols, Walter S. "Fraternal Insurance in the United States: Its Origin, Development, Character and Existing Status." *Annals of the American Academy of Political and Social Science* 70 (March 1917): 109–22.

Norton, Mary Beth, David M. Katzman, Paul D. Escott, Howard P. Chudacoff, Thomas G. Patterson, and William M. Tuttle. *A People and a Nation*. Boston: Houghton Mifflin, 1982.

"Notes: Charities and Social Problems." *Annals of the American Academy of Political and Social Science* 18 (1901): 183.

O'Connor, James. *The Fiscal Crisis of the State.* New York: St. Martin's Press, 1973.

Offe, Claus. *Contradictions of the Welfare State.* Cambridge: MIT Press, 1984.

"Ohio Joins Pension States." *American Labor Legislation Review* 23 (March 1923): 191.

"Old Age Pension Plan for Ashland Employees." *Electric Railway Journal* 63 (12 January 1924): 80.

Oliver, John W. *History of the Civil War Military Pensions, 1861–1885.* History Series 1. Madison: University of Wisconsin, 1917.

Olson, Laura Katz. *The Political Economy of Aging.* New York: Columbia University Press, 1982.

Oppenheimer, Martin. *White Collar Politics.* New York: Monthly Review Press, 1985.

Orloff, Ann Shola. The Politics of Pensions: A Comparative Analysis of the Origins of Pensions and Old Age Insurance in Canada, Great Britain and the United States, 1880s–1930s." Ph.D. diss., Princeton University, 1985.

Orloff, Ann Shola, and Theda Skocpol. "Why Not Equal Protection? Explaining the Politics of Public Social Spending in Britain, 1900–1911, and the United States, 1880s–1920s." *American Sociological Review* 49 (December 1984): 726–50.

Pampel, Fred, and Jane Weiss. "Economic Development, Pension Policies, and the Labor Force Participation of Aged Males: A Cross-National Longitudinal Analysis." *American Journal of Sociology* 89 (1983): 350–72.

Parker, Florence E. "Experience under State Old-Age Pension Acts in 1933." *Monthly Labor Review* 39 (August 1934): 255–72.

Parkin, Frank. *Class Inequality and Political Order.* New York: Praeger, 1971.

Parsons, G. Chauncey. "Old Age Pensions on a Sound Basis." *American Machinist* 780 (15 August 1934): 567–68.

"Pensions for Industrial Workers a Problem for Executives Today." *American Machinist* 64 (18 February 1926): 298.

"Pensions Stir Labor Unions." *Locomotive Engineers Journal* 60 (February 1926): 408.

Perlman, Mark. "Labor in Eclipse." In *Change and Continuity in Twentieth Century America: The 1920s,* ed. John Braeman, Robert Bremner, and David Brody. Columbus: Ohio State University Press, 1968.

Perlman, Selig, and Philip Taft. *History of Labor in the United States, 1896–1932.* New York: Macmillan, 1935.

Perrin, Guy. "Reflections on Fifty Years of Social Security." *International Labour Review* 99 (February 1969): 249–89.

Peterson, Florence. *American Labor Unions.* New York: Harper and Row, 1945.

Pflug, Warner. *The UAW in Pictures.* Detroit: Wayne State University Press, 1971.

"Phelps Dodge Modified Employees' Pension System at Bisbee." *Mining News* 116 (15 December 1923): 1042.

Phillipson, Chris. "The State, the Economy and Retirement." In *Old Age and the Welfare State,* ed. Anne Marie Guillemard. Beverly Hills, Calif.: Sage, 1983.

Piccarello, Louis. "The Administration of Public Welfare: A Comparative Analysis of Salem, Danvers, Deerfield and Greenfield." *Historical Journal of Massachusetts* 10 (June 1982): 30–42.

————. "Social Structure and Public Welfare Policy in Danvers, Massachusetts: 1750–1850." *Essex Institute Historical Collections* 118 (October 1982): 248–63.

Piore, Michael, and Charles F. Sabel. *The Second Industrial Divide.* New York: Basic Books, 1984.

Piven, Frances Fox, and Richard A. Cloward. *Regulating the Poor: The Functions of Public Welfare.* New York: Vintage Books, 1971.

Poggi, Gianfranco. *The Development of the Modern State: A Sociological Introduction.* Stanford, Calif.: Stanford University Press, 1978.

Potter, David. *The South and the Concurrent Majority.* Baton Rouge: Louisiana State University Press, 1972.

Poulantzas, Nicos. *State, Power, Socialism.* London: NLB, 1978.

A Promise Made, a Promise Kept: The Story of the UAW Pension Program. Detroit: UAW Education Department, Solidarity House, 1978.

"Public Assistance." *Social Security Bulletin* 10 (December 1947): 29–30.

"Public Pensions for Aged Dependents." *Monthly Labor Review* 22 (June 1926): 1–9.

Quadagno, Jill. *Aging in Early Industrial Society: Work, Family and Social Policy in Nineteenth Century England.* New York: Academic Press, 1982.

————. "From Poor Laws to Pensions: The Evolution of Economic Support for the Aged in England and America." *Milbank Memorial Fund Quarterly* 62 (Summer 1984): 417–46.

————. "State Structures and the Administration of Old Age Assistance." Paper presented to the Social Science History Association, Toronto, October 1984.

————. "Welfare Capitalism and the Social Security Act of 1935." *American Sociological Review* 49 (October 1984): 632–47.

"Railway Pension Bill Approved by President." *Railway Age* 97 (1934): 6.

Raushenbush, Stephen. *Pensions in Our Economy.* Washington, D.C.: Public Affairs Institute, 1955.

Renaud, E. R. "Old Age Pensions on a Sound Basis—Discussion." *American Machinist* 78 (October 1934): 735.

Riebenack, M. "Pennsylvania Railroad Pension Departments: Systems East and West of Pittsburgh and Erie, Pa. Status to and Including the Year, 1907." *Annals of the American Academy of Political and Social Science* 33 (1909): 258–64.

Rimlinger, Gaston V. *Welfare Policy and Industrialization in Europe, America and Russia.* New York: John Wiley, 1971.

Robbins, Hayes. "Clearances Needed in Railroad Pension Financing." *Railway Age* 89 (1930): 485.

Ross, David F. "State and Local Governments." In *Employment of Blacks in the*

South, ed. Ray Marshall and Virgil L. Christian. Austin: University of Texas Press, 1978.

Rothman, David. *The Discovery of the Asylum.* Boston: Little, Brown, 1971.

Rubinow, I. M. *The Quest for Security.* New York: Henry Holt, 1934.

————. *Social Insurance.* New York: Henry Holt, 1913.

Ruggie, Mary. *The State and Working Women: A Comparative Study of Britain and Sweden.* Princeton: Princeton University Press, 1984.

Russel, Robert Royal. *Economic Aspects of Southern Sectionalism, 1840–1861.* Studies in the Social Sciences, vol. 11, no. 1. Urbana: University of Illinois, 1922; reprinted New York: Arno Press, 1973.

Sanders, Daniel. *The Impact of Reform Movements on Social Policy Change: The Case of Social Insurance.* Fairlawn, N.J.: R. E. Burdick, 1973.

Sanders, Heywood T. "Paying for the Bloody Shirt: The Politics of Civil War Pensions." In *Political Benefits,* ed. Barry Rundquist. Lexington, Mass.: Lexington Books, 1980.

Schlesinger, Arthur. *The Coming of the New Deal.* Boston: Houghton Mifflin, 1958.

Schmidt, Emerson P. "Industrial Pensions and Trade Unions." *American Federationist* 36 (1929): 414–19.

Schulz, James. *The Economics of Aging.* New York: Van Nostrand Reinhold, 1985.

————. "To Old Folks with Love: Aged Income Maintenance in America." *Gerontologist* 5 (October 1985): 464–71.

Schulz, James H., and Thomas D. Leavitt. *Pension Integration: Concepts, Issues and Proposals.* Washington, D.C.: Employee Benefit Research Institute, 1983.

Seager, Henry Rogers. *Social Insurance: A Program of Reform.* New York: Macmillan, 1910.

Shaffer, Alice, Mary Wysor Keefer. *The Indiana Poor Law.* Chicago: University of Chicago Press, 1936.

Shalev, Michael. "The Social Democratic Model and Beyond: Two Generations of Comparative Research on the Welfare State." In *Comparative Social Research Annual,* vol. 6, ed. Richard F. Tomasson, pp. 319–20. Greenwich, Conn.: JAI Press, 1983.

Shefter, Martin. "Party, Bureaucracy and Political Change in the United States." In *Political Parties: Development and Decay,* ed. Louis Maisel and Joseph Cooper., Beverly Hills, Calif.: Sage, 1978.

Skocpol, Theda. "America's Incomplete Welfare State: The Limits of New Deal Reforms and the Origins of the Present Crisis." Paper presented to the American Sociological Association, San Antonio, 1984.

————. "Political Response to Capitalist Crisis: Neo-Marxist Theories of the State and the Case of the New Deal." *Politics and Society* 10 (1980): 155–201.

Skocpol, Theda, and Edwin Amenta. "Did Capitalists Shape Social Security?" *American Sociological Review* 50 (1985): 572–75.

Skocpol, Theda, and John Ikenberry. "The Political Formation of the

American Welfare State in Historical and Comparative Perspective." *Comparative Social Research* 6 (1983): 87–147.

Skowronek, Stephen. *Building a New American State: The Expansion of National Administrative Capacities, 1877–1920.* Cambridge: Cambridge University Press, 1982.

Slichter, Sumner H. "The Current Labor Policies of American Industry." *Quarterly Journal of Economics* 43 (May 1929): 293–435.

Slocum, H. W. "Pensions: Time to Call a Halt." *Forum* 12 (January 1892): 646–51.

Smith, Mary Roberts. "Almshouse Women." *American Statistical Association* 31 (September 1895): 219–62.

Snydor, Charles S. *The Development of Southern Sectionalism, 1819–1848.* Baton Rouge: Louisiana State University Press, 1948.

"Social Security," *Congressional Quarterly Almanac* 14 (1958): 157.

"Social Security Act, H.R. 6000–P.L. 734, Summary." *Congressional Quarterly Almanac* 6 (1950): 165–74.

"Social Security Extension, H.R. 6000, Summary." *Congressional Quarterly Almanac* 5 (1949): 289.

Sombart, Werner. *Why Is There No Socialism in America?* White Plains, N.Y.: M. E. Sharpe, 1976. Originally published 1902.

Squier, Lee Welling. *Old Age Dependency in the United States.* New York: Macmillan, 1912.

Stanwood, Edward. *American Tariff Controversies in the Nineteenth Century.* Vol. 1. Boston: Houghton Mifflin, 1903.

Stark, Louis. "Labor on Relief and Insurance." *Survey Magazine,* 1931, pp. 186–87.

Stephens, John. *The Transition from Capitalism to Socialism.* London: Macmillan, 1979.

Stevens, Albert C. *Cyclopedia of Fraternities.* New York: E. B. Treat, 1907.

Stevens, Beth. "Blurring the Boundaries: How Federal Social Policy Has Influenced Welfare Benefits in the Private Sector." In *The Politics of Social Policy in the United States,* ed. Ann Orloff, Margaret Weir, and Theda Skocpol. Princeton: Princeton University Press, 1988.

———. "New Ties That Bind: The Development of Employer-Sponsored Welfare Benefits." Paper presented to the American Sociological Association, San Antonio, 1984.

Sundquist, James. *Politics and Policy: The Eisenhower, Kennedy and Johnson Years.* Washington, D.C.: Brookings Institution, 1968.

Swope, Gerard. "The Stabilization of Industry." In *America Faces the Future,* ed. Charles Beard. Boston: Houghton Mifflin, 1932.

Sydnor, Charles. *The Development of Southern Sectionalism, 1819–1848.* Baton Rouge: Louisiana State University Press, 1948.

Terrill, Tom E. *The Tariff, Politics, and American Foreign Policy, 1874–1901.* Westport, Conn.: Greenwood Press, 1973.

Therborn, Goran. "The Rule of Capital and the Rise of Democracy." In *States and Societies,* ed. Thomas Held, James Anderson, Bram Gieben, Stuart

Hall, Laurence Harris, Paul Lewis, Noel Parker, and Ben Turok. New York: New York University Press, 1983.

Thornton, J. Mills. *Politics and Power in a Slave Society: Alabama, 1800–1860.* Baton Rouge: Louisiana State University Press, 1978.

Tilly, Charles. *Big Structures, Large Processes, Huge Comparisons.* New York: Russell Sage Foundation. 1984.

——. *From Mobilization to Revolution.* Reading, Mass.: Addison-Wesley, 1978.

Tomasson, Richard F. "Government Old Age Pensions under Affluence and Austerity: West Germany, Sweden, the Netherlands and the United States." *Research in Social Problems and Public Policy* 3 (1984): 217–72.

Tomlins, Christopher. *The State and the Unions: Labor Relations, Law, and the Organized Labor Movement in America, 1880–1960.* Cambridge: Cambridge University Press, 1985.

Townsend, Francis E. *New Horizons.* Chicago: J. L. Stewart, 1943.

Trempe, Rolande. "The Struggles of French Miners for the Creation of Retirement Funds in the Nineteenth Century." In *Old Age and the Welfare State,* ed. Anne Marie Guillemard. Beverly Hills, Calif.: Sage, 1983.

"U.S. May Take over Railroad Pension Plans." *Railway Age* 97 (1934): 143.

Vale, Vivian. *Labour in American Politics.* London: Routledge and Kegan Paul, 1971.

Vanderlip, E. A. "Insurance from the Employer's Standpoint." *Proceedings of the Thirty-third National Conference of Charities and Corrections,* 1906, pp. 457–64.

Walker, John H. "Labor's Point of View." In *The Care of the Aged,* ed. I. M. Rubinow. New York: Arno, 1980. Originally published 1930.

Wall, Bennett H., and George S. Gibb. *Teagle of Jersey Standard.* New Orleans: Tulane University Press, 1974.

Wallerstein, Immanuel. *The Capitalist World Economy.* Cambridge: Cambridge University Press, 1979.

Warner, John DeWitt. 1893. "Half a Million Dollars a Day for Pensions." *Forum* 15 (June 1893): 439–51.

Wedge, D. B. "Why the Government in Pensions." *American Machinist* 70 (3 January 1929): 2.

"Welfare Work for Employees in Industrial Establishments." *Bulletin of the U.S. Bureau of Labor Statistics* 250 (1919): 107–12.

"What Business Thinks." *Fortune,* October 1939, pp. 52, 90.

Wiebe, Robert H. *Businessmen and Reform: A Study of the Progressive Movement.* Chicago: Quadrangle Books, 1968.

Wilensky, Harold. *The Welfare State and Equality: Structural and Ideological Roots of Public Expenditures.* Berkeley: University of California Press, 1975.

Williamson, John, and Jane Weiss. "Egalitarian Political Movements, Social Welfare Effort and Convergence Theory: A Cross-National Analysis." *Comparative Social Research* 2 (1979): 289–302.

Wilson, Graham K. *Unions in American National Politics.* London: Macmillan, 1979.

Wisner, Elizabeth. *Social Welfare in the South: From Colonial Times to World War I*. Baton Rouge: Louisiana State University Press, 1970.

Witte, Edwin. *The Development of the Social Security Act*. Madison: University of Wisconsin Press, 1963.

Wolman, Leo. *The Growth of Trades Unions, 1880–1923*. New York: National Bureau of Economic Research, 1924.

Wolters, Raymond. "The New Deal and the Negro." In *The New Deal*, ed. John Braeman, Robert H. Bremmer, and David Brody. Columbus: Ohio State University Press, 1975.

Woodward, C. Vann. *Origins of the New South, 1877–1913*. Baton Rouge: Louisiana State University Press, 1951.

Woofter, Thomas J. *Landlord and Tenant on the Cotton Plantation*. Washington, D.C.: Works Progress Administration, 1936.

Wright, Gavin. *The Political Economy of the Cotton South: Households, Markets, and Wealth in the Nineteenth Century*. New York: W. W. Norton, 1978.

Zald, Mayer, and John McCarthy. "Resource Mobilization and Social Movements: A Partial Theory." *American Journal of Sociology* 82 (May 1977): 1212–41.

———. "Social Movement Industries: Competition and Cooperation among Movement Organizations." *Research in Social Movements, Conflicts and Change* 3 (1980): 1–20.

Zeichner, Oscar. "The Legal Status of the Agricultural Laborer in the South." *Political Science Quarterly* 55 (1940): 412–28.

GOVERNMENT DOCUMENTS

Massachusetts. Commission on Old Age Pensions, Annuities, and Insurance. *House Report No. 1400*. Boston, January 1910.

U. S. Bureau of the Census. *Population: Characteristics of the Population*. Part 1. *United States Summary, Reports to the States*. Washington, D.C.: Government Printing Office, 1940.

———. *Biennial Census of Manufacturers, 923*. Washington, D.C.: Government Printing Office, 1926.

U.S. Bureau of Research and Statistics. *Trends in Public Assistance, 1933–1939*. Bureau Report no. 8. Washington, D.C.: Social Security Board, 1940.

U.S. Congress. *Annals of the Congress of the United States, 1789–1824*. 42 vols. Washington, D.C., 1834–56.

———. *Biographical Directory of the American Congress, 1774–1971*. Washington, D.C.: Government Printing Office, 1971.

———. *Congressional Record*. Washington, D.C.: Government Printing Office, 1882, 1887, 1888, 1890, 1906, 1949, 1954.

———. *Register of Debates in Congress*. Washington, D.C., 1832.

U.S. Congress. House. *The Raum Investigation*. H. Rept. 3732. Washington, D.C.: Government Printing Office, 1890.

U.S. Congress. House. Committee on Ways and Means. *Hearings on H.R. 6000: Social Security Revision*. 81st Cong., 2d sess. Washington, D.C.: Government Printing Office, 1950.

U.S. Congress. House. Committee on Labor. *Old Age Pensions.* 71st Cong., 2d sess. Washington, D.C.: Government Printing Office, 1930.

U.S. Congress. House. Committee on Ways and Means. *Hearings on H.R. 5710: Amendments to the Social Security Act.* Washington, D.C.: Government Printing

————. *Hearings on H.R. 6635.* 76th Cong., 1st sess. Washington, D.C.: Government Printing Office, 1939.

U.S. Congress. House. Subcommittee of the Committee on Labor. *Hearings on H.R. 2827: Unemployment, Old Age and Social Insurance.* 74th Cong., 1st sess. Washington, D.C.: Government Printing Office, 1935.

U.S. Congress. Senate. Committee on Finance. *Hearings on S. 1130: Economic Security Act, a Bill to Alleviate the Hazards of Old Age Unemployment, Illness and Dependency, to Establish a Social Insurance Board in the Department of Labor, to Raise Revenue, and for Other Purposes.* 74th Cong., 1st sess. Washington, D.C.: Government Printing Office, 1935.

————. *Hearings on S. Con. Res. 4: A Concurrent Resolution Calling for the Amendment of Certain Provisions of the Social Security Act.* 75th Cong., 1st sess. Washington, D.C.: U.S. Government Printing Office, 1937.

U.S. Congress. Senate. Subcommittee of the Committee on Interstate Commerce. *Hearings on S. 3151: Retirement System for Employees of Carriers.* 74th Cong., 1st sess. Washington, D.C.: Government Printing Office, 1935.

U.S. Congress. Senate. Subcommittee of the Committee on Pensions. *Hearings on S. 3257: A Bill to Encourage and Assist the States in Providing Pensions to the Aged.* 71st Cong., 2d sess. Washington, D.C.: Government Printing Office, 1931.

U.S. Social Security Administration. *Social Security Bulletin, Annual Statistical Supplement.* Washington, D.C.: Government Printing Office, 1982.

Archival Collections

American Association for Social Security Archives, Cornell University, Ithaca, N.Y.

Archives of Labor History and Urban Affairs, Walter P. Reuther Library, Wayne State University, Detroit, Mich. Collections of Arthur Hughes, Katherine Ellickson, UAW Local 9, Lillian Hatcher.

Arthur Altmeyer Papers, CES file 2, box 1. Historical Society of Wisconsin Library, Madison, Wisc.

Columbia University Oral History Collection, Butler Library, New York. Memoirs of Nelson Cruickshank, Frank Bane, Katherine Ellickson, Thomas Eliot, Marion Folsom, Jane Hooey.

Federal Archives and Records Center, Suitland, Md. RG 47, Chairman's Files.

Franklin Delano Roosevelt Papers, FDR Library, Hyde Park, N.Y. Official Files, 494a.

National Archives, Washington, D.C. RG 47, Records of the Executive Director, State Files, Chairman's Files.

PERIODICALS AND JOURNALS

The Eagle Magazine, 1922, 1923, 1924.

Illinois State Federation of Labor. *Weekly News Letter*, 17 March 1923.

National Tribune, 1884, 1887.

Odd Fellows Magazine, 1925.

Pennsylvania Manufacturers' Association. *Monthly Bulletin*, 1 May 1927.

Proceedings of the American Federation of Labor, 1928, 1929.

Proceedings of the Annual Convention of the Brotherhood of Locomotive Firemen and Enginemen, 1928.

Proceedings of the Convention of the Brotherhood of Railroad Trainmen, 1919.

Proceedings of the International Typographical Union, 1928.

Proceedings of the Ninth Annual Convention of the Arkansas State Federation of Labor, 1911.

Proceedings of the Seventeenth Annual Convention of the California State Federation of Labor, 1916.

Reports of Officers of the International Typographical Union, 1921, 1925, 1926, 1929, 1931, 1932, 1934, 1935.

United Mine Workers Journal, 1918, 1919, 1920.

Index

Achenbaum, W. Andrew, 21
Advisory Council on Economic Security, 111, 113
AFL: attitude toward industrial
unionism, 12, 155–56; coalition
with Eagles, 66–72; cooperation
with Social Security Administration, 172; factionalism within,
156–58; membership increases in,
54; on private pensions, 55, 93,
160; refusal to admit blacks, 16;
stance on political action, 60;
stance on tariffs, 41; on state pensions, 53, 61–63, 71–72, 108, 147;
support for Democratic party, 63.
See also Craft workers; Labor
movement; Organized labor
AFL-CIO: factionalism within, 174,
183; merger of, 169; stance on social security expansion, 173; ties to
Democratic party, 172–73. *See also*
Craft workers; Labor movement;
Mass-production workers; Organized labor
Aged: institutional care of, 53; need
for public aid, 51; public concern
for, 27; treatment under poor law,
24, 26; support for Townsend
plan, 108. *See also* Older workers
Agricultural Adjustment Act, 142
Agriculture: black employment in,
116; contrast between North and
South, 31; cotton base in South, 18,

30, 33, 47; impact on southern wel-
fare, 28; mechanization of, 142,
151, 188; under plantation mode
of production, 15, 23
Aid to Families with Dependent Chil-
dren, 149
Alber, Jens, 3
Almshouses, 27–28
Altmeyer, Arthur, 110, 111, 120
Amalgamated Clothing Workers,
155
Amenta, Edwin, 100, 122
American Anti-Boycott Association,
60
American Association for Labor Leg-
islation, 65, 99, 110, 111
American Association for Old Age
Security, 103
American Association for Social Se-
curity, 119
American exceptionalism, 2, 10, 15,
179–88
American Labor Legislation Review, 63
American plan, 88–89
Armstrong, Barbara, 111
Arrears of Pension Act, 38
Association of Railway Executives, 73
Auto Worker, 163

Bensel, Richard, 39
Beveridge Report, 2
Blacks: access to private pensions, 93;
benefit levels of, 21, 34; exclusion

247